Ashraf's Advice L

Great I........

of Fiqh©

A study of the Lives & Contributions of

Imām Aboo Haneefah 爨
Imām Mālik 爨
Imām Shāfi'ee 爨
Imām Ahmad ibn Hambal 爨

'The Rahmat (Mercies) of Allah 爨 descends upon those occasions when the virtues of His sāleh (pious) servants are related.'

'Allamāh Ibne Jawzee 爨

Allah 🪷 mentions in the Glorious Qur'ān:

'He grants Hikmah (wisdom - the knowledge & understanding of the Qur'ān & Sunnah) to whomsoever He wills, and he, to whom Hikmah is granted, is indeed granted abundant good...' (2:269)

Abdullah bin 'Umar 🪷 narrates...

'Once when Nabee 🪷 passed by two groups in the Masjid, He commented, 'Both groups are on khair (virtue); however one is superior to the other. The group which is engaged in du'aa (supplication), dhikr (remembrance of Allah 🪷) and meditation are calling Allah Ta'ālā and are enveloped in His Rahmat (Mercies). If Allah wishes, He blesses them or if He wishes he may deprive them.

However, this second group, who are engrossed in the acquisition of fiqh and 'ilm (deeni knowledge) and who teach masā'eels & ahqāms (deeni rulings and commands) to the unknowing are superior. Moreover, I too was sent as a mu'allim (tutor).' So saying, Nabee 🪷 sat down with the (second) group (of scholars and students).' (p37, Episodes...)

Ashraf's Advice Upon the Four

Great Imāms

ISBN-1-9026-2703-2

Revised Second Edition

Based Upon the Teachings

of...

'Allamah Muhammad bin Yousuf Salehee Damasqee,
Shaykh Badre 'Ālam Meerathi, Shaykh Muheebullah Nadwee,
Shaykh Ashraf 'Ali Thānwi, Shaykh-ul-Hadeeth Zakariyyā,
Shaykh Anwar Shah Kashmiree, Shaykh 'Abdullah Madanee,
Shaykh Maseehullah Khan, Shaykh 'Abdu'l-Qayyum Haqqanee
Shaykh Mufti Aashiq 'Ellahi Madanee, Shaykh Muhammad Qasim Nanotwee,
Shaykh Mufti Muhammad Shafee, Shaykh Mufti Azeez-ur-Rahman,
Shaykh Abul Hasan 'Ali Nadwee, Shaykh Muhammad Haneef Gangohi, ,
Shaykh Abdur Raoof Lajpoori, Shaykh Qadhi Athar Mubarkapooree
Shaykh Yousuf Darwan, Shaykh Mufti Taqee 'Uthmānee

Patron

Shaykh Muhammad Saleem Dhorat

Prepared & Published by

Maulāna Yousuf, Hāfiz Maseehullah, Hāfiz Muhammad 'Abdullah & Hāfiz Aslam Patel

BA (Hons) Arch. Studies, Dip. Arch.

Ashraf's Amānat©

PO Box 12, Dewsbury, W. Yorkshire, UK, WF12 9YX
Tel: (01924) 488929

www.ashrafsamanat.org

ഇൻൽ

Copyright Notice

Recommended Retail Price:
£6.00 (UK); €10.00 (Europe); $11.00 (USA)

All proceeds received by Ashraf's Amānat© from sales fund new works.

Ashraf's Amānat & Copyright

haykh Mufti 'Abdur Raheem Lajpoori ۞ writes in *Fatāwā Raheemeeyah (Vol. 3)… 'Any book comes into existence after the toil and labour of the writer, accordingly the foremost right of publishing it belongs to him alone. Moreover, besides the intention of propagating Knowledge of Deen, the author has the right to derive profit from his writings. Accordingly, until the author's interest is connected with the book, nobody else has the right to publish it. Other people who publish a popular book without (written permission from the author) do so only out of selfish commercial interest. Their argument of propagating the Knowledge of Deen (and being of benefit to Muslims) is baseless because if this was a true intention of theirs then what prevents them from buying the Kitāb in large quantities from the author and distributing it for the purpose of thawāb? Similarly, although everybody has the right to adopt a particular title for his (Jamā'at), nevertheless when a certain person has adopted a title for his activity and his finances are bound with the said title…then no one else has the right to use this very title for his business…'*

shraf's Amānat© is a School of Islāmic English Writing. Through Tawfeeq from Allah ۞, we attempt to present authentic Teachings of Pious Scholars in the Light of the Qur'ān and Hadeeth for the benefit of western educated Muslims. Our work is ongoing; new titles are under preparation and would be assisted by your support & du'aa. If you wish to order our books or support our work please write or send Lillah donations to:

Ashraf's Amānat©
PO Box 12,
Dewsbury,
W. Yorkshire, UK,
WF12 9YX
Tel: (01924) 488929
email:info@ashrafsamanat.org

Or

Bank Sort Code: 40 -19 -17
Account Number: 91367765
Account Name: Ashraf's Amanat
Bank: HSBC
Branch: Market Place,
Dewsbury,
W. Yorkshire,
UK, WF13 1DH

Salāt & Salāms upon our Beloved Nabee ﷺ

Permission & Du'aa's

Shaykh Mufti
Muhammad Taqee 'Uthmānee

dāmat barakātuhum

Member Shar'eeat Appellate Bench
Supreme Court of Pakistan
Deputy Chairman, Islāmic Fiqh Academy [OIC] Jeddah
Vice-President, Darul Uloom Karachi

Assalamu Alaikum,

Editor,

Ashraf's Amānat© of Dewsbury

8th Zil Hijjah 1420

(14th March 2000)

am pleased to give you permission for translating some of my discourses in *Islāhi Khutbaat*...If you undertake a new translation, you are permitted from my side.

May Allah ﷻ approve your efforts and make them beneficial for the Ummah.

Āmeen, Was-salām,

(Shaykh Mufti)

Muhammad Taqee 'Uthmānee

Salāt & Salāms upon our beloved Nabee ﷺ

Introduction

Shaykh Muhammad Saleem Dhorat

Principal & Senior Lecturer in Hadeeth, IDA, Leicester

Alhamdulillah, both the Glorious Qur'ān and Hadeeth are present in their original form. However, the need arose for a group in the Ummah who would strive to ascertain daily practicalities from words of the Glorious Qur'ān and ahadeeth. When you awake, do this; if so-and-so occurs during salāh, it is permissible; however, should such-and-such take place, the salāh is void. There are 'x' *farā'idh* and *sunnahs* in salāh, wudhu, etc., etc.

Allah ﷻ through His infinite Mercies and Favours created a group known as the *fuqahā-e-ezām* (jurists), who have deduced commands and rulings from the Glorious Qur'ān and ahadeeth, thus allowing us to achieve success both in dunya and the Ākhirah.

The intention of this book is to create awareness amongst Western Muslims of the lives and contributions of these successors of our Prophet ﷺ and the importance of their taqleed. We are delighted to be part of this Kitab published by Ashraf's Amānat©. It is another bouquet prepared with great care for Muslims living in western society. May Allah ﷻ accept and bless the efforts of all those associated with this Kitab, especially Shaykh Yusuf Darwan, Shaykh Rasheed Kola, Shaykh 'Abdur Ra'oof Lajpoori, Shaykh Yousuf ibn Hāfiz Abdus Salām Sacha and all others who have advised the author Aslam Patel.

Salāt & Salāms upon our beloved Nabee 🕌

Foreword

Shaykh Yusuf A. Darwan

Senior Lecturer in Tajweed & Hadeeth, Dewsbury, UK

Success in both this world and the Ākhirah is attainable only through adherence to Deen. For a person to follow Deen, knowledge is conditional and is the first step to success, action and propagation of Deen are the next two steps.

There is a scarcity of well-written, informative and understandable Islāmic literature available in the English language. Muslim youth are highly vulnerable to western influences. It is therefore imperative to present them with the true teachings of Islām.

Through the infinite Mercy & Grace of Allah 🕌, Ashraf's Amānat© of Dewsbury have published a series of beneficial Islāmic books. May Allah 🕌 grant them Tawfeeq to progress in this noble and rewarding endeavour and bless them with continuous ikhlaas and steadfastness. May Allah 🕌 make these publications beneficial and informative especially for our younger Muslim brothers and sisters and grant all readers the Tawfeeq to appreciate, learn and practice thereupon. We hope and pray to Allah 🕌 that this latest publication 'Great Imāms & Taqleed' is just one of many more topics to be covered by brother Aslam of Ashraf's Amānat. Āmeen, Was-salām

(Shaykh) **Yusuf A. Darwan**

What other Senior Scholars & Mashāikh have said about Ashraf's Amānat...

Shaykh 'Abdullah Kapodrawi of Canada...

'These publications contain the works of our pious predecessors upon which we have full confidence. May Allah ﷻ grant greater barakat.'

Shaykh Mufti Taqee 'Uthmānee of Darul Uloom Korangi...

'May Allah ﷻ approve your efforts and make them beneficial for the Ummah.'

Shaykh 'Abdul Hameed Isaac of South Africa...

'I am sure and, it is my du'aa, that by this great work Muslims living in western countries or whose mother tongue has become English, will be able to appreciate the great treasures of Islāmic Knowledge...'

Shaykh Mufti Rafee 'Uthmānee of Darul Uloom Korangi...

'Mashā'Allah! Excellent set of publications...'

Shaykh Ahmad Sadeeq Desai of South Africa...

'May Allah ﷻ accept your service & increase your Deeni activities.'

Shaykh Mufti Zubayr Bhayat of South Africa...

'Mashā'Allah! The work being undertaken is extremely good & much needed...'

Shaykh Dr. Ismā'eel Mangera of South Africa...

'May Allah ﷻ fulfil your wishes to serve the Ummah. May your publications be a means of spreading the teachings of our akābir to others, young and old.'

Shaykh Dr. Muhammad Sābir of Sakkar...

'Mashā'Allah...the heart is pleased...this work is undoubtedly due to the sincerity of our cherished predecessors...'

Shaykh 'Abdur Rahmān Mangera of USA...

'Bringing into English the spirit of the work of our pious predecessors is a very noble deed. May Allah ﷻ accept it.'

Shaykh Mufti Saiful Islam of UK...

'Alhamdulillah! The work being produced is very good!'

Contents

Chapter One

'ILM, FIQH & THE FUQAHĀ

Chapter Two

IMĀM ABOO HANEEFAH

Chapter Seven

SCHEMES OF ENEMIES

Chapter Eight

KITÃBULLAH & RIJÃLULLAH

Chapter Nine

ISTIFTA'~ STATEMENTS OF SCHOLARS

'ILM, FIQH

&

THE FUQAHÃ

*O*ur Jurists relate, 'The 'crop' of fiqh was sown by 'Abdullah ibn Mas'ûd ﷺ; 'Alqamah ﷺ irrigated it; Ibrãheem Nakha'ee ﷺ harvested it; Hammad ﷺ segregated it; Imãm Aboo Haneefah ﷺ milled it; Imãm Aboo Yousuf ﷺ kneaded it; Imãm Muhammad ﷺ thereafter baked the bread...and the rest of us are eaters!'

(p43, Episodes...)

'Ilm, Fiqh & the Fuqahā

Imām Aboo Haneefah 🕮 defined *Fiqh* as:

'The (Deeni) knowledge possessed by a person whereby he is able to ascertain and differentiate between what is of benefit and harm to him...'   (p33, Episodes...)

Who is a Faqeeh? A person well acquainted with Deeni 'Uloom and Faculty of *Baseerat* (spiritual vision) whereby he is able to ascertain daily *marhalas* (rulings and practicalities) from words of the Glorious Qur'ān, Ahadeeth and the teachings of our pious predecessors. In reality, a Faqeeh removes the veil of ignorance and guides the Ummah upon *Seeratul Mustaqeem*. Accordingly, Allah 🕮 has described the Faqeeh as His *Khaleefh* (deputy) and *wārith* (inheritor) of the Prophets 🕮 in the Glorious Qur'ān,...

'O you who believe! Obey Allah and obey the Messenger and those of you (Muslims) who are in authority...' (4:59)

Hāfiz Ibn Qayyum 🕮 comments, 'From this Verse, it becomes compulsory to obey and follow the *fuqahā* and *mujtahideen*, moreover, according to 'Abdullah ibn Abbas, Jabir bin 'Abdullah, Hasan Basree 🕮, the *'Ulul Amr'* (authorities) referred to in this Ayah does not imply to rulers but the *fuqahā* of Islām.' Regarding the importance of 'ilm, Allah 🕮 mentions,

'And it is not (proper) for the believers to go out to fight (jihād) all together. Of every troop of them, a party only should go forth, so that they (who are left behind) may get instructions in (Islāmic) religion, whereby they may warn their people when they return to them; so that they may beware (of evil).'   (Glorious Qur'ān, 9:122)

Fiqh of the Sahābāh ﷺ

haykh Qādhi Athar ﷺ relates, 'During the blessed time of Nabee ﷺ the fountainhead of Sharee' *ahqāms* (commands) were the Glorious Qur'ān and Sunnah. After the death of Nabee ﷺ, new *masā'eels* were still deduced from these sources and, when the need arose, the statements and decrees of those Companions was accepted who were unanimously regarded as authorities in Deeni 'Uloom.

These people were those, who were 'Alim's (scholars) of the Glorious Qur'ān, who had written down *Wahee* and had studied under the direct patronage of Nabee ﷺ. As a result, they had become experts of Qur'ānic meaning and sciences (*mafhum, nasikh & mansukh*). Such authorised Sahābāh ﷺ were known as *Qurra.'* This title differentiated the 'Alim from the non-scholar. Amongst the Sahābāh ﷺ, there were approximately 130 such authorised men and ladies. Of these, 7 Sahābāh ﷺ are known as *mukathireen* - those who passed *fatawas* (decrees) in large numbers. They are:

1) 'Umar bin Khattab ﷺ
2) 'Ali bin Abee Taalib ﷺ
3) 'Abdullah bin Mas'ûd ﷺ
4) Umm al-Mu'mineen 'Ā'ishah ﷺ
5) Zayd bin Thaabit ﷺ
6) 'Abdullah bin 'Umar ﷺ
7) 'Abdullah bin 'Abbas ﷺ

The *fatawas* of the latter alone have been compiled in 20 volumes. Moreover, there were 13 other Sahābāh ﷺ, known as the *mutawasiteen...*

1) Aboo Bakr Siddeeq ﷺ
2) Umm al-Mu'mineen Umme Salamah ﷺ
3) Anas bin Malik ﷺ
4) Aboo Sa'eed Khudree ﷺ
5) Aboo Hurayrah ﷺ
6) 'Uthmān bin 'Affān ﷺ
7) 'Abdullah bin 'Amr-ul-'As ﷺ
8) 'Abdullah bin Zubayr ﷺ
9) Aboo Moosaa Ash'aree ﷺ
10) Sa'ad bin Abee Waqqas ﷺ
11) Salman Farsee ﷺ
12) Jabir bin 'Abdullah ﷺ
13) Mu'adh bin Jabal ﷺ

These scholars had also issued decrees, though in lesser numbers.

Ashãb-ul-Hadeeth & Ashãb-ul-Fiqh

After the era of the four *Khulafaa-e-Rasheedeen* (10-40AH/c. 650CE), two new titles were introduced for the *Qurra* (scholars). Many Sahābāh ﷺ were more inclined towards Hadeeth, its kitabs, *sanad* (chain of narration) and *matan* (words and meanings). These scholars were titled *Ashab-ul-Hadeeth*, the *markaz* (headquarters) of which were, of course, Makkah and Madeenah. There were also those Sahābāh ﷺ who preferred and gave precedence to memorising Hadeeth and deducing meanings and *mafaheem*, accordingly such scholars were known as *Ashab-ul-Fiqh*. Their *markaz* was Kufa in Iraq. The students of both groups, as we shall study, would soon illuminate the whole world with both *'Ilm* and *Nûr-e-Nabbuwwat*.

Kufa

A Centre of Deeni 'Uloom

*K*ufa - the renown centre of Islāmic 'Uloom (knowledge) in Iraq was founded in 17 AH (640 CE) under the supervision of *Ameerul Mu'mineen* 'Umar ﷺ. Some elite of Arabian society settled here and for their moral and spiritual well-being 'Umar ﷺ dispatched the famous Scholar 'Abdullah ibn Mas'ûd ﷺ...

> '(O people of Kufa)! We also are in need of 'Abdullah ibn Mas'ûd ﷺ, however, giving priority to your needs, I am sending him for the benefit of your t'āleem.'

(p599, Seerah Sahābāh)

For the next twenty years, 'Abdullah ibn Mas'ûd ﷺ imparted *masā'eels* and Teachings of the Glorious Qur'ān. The result of this unselfish toil and effort? Some 4,000 'Ulamā and Muhadditheen were born and graduated in this new town! When 'Ali ﷺ observed this display of 'Uloom, he commented,

> 'May Allah grant Ibn Mas'ûd further goodness, for he has filled this locality with 'Ilm...and his students are the lamps of this city!'
> (ibid.)

Great 'Ulamā of the calibre of Sa'eed bin Jabeer ﷺ (a student of 'Abdullah ibn 'Abbas ﷺ) and Sh'ābee ﷺ were present. When the famous Ibrāheem Nakha'ee ﷺ (a student of Sa'eed bin Khudree and 'Āishāh Sideeqa ﷺ) died here in 90 AH, the comment was heard,

> 'You have buried one of the greatest Faqeeh today...higher than all...the Scholars of Basra, Kufa and Arabia!'

The 'Ilmi rank and Superiority of Kufa

The 'Ilmi rank and superiority of Kufa may be gauged from the fact that only 3,000 Sahābāh ♣ settled in the whole of Egypt, whilst in Kufa alone, 1,500 Sahābāh were resident; of whom 70 were veterans of Badr and 300 were *Ashab-Bay'at-ar-Ridhwan* (those noble souls who had pledged allegiance to Nabee ♣ at al-Hudaybiyyah in 6 AH). However, despite this large presence, there were 33 other Muftis born in Kufa who were authorized to pass *fatwās*. When a person was asked why he visited 'Alqamah ♣ (one of the greatest Scholars and deputy of Ibn Mas'ûd ♣) instead of the other Sahābāh still living in Kufa, he replied,

> *'I have personally observed these very same Sahābāh visiting 'Alqamah to seek Masā'eel.'*   (ibid.)

Regarding Shurayh ♣, the famous Chief Qādhi (Judge) of Kufa, 'Ali ♣ commented,

> *'O Shurayh! Arise and arbitrate, because you are the highest ranking Judge of Arabia!'*   (ibid.)

In essence, whilst Madeenah Munawwarah possesses the soil upon which descended *wahee* and houses the Grave of our Nabee ♣, in comparison, Kufa holds the honour of imparting the Teachings of Hadeeth. During the early era of the Tābi'een, there were 4,000 students of Hadeeth studying here, with 400 Fuqahā teaching. Imām Bukhāree ♣ commented,

> *'I am unable to remember how many times I must have visited Kufa to acquire Hadeeth.'*   (ibid.)

Even today, if one studies the books of Fiqh and Hadeeth, one cannot fail to notice the numerous occasions when the name of one of the narrators has Kufa adjoined.

'Abdullah bin Mas'ud ﷺ

A llah ﷻ mentions in the Glorious Qur'ān:
'And the foremost to embrace Islām of the Muhājirûn (Muslim Migrators from Makkah) and the Ansār (Muslim Helpers of Madeenah) and also those who followed them exactly (in Faith): Allah is well-pleased with them as they are well pleased with Him. He has prepared for them Gardens under which rivers flow (in Paradise)...to dwell therein forever. That is the supreme success.' (9:100)

Shaykh Abu Yusuf *dāmat barakātuhum* relates, 'One of the reasons for highlighting the personality of Sayyidina 'Abdullah ibn Mas'ud ﷺ is that unfortunately it has become a fashionable trend nowadays, amongst certain people to criticize and, at times, to abuse some members of the Sahābāh ﷺ. Certain people, such as the *Rawafidh*, have always been known to abuse the Sahābāh and, not just one or two, but almost all of them. However, of recent, certain people who claim to be from amongst the *Ahl-us-Sunnah-wal-Jamaah* have also been responsible for attacking the Sahābāh and especially 'Abdullah ibn Mas'ud ﷺ. One reason is that people wish to attack Hanafee Fiqh and everything based upon it: the laws; the methods of performing *ibaadaat*, etc.

Moreover, some people, partly rightfully, though not entirely correctly, consider the only foundation for some of the laws of Hanafee Fiqh to be the sayings of 'Abdullah ibn Mas'ud ﷺ. Therefore, they wish to cut from the root and attack its very foundation. If it is possible for such misguided people to show that 'Abdullah ibn Mas'ud ﷺ was forgetful, senile, neglectful and quite errant on many issues (and regrettably all these vile epithets *are* being used), then the very foundation of Hanafee Fiqh is destroyed.

Surprisingly, all this venom is not coming from the *Rawafidh*, but from people who claim to be members of the *Ahl-us-Sunnah-wal-Jamaah* and followers of the Sunnat & Hadeeth of Rasoolullah ﷺ. Such people, with supposedly sound *aqaaid* (beliefs), are trying to besmirch a personality of the calibre and rank of 'Abdullah ibn Mas'ud ﷺ. Another shocking facet of those who discuss the competence and personality of this noble Companion is their complete lack of knowledge of religion! If one were to engage such criticisers in a dialogue about any aspect of Deen, they would be hard-pressed to say anything; yet such people are somehow and for some reason able to comment on the character and knowledge of 'Abdullah ibn Mas'ud ﷺ.

Many people who embrace religion, or begin to practice after some time, they sadly become entrapped in debates and discussions with protagonists who do not care to teach such gullible 'newcomers' the basics of Deen. Rather they are indoctrinated with controversies; therefore from the beginning they pick-up the name of Ibn Mas'ud and all they know is that only certain people follow him; his hadeeth and fatawas are at variance with the other Sahābāh, etc, etc!

It is extremely dangerous for anyone, no matter how scholarly such a person may be, to loosen his tongue about 'Abdullah ibn Mas'ud ﷺ. We should fear Allah and fear for our own Imān.'   *(Courtesy of Islamic Shariah Institute)*

Early Life of Ibn Mas'ud ♦

haykh Mueenuddeen Nadwee ♦ relates, 'Abdullah ibn Mas'ud ♦ accepted Islām at a time when the Jamā'at of Muslims in Makkah numbered a handful and nobody besides the noble personality of our Nabee ♦ dared to recite the Glorious Qur'ān loudly (for fear of being persecuted).

When the propagation of Deen had commenced in Makkah, one day Nabee ♦ and his close companion Aboo Bakr ♦ were travelling through the outskirts where goats were being grazed. They met a young shepherd 'Abdullah ibn Mas'ud ♦ and Aboo Bakr ♦ asked, 'If you have some milk, kindly quench our thirst?' The young shepherd replied, 'I am unable to offer you milk for (these goats) are the *amānah* of another.' Nabee ♦ commented, 'Why, do you have such a goat which has not given birth to a kid?' Ibn Mas'ud ♦ replied, 'Yes,' and presented a goat. Nabee ♦ prayed and thereafter stroked the animals empty udder...upon which they became full of milk! Aboo Bakr ♦ milked the goat and all three present drank milk one after the other to their hearts content. Thereafter, Nabee ♦ commanded the udder, 'become dry!' whereupon it returned to its original state. (Vol. 2, p276, Seerah..)

The young Ibn Mas'ud ♦ was so influenced by this incident he requested, 'Teach me the 'Uloom of this Glorious (Qur'ān).' Nabee ♦ replied,

'You are a t'aleem yaftah (educated) child.' (ibid.)

From this day, he entered the company of Nabee ♦, acquiring *tarbiyyah* and 'Uloom.

Student & Khādim of Nabee 🌸

Day and night, at home and on journeys, 'Abdullah ibn Mas'ud 🌸 was fortunate to stay in the company of Nabee 🌸 and is regarded as his close student and *khādim*. Placing *miswak*, shoes, leading the conveyance during journeys, etc., were his duties. Accordingly, he became aware of such knowledge which led to him being highly respected and esteemed even amongst the Sahābāh 🌸. Aboo Moosa Ash'aree 🌸 narrates,

> 'When we arrived from Yemen and had stayed for a few days in Madeenah, we observed 'Abdullah ibn Mas'ud 🌸 coming and going from the residence of Nabee 🌸 so regularly, that (for some time) we assumed him to be a family member.'   (p287, ibid.)

This constant presence in the company of Nabee 🌸 resulted in 'Abdullah ibn Mas'ud 🌸 becoming possibly the greatest 'Alim of the Glorious Qur'ān...

> 'Seventy surahs I have acquired and learnt directly from the auspicious Lips of the Recipient of Wahee and Ilhaam...there is no Ayah of the Glorious Qur'ān regarding which I do not know when, where and why it was revealed...should any person possess more 'Uloom of the Glorious Qur'ān than myself, then I would journey to meet him.' 'All the Sahābāh are aware that I am the most knowledgeable 'Alim of the Glorious Qur'ān though I am not the best amongst them.'   (ibid.)

Nabee 🌸 commented,

> 'Acquire the Glorious Qur'ān from four people: Abdullah ibn Mas'ud, Salem, Mu'āz and Ubay bin Ka'āb.' (p289, ibid)

Caution of Ibn Mas'ud in Narrating Hadeeth

haykh-ul-Hadeeth Zakariyyā 🌸 relates, 'Nabee 🌸 also commented:

'If I were to appoint somebody as Ameer without consultation, it would be 'Abdullah ibn Mas'ud.'

'You (Ibn Mas'ud) have permission to attend at all times.'

'Whomsoever wishes to recite the Glorious Qur'ān as it was revealed should recite it in the manner recited by 'Abdullah ibn Mas'ud.'

'Regard whichever hadeeth Ibn Mas'ud relates to you to be true.'   (p107, Stories…)

Despite these Prophetic endorsements, Aboo 'Amr Shaybanee 🌸 relates,

'I stayed for one year with Ibn Mas'ud 🌸; never did I hear him substantiate any statement towards Nabee 🌸. Whenever he did refer a matter towards a comment of Nabee 🌸, his body would start to tremble.'   (ibid.)

This was the caution of (Ibn Mas'ud 🌸 and the other) Sahābāh 🌸 in relating hadeeth because Nabee 🌸 has warned:

'Whomsoever falsely attributes something towards me, should prepare his abode in Hell.'   (ibid.)

Ibn Mas'ud 🌸 and the other Sahābāh were so wary of even accidentally relating something towards Nabee 🌸, whereas nowadays, without any research or qualification, people blurt out hadeeth and then have the audacity to vilify and criticise these noble Sahābāh!'

Nabee 🌸 also commented,

'Fear Allah regarding my Sahābāh. Do not make them a

target for vilification. Whomsoever loves them, loves them for my sake and; whomsoever hates them, hates them because of hatred for me. Whomsoever vexes them has vexed me and, whomsoever vexes me has vexed Allah. And whomsoever vexes Allah, soon will (such a person) be apprehended in (His) grip.'

'Regarding my Sahābāh, whomsoever shows partiality for my sake, will be able to reach me at the Fountain of Kauthar (on the Day of Qiyāmah). Moreover, whomsoever does not show partiality towards them for my sake, will not be able to reach me at the Fountain; such a person will only observe me from afar.' (p200, Virtues)

$\mathcal{S}$hah Abdul Azeez Dehlwee 🕮 writes,

'It is a firm belief of the Ahl-e-Sunnah that all the Sahābāh were 'ādil (just). This word has been employed repeatedly and, when my respected father Shāh Waleehullah Muhaddith Dehlwee 🕮 discussed this issue it became apparent that the word 'adālat is not used to imply some general quality, but it is used specifically for riwāyat (narration of) hadeeth. Nothing else is implied. The reality of this 'adālat is total abstention from falsehood in narrating hadeeth. We have carefully studied the seerahs of the Sahābāh...to the extent of scrutinising even the lives of those Sahābees who became involved in mutual disputes; we have come to understood that even they considered the malpractice of attributing anything (false) towards Nabee 🕮 as a grave criminal wrong. This is why they strenuously refrained.' (Vol.5, p24, Seerah)

Despite extreme caution in quoting hadeeth, 'Abdullah ibn

Masʿud ﷺ prophetic training and appointment as a *Muʿallim* (tutor) for the Ummah resulted in him narrating a staggering 848 ahadeeth; of which 64 appear in both Bukhāree & Muslim Shareef; whilst 21 appear in Bukhāree and 35 appear in Muslim. ʿAbdullah ibn Masʿud ﷺ is also acknowledged by scholars as being one of the founding Sahābāh of the science of Fiqh, especially that of the Hanafee School. When he was appointed the *Qādhi* of Kufa, the responsibility of imparting *tāleem* of Deen was also delegated to him. Accordingly, he established a *halqah-e-dars* (lecture programme) wherein fiqh *masāʿeels* were deduced and propagated. Within a short time, the whole of Iraq became his followers in fiqh.

Ijmā of the Ummah & the Tābiʿeen

Nabee ﷺ commented, 'In my Ummah, those people are the best who have met me (i.e. my Sahābāh); thereafter, those who have met them (i.e. the Tābiʿeen); then those who have met them (the Tabeʾ Tābiʿeen).'

(Vol. 7, p11, Seerah Sahābāh)

With regards to physical, *ʿilmi* and practical *khidmat* (aid) of Deen, it is obvious that the recipients of the praises in this hadeeth are the three groups of *Khairul Qurun* (Golden Early Age of Islām, c624-850CE): the Sahābāh; the Tābiʿeen; (and their students) the Tabeʾ Tābiʿeen. Islām was most respected, glorious, powerful and dominant during this period. Why? Because, these noble souls had directly benefited and acted upon the Teachings of our Nabee ﷺ. Hāfiz Abul Fadhl ʿIraqee ﷺ defines a Tābiʿee as that person who had met a Sahābee ﷺ even though he was not able to stay in his company.

'Alqamah (ibn Mas'ud) ﷺ

uring the Khilaafat of 'Umar bin 'Abdu'l-Azeez ﷺ (98-101AH), he had, with prudence and caution initiated the compilation in writing of Ahadeeth. This proved to be the catalyst for the great Islāmic 'Ilmi literary publication revolution which was to follow.

Amongst the numerous students of 'Abdullah ibn Mas'ud ﷺ, 'Alqamāh bin Qais (d. 62 AH) ﷺ, who was born during the time of Nabee ﷺ occupies a distinguished rank and is regarded as one of the leading Tābi'een. He was fortunate to study from leading Sahābāh such as: *Umm al-Mu'mineen 'Ā'ishah,* 'Umar, 'Ali, Hudhayfah ibn al-Yaman, Salmān al-Fārsi, Aboo Darda Ansāri, etc., ﷺ. However, it is from Ibn Mas'ud ﷺ that he derived the greatest benefit and who relates, 'Whatever I know and read, all of it 'Alqamāh also knows and reads.' (Vol.7 p395, Seerah) Leading scholars have testified to the *'Ilmi* excellence of 'Alqamāh ﷺ. He was unique in commanding expertise in the 'Uloom of the Glorious Qur'ān, Hadeeth and Fiqh. Hāfiz Zahabee ﷺ relates, 'He was a faqeeh and Imām...' Ibn Mas'ud ﷺ would ask 'Alqamāh ﷺ to recite the Glorious Qur'ān and comment...

> *'May my parents be sacrificed upon you! Keep reciting with a sweet voice for I have heard Rasoolullah ﷺ say, 'Husne Sawt (good voice) is the zeenat (beauty) of the Qur'ān.'*
> (p396, ibid.)

'Alqamāh ﷺ also possessed an outstanding memory, whatever he studied once would be remembered lifelong as if scribed on paper. Accordingly, his stay in the company of leading Sahābāh allowed him to build a huge treasure-house of hadeeth and earn the title *kaseer-ul-hadeeth* and the accolade, 'Alqamāh Ibn Mas'ud.' His status was so elevated that after the death of 'Abdullah ibn Mas'ud ☙, not only the laity, but also senior Sahābāh would approach him to seek *masā'eel* - a great acknowledgement for a Tābi'ee. In character and behaviour...

> *'Abdullah ibn Mas'ud ☙ was a reflection of Nabee ☙ in character, habit and disposition. And, 'Alqamāh was a reflection of Ibn Mas'ud ☙...and whomsoever had not observed the (Nabee & Sahābee) could observe their mirror image in the behaviour and personality of 'Alqamāh ☙.'*
>
> (p398, ibid.)

Recitation of the Glorious Qur'ān was his preoccupation. He would complete a *khatam* (recitation) every six days and sometimes in one night. Once when he arrived at the Ka'bah in Makkah, he completed one *khatam* whilst making Tawaf! He was also fortunate to be a member of the Jamā'at which enacted the Prophesy of Nabee ☙ in 32 AH, by storming Constantinople with Ameer Mu'aweeyah ☙. Despite his huge popularity, he abhorred fame and publicity preferring to teach in seclusion. When he was about to pass-away in Kufa in 62 AH, he requested:

> *'At the time of death, make talqeen of the Kaleemah so that my final words are 'There is no God but Allah...' and do not notify people of my death, for people may resort to acts of ignorance. Make haste in my burial...'* (p401, ibid.)

This servant of Islām left hundreds of students of whom his nephews Ibrāheem Nakha'ee ☙ and Aswad bin Yazeed ☙ are the most famous deputies.

Ibrāheem Nakha'ee ﷺ

uring childhood, Ibrāheem Nakha'ee ﷺ was fortunate to attend the *majlis* of *Umm al-Mu'mineen* 'Ā'ishah ؤ with his paternal uncle 'Alqamah ؤ and maternal uncle Aswad bin Yazeed ؤ. The company of such noble and distinguished 'Ilmi personalities from a young age nurtured him to become one of the leading scholars of his era. He was an accomplished Hāfiz of hadeeth who studied under such leading scholars as 'Alqamah, Aswad, Masrooq, Hammam, Qādhi Shurayh, etc., ؤ. However, it is in the science of fiqh wherein he became an Imām earning the titles, *Faqeeh-e-'Iraq* & *Faqeeh-e-Kufa*. He was held in such high esteem that leading scholars of the time would divert people towards Ibrāheem Nakha'ee ؤ and ask to be informed of his reply. Despite these excellences, he was reluctant to mention his 'Uloom. He would never reveal his knowledge without being asked, for he considered Deeni 'Ilm to be a grave responsibility commenting:

'There was once a time when people were afraid to make Tafseer of the Glorious Qur'ān whilst nowadays whomsoever wishes appoints himself as a mufassir. Personally, I wish that I did not have to make a single 'Ilmi statement...woe upon the day I qualified as a Faqeeh, for I have observed people who, when in a gathering, would not even reveal their most treasured ahadeeth...Remember, whomsoever utters even a single statement to incline people towards him, then as a consequence he will fall straight into Hell. What then to say of a person, whose intention from beginning to end is corrupted?' (p21, ibid.)

Despite his esteem and respect, he was the model of humility. Informal and simple in living, he would not even lean against anything when sitting down. Sometimes, he would even lift and carry the load of others saying, 'I do so to acquire reward in the Ākhirah.' Nevertheless, he commanded such awe that people behaved in his presence as if standing before a king. He mingled with laity and nobles alike, aiding anybody where possible, however, he made a point of distancing himself from tyrants. Accordingly, he acquired the wrath and enmity of the notorious Hajjaj bin Yousuf...and Ibrāheem Nakha'ee ﷺ did not hesitate to verbally lambaste him in public. When the time of his own death neared in 96 AH at the age of 50 years, he appeared apprehensive. Upon being asked, he replied,

> *'What greater danger is there than the present? For Allah's courier will be arriving with news of either Jannah or Hell. In lieu of (the fear of) this message, I prefer to stay in this present condition until the Day of Qiyāmah.'*   (ibid.)

Ibrāheem Nakha'ee's Pearls of Wisdom

1) *Whatever seerah (lifestyle) a man adopts for 40 years, then he is unable to change therefrom (unless Allah Wills otherwise).*

2) *After the nemat of Imān, the highest bounty bestowed to man is the ability to make sabr (patience) upon difficulties. This is why he did not consider it preferable to even mention illness saying, 'When an ill person is asked about his health, he should firstly say that, 'he is better,' and thereafter relate his state because to complain is also against the shan (feature) of sabr.*   (p26, ibid.)

Amongst his students is Hammad bin Sulaiman (d. 120 AH), the famous ustadh of Aboo Haneefah ﷺ.

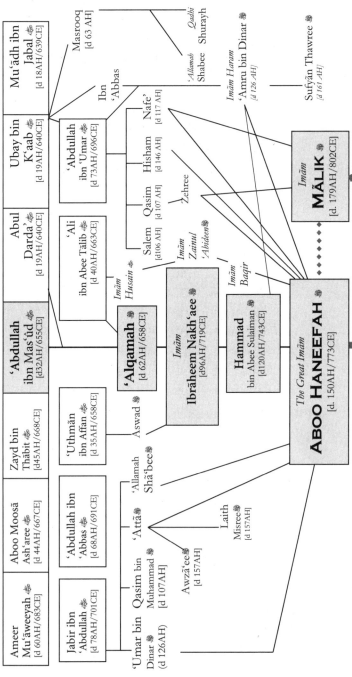

Fig 1: 'Ilmi Tree
of the Fuqaha
& Muhadditheen

Prophet Sayyidina
MUHAMMAD ﷺ
(d. 11AH/632CE)

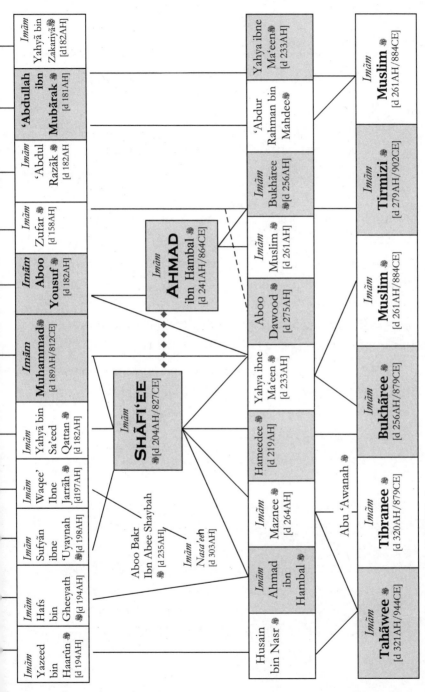

The Two Avenues of Da'wah

Da'wah (propagation) of Deen received through our Nabee ﷺ may be divided into two categories:

1) Tableegh (propagation & preservation) of the *Statements* of Nabuwwat.

2) Tableegh & Tashreeh (explanation) of the *Meanings* of the Statements of Nabuwwat.

The group which carry out the first task are known as *Muhadditheen*, whilst those who discharge the second responsibility (the elucidation of 'Ilm) are known as the *Fuqahā*. It is to this second group that the Qur'ānic term *'Ulul Amr'* applies. Why? Imām Jawzee ﷺ comments,

> *'Understand well! There appears fine and intricate matters in ahadeeth, which only those 'Ulamā are able to appreciate and comprehend who are Fuqahā...'*

Moreover, Nabee ﷺ commented,

> *'One Faqeeh is harder upon Shaytān than a thousand 'ābids (pious worshippers).'*

> *'With whomsoever Allah Ta'ālā desires Khair (goodness), He bestows upon him Tafaqquh fid Deen (understanding and fah'm of Deen).'*

> *'In my Ummah, two groups are such that when they behave properly the masses too behave properly, but when they misappropriate, the laity too misbehave. One group is the rulers, whilst the other group is that of the Fuqahā.'*

(p35-41, ibid.)

Chapter Two

ABOO

HANEEFAH

The Great Imām

(80—150 AH ~ 703—773 CE)

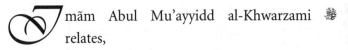

Imām Abul Mu'ayyidd al-Khwarzami ☀
relates,

'Imām Aboo Haneefah ☀ scrutinized every
branch of Deeni 'Ilm, until he (amassed) mountains of
'uloom. Thereafter, he (tackled) fiqh...which was
submerged in deep valleys and restricted to an elite few.
His benevolent temperament and the patronage of
Hammād bin Sulaiman ☀ enabled him to congregate
this 'uloom and present it (in the form of fatwās) for
the benefit of servants of Allah ☀.

Within a short time, because of his fiqh, he soared to
such heights that the hopes of all enviers were dashed.
Even deviated sects were constrained to follow him....
and the Great Imām ☀ guided them also towards the
Path of Haqq. Allah ☀ has Spoken the truth,

'For every nation, there is a Guide.'

(p237, Tazkiratul...)

Introduction

haykh Mufti 'Ashiq 'Ellahi Madanee 🌸 relates, 'It is
indeed a great Favour of Allah 🌸 upon this Ummah of
Muhammad 🌸 that He has undertaken to Protect His Kitāb
(the Glorious Qur'ān). There have always been 'Ulamā's
present to preserve, who have remembered and understood the
words and meaning of the Glorious Qur'ān - deducing
commands therefrom. Moreover, in order to accomplish this
task it was also necessary to preserve the *aqwāl* (statements),
af'āl (actions) and *taqreerāt* (lectures) of Nabee 🌸.

For this Allah 🌸 created such a Jamā'at of men who preserved
ahadeeth and passed it unto those students who became
leading 'ulamā's and propagators. They toiled to deduce
masā'eels from the Glorious Qur'ān and the Sunnah of Nabee
🌸. They comprehended and understood *nashikh* (annulments)
and *mansukh* (abolitions), clarified any apparent *ikhtilaf*
(differences). These people are known as the *A'imma-e-
Mujtahideen* and, although there were many, four amongst
them are synonymous: the Great Imām Aboo Haneefah 🌸 of
Kufa (d 150AH), his contemporary Imām Mālik 🌸 of
Madeenah (d 179AH); both of them met and benefited from
each other.

Thereafter arrived Imām Shāfi'ee 🌸 of Makkah (d 204 AH)
who studied Hadeeth from Imām Mālik 🌸. Imām Shāfi'ee 🌸
later travelled to Iraq and acquired expertise in fiqh from
Imām Muhammad 🌸, the distinguished student of the Great

Imām. Similarly, the fourth *A'imma*, Imām Ahmad ibn Hambal ﷺ (d 241 AH) was a student of Imām Shāfi'ee ﷺ who travelled to the Great Imām's other deputy, Imām Aboo Yousuf ﷺ. Imām Bukhāree ﷺ - who is titled *Ameerul Mu'mineen fil Hadeeth,* also studied Hanafee Fiqh. His comments are related in *Fathul Baree,*

> *'When I was 16 years old, I studied the kitabs of Ibn Mubārak ﷺ and Wakee' ﷺ, acknowledging the works of this School.'*

Both 'Abdullah ibn Mubārak ﷺ and Wakee' Ibne Jarrāh ﷺ are students of the Great Imām ﷺ. What need was there for all these later authorities to visit Kufa? Undoubtedly, it was to benefit from the 'Uloom of the Great Imām ﷺ. Modernists and enemies conveniently overlook this reality in an attempt to undermine the achievements of the Great Imām ﷺ. But, 'Whomsoever is jealous of light from the sun and, attempts to produce an alternative is in great danger.' Many have tried (in vain) to lower the esteem of the Great Imām ﷺ but are constrained to acknowledge,

> *'The high rank of Aboo Haneefah ﷺ is Divinely Bestowed - whomsoever Allah ﷻ elevates - none is able to lower him.'*
>
> (p19-30, Tazkiratul...)

Abdullah ibn Mubārak ﷺ commented,

> *'If we do not come across any explicit text of Nabee ﷺ or of the Sahābāh ﷺ on any religious issues, then according to us, the opinion of Imām Aboo Haneefah ﷺ is just like the Hadeeth of Rasoolullah ﷺ (as it would never contradict the Sunnah).'*
>
> (p9, Sunnah &...)

Birth of the Great Imām 爨

What is achieved if you are changed by the era (ẓamānah)?

For a great person is he who 'changes' the ẓamānah!'

mām Aboo Haneefah 爨 was born in 80 AH (703 CE), in Kufa, Iraq, during the rule of 'Abdul Malik bin Marwan. His real name is No'maan and Aboo Haneefah is his *kunyat*. Some weak reports base this title upon a daughter Haneefah, whilst others dispute this and say he had only one son named Hammad 爨 after his Ustadh. Other historians suggest 'Haneefah' is an 'Iraqee word for an ink pen whilst the most plausible explanation suggest *Haneefah* is based upon an Ayah from the Glorious Qur'ān.

Imām Aboo Haneefah's 爨 grandfather Zutā is reported to be of Persian origin and had converted to Islām. When the Great Imām's father Thabit 爨 was born, he was presented into the company of 'Ali 爨 who made du'aa for *barakat* (blessings). Thabit bin Zutā 爨 was a pious, intelligent and cultured person.

Thabit's son, Imām Aboo Haneefah 爨 was of average height, extremely handsome in appearance with an elegant beard, well civilised and mannered with a sweet voice. He was able to converse with great clarity and insight; commanding great awe and respect. He dressed elegantly, wore good shoes and was always clean and well perfumed. By nature, he spoke little and refrained from futile talk and acts.

Bashārat-e-Nabawee

Glad Tidings & Prophesy of Nabee

Shaykh 'Abdu'l-Qayyum Haqqānee *hafizahullah* relates from Saheeh Muslim...

'Aboo Hurayrah narrated, 'We were present in the Company of our Nabee when Sûrah Al-Jumu'ah (of the Glorious Qur'ān) was revealed and Nabee read out the Ayah:

'And (He has sent Prophet Muhammad also to) others amongst them (Muslims) who have not yet enjoined them (but will come). And He (Allah) is the All-Mighty, the All-Wise.'   (62:3)

From amongst those present, a person requested, 'O Rasoolullah ! Who are these 'other' people who have not yet joined us?'

Nabee briefly maintained silence, whereupon the questioner repeated his query. Placing his auspicious hand upon the shoulders of Salman al-Farsee , our Nabee commented:

'If Imān be near the Seven Stars and the Arabs are unable to stake it, even then one of his (Persian) people will be able to claim it.'   (p193, Episodes)

'Allamah Jalālluddeen Suyutee and Hāfiz Ibn Hajar and other 'Ulamā relate this as an authentic Hadeeth, similar to the Prophetic Prophesies relating to the appearance of Imām Mālik and Imām Shāfi'ee .

Meeting some of the Sahābāh ﷺ

mām Aboo Haneefah ﷺ was fortunate to meet in Kufa the famous Anas bin Mālik ﷺ, the Close Khādim (associate) of our Nabee ﷺ.

Shaykh Badre 'Ālam ﷺ mentions the names of four Sahābees whom the Imām met:

1) Anas bin Mālik ﷺ ~ in Kufa

2) Abdullah bin Abee Awnee ﷺ ~ also in Kufa

3) Suhayl bin Sa'd al Sa'dee ﷺ ~ in Madeenah

4) Abul Tufayl Amir bin Wathila ﷺ - in Makkah

Other scholars have reported the Great Imām's meeting with the following Sahābāh also: 'Umar bin Hāreeth ﷺ, 'Abdullah bin Hāreeth bin Jaz'a ﷺ, Jabir bin 'Abdullah ﷺ, Abdullah bin Anais ﷺ, Watheelah bin Asqaa' ﷺ, M'uaqqal bin Yasaar ﷺ and 'Ā'ishāh binte 'Ajru ﷺ.

Once Imām Aboo Haneefah ﷺ entered the company of Imām J'āfar bin Muhammad Sādeeq ﷺ who commented,

> *'It appears that you will be reviving and rejuvenating the Sunnahs of my Grandfather (Nabee) ﷺ. You will become a shelter for every distressed person, the anguish of every complainant will be addressed; when the bewildered and depressed will stand aghast...they will walk in your shadow; when all appears lost, you will nurture and guide towards the Clear and Straight Path.'* (p77, Tazkiratul)

Youth & Tālib 'Ilmi (Student) Phase

$\mathcal{A}$lthough Imām Aboo Haneefah 🕮 grew up in Kufa at a time when a number of Sahābāh 🕮 were still present, nevertheless nobody inclined him towards Deeni Knowledge. He therefore spent his early youth in trade. Once the young Aboo Haneefah 🕮 was passing the residence of Imām Sh'ābee 🕮 when he called him over, 'Where are you off to?' 'To such-and-such a place,' replied Aboo Haneefah 🕮. Imām Sh'ābee 🕮 commented, 'I am not asking about the bazaar, but of the 'Ulamā...incline towards 'Ilm and the Company of the 'Ulamā; for I perceive promise and talent within you!'

This 'divinely inspired' message so influenced the young Aboo Haneefah 🕮 that he immediately stopped visiting the bazaar and debating (in which he was an expert) and commenced Deeni Studies at 20 years of age.

One day, a women arrived and asked a question, 'A man has a wife whom he wishes to divorce in accordance to the teachings of the Sharee'ah, what is the correct way?' Embarrassed at being unable to answer, the young Aboo Haneefah 🕮 replied, 'Ask Hammād bin Abee Sulaiman and let me also know the answer.' When the lady returned and conveyed Hammād's 🕮 reply, immediately Aboo Haneefah 🕮 picked up his shoes and proceeded to Hammād's 🕮 *Majlis* which was in the same neighbourhood. Within a short time, he amassed a wealth of knowledge, fully understanding, remembering and revising the *masā'eel* which Hammād 🌸 daily imparted. He was so impressed by Aboo Haneefah's 🌸 quest, dedication, memory, intelligence and comprehension that he ordered, 'None except Aboo Haneefah is to sit in front of me!' For 20 years, Aboo Haneefah 🌸 diligently attended these lectures and when the need arose for Hammād 🌸 to depart for Basra, he deputed Aboo Haneefah 🌸 in his place for 2 months. During his absence, Aboo Haneefah 🌸 replied to over 80 *masā'eels,* carefully writing them down. Upon Hammād's 🌸 return, these replies were presented to him; he agreed with 40 and amended the others.

Other Prominent Ustādhs of the Great Imām 🌸

Shaykh Mufti Taqee 'Uthmānee *dāmat barakātuhum* relates, 'Amongst the Great Imām's prominent ustadhs are those who are regarded as *'Pillars of the Ilm of Hadeeth'* during the era of the Tābi'een. Imām Sh'ābee 🌸 is reported to have learnt Hadeeth (by memory) from over 500 Sahābāh. Once he was relating one of the *ghazwāt's* (battles) of our Nabee 🌸, when the Sahābee 'Abdullah bin 'Umar 🌸 passed by and overhearing the narration commented, 'I was personally with Nabee 🌸 in these *ghazwāt's,* however, Sh'ābee has more knowledge of these *ghazwāt's* than I have.' Ali bin Al-Madanee 🌸 relates,

> *'The 'Ilm of Ibn Mas'ûd's* 🌸 *'uloom terminates upon* '*Alqāmah, Aswad, Harith, 'Amru and 'Ubaydah bin Qais* 🌸*. And the 'Uloom of these noble personalities ends upon two people: Ibraaheem Nakha'ee* 🌸 *and 'Amir Sh'ābee* 🌸 *(and both are regarded as Ustadhs of the Great Imām* 🌸*).'*

(Vol.1, p. 94, Dars-e-Tirmizee)

Teaching Career & Ifta'ā

n 96 AH, after the death of Ibrāheem Nakha'ee ﷺ, the gaze of Kufan's turned towards Mufti Hammad bin Aboo Sulaiman ﷺ. When he died in 120AH/743CE, despite efforts to succeed his son, other 'Ulamā proposed and approached the relatively young Aboo Haneefah ﷺ, who replied, 'I do not wish to see Deeni 'Uloom ending or suffering (by unnecessary delays and turmoil).' So saying, he bravely accepted the post of *Tadrees* (teaching) and *Ifta'ā* (passing of official rulings and decrees). The Great Imām ﷺ was wealthy and independent by trade; generous and benevolent by nature; he therefore devoted his full energies towards the backbreaking task of solving and caring for the problems of the masses. Abul Waleed ﷺ relates,

> *'Undoubtedly the Great Imām ﷺ was young in age, nevertheless people found in him all those great qualities which were lacking in his contemporaries and even predecessors. Consequently, they disassociated from others and inclined towards him, now great 'Ulamā's attended his company and subsequently great Scholars of the calibre of Aboo Yousuf, Asad bin 'Amru, Qāsim bin Mu'an, Zufar bin Hazeel ﷺ...were born in Kufa. The Great Imām ﷺ taught them 'Ilm of Fiqh with great dedication, affection and compassion.'* (p238, Tazkiratul...)

As the Great Imām's ﷺ popularity, fame, appeal and support increased so did the enmity of enviers...

> *'You will only find people of true excellence being envied, for those bereft of virtues & good character have no hasid!'*

Divine Selection

Despite his huge popularity, Aboo Haneefah 🌸 shunned publicity, preferring to keep aloof and adopted a low profile. However, Allah 🌸 had willed differently, the Great Imām 🌸 observed a dream wherein he was digging the Blessed Grave of our Nabee 🌸, collecting the bones and placing them upon his chest. Terrified at having viewed such a dream, he cried and was deeply saddened. He completely stopped teaching...people began to visit him assuming some illness. Eventually, they found out the reason for his aloofness and related this dream to the famous Imām and interpreter of dreams 'Allamah Muhammad Ibn Sireen 🌸, who replied,

'If what you relate is haqq, then in matters of the Sunnah, you will undertake such tasks which nobody before you has achieved, moreover you will delve very deeply into 'Ilm.'

In another dream, our Nabee 🌸 appeared and commanded,

'O Aboo Haneefah! Allah Ta'ālā has created you for reviving my Sunnah, never make an intention to seclude and remain aloof.' (p56, Episodes…)

As soon as the Great Imām 🌸 heard these *bashaarats* (glad tidings), he felt revitalized and launched himself body and soul in the service of Deeni 'Ilm and the creation of Allah 🌸.

'The Great Imām's daytime was spent in dars, tadrees and the service of creation for waqf,

Whilst nights were spent in the worship of Allah Ta'ālā for waqf.'

(p62, ibid.)

Worshipper of the Night

aqee' ❀ commented, 'I have never met an 'alim who was a greater faqee' or who prayed salāh better than Imām Aboo Haneefah ❀.' The Great Imām ❀ was the epitome of piety, *taqwa, zuhd* (abstention), an affectionately mild temperament and ever-willing to help his Muslim brethren. Asad bin 'Amr ❀ relates,

> *'For forty years, Imām Aboo Haneefah ❀ performed Fajr Salāh with the same wudhu with which he had prayed 'Esha Salāh...he generally completed the whole of the Glorious Qur'ān during the night in one rakaat!'* (p56, ibid.)

After Zuhr, he used to sleep for a while, citing how our Nabee ❀ had advised to seek help for awakening at night (for Tahajjud) by sleeping *qailullah* (mid-day nap). In Ramadhān, his routine changed, whereby he completed one *khatm* of the Glorious Qur'ān by day and one by night...with some reports recording over 70 *khatms* during the blessed month!

When the Great Imām ❀ passed-away, his neighbour's little child asked, 'Father! Upon Imām Aboo Haneefah's ❀ balcony there was a pillar visible, what has happened to it?' With sorrow, the neighbour replied,

> *'Dear child! There was no column there, rather the pillar of the Sharee'ah, Imām Aboo Haneefah ❀ used to pray to Allah ❀ the whole night upon that balcony. Now the column has fallen...in that the Great Imām ❀ has passed-away.'*

Imām Aboo Yousuf ❀ relates, 'Once I was walking with Imām

Aboo Haneefah ❀ when some people upon observing us, pointed towards the Great Imām ❀ and commented, 'This is the very Imām Aboo Haneefah ❀ who worships Allah ﷻ the whole night, never sleeping!' This statement reached the ears of the Great Imām ❀ who commented,

> *'Subhānallah! Do you not hear what Allah ﷻ has spread about me amongst people? Therefore, how shameful would it be if these qualities were not within us. Wallah! These people are not saying anything about me which is untrue!'*

Recitation of Whole Qur'ān in the Ka'bah

Whilst Imām Aboo Haneefah ❀ performed a total of 55 Hajj during his life; on the last occasion, he requested and was granted permission from the *khuddam* (supervisors) of the Holy Ka'bah to enter the *Baytullah*. Once inside, he commenced two rakaats salāh wherein he completed a *khatm* of the Glorious Qur'ān. Thereafter, he made du'aa,

> *'O Allah! This weak servant testifies to Your Perfect Ma'arifat (Quality of Greatness and Knowledge) as is Your right to be recognised. However, as is Your right and Sovereignty to be worshipped I have been unable to do so. Therefore, O Creator, overlook the faults of this weak servant through the Glory and Majesty of Your Perfect Honour and Greatness.'*

From a corner of the Holy Ka'bah, an unseen voice was heard,

> *'O Aboo Haneefah! You have recognised Us as was Our due; moreover, in the way that you have rendered service to Our Deen, have We forgiven you and all those who follow your Mazhab (creed). And, whomsoever, until Qiyāmah follows you, We have forgiven all of them also.'*

Foundation & Feature of the Hanafee School of Fiqh

Imām Aboo Haneefah ﷺ relates,

'(In formulating Deeni Masā'eel), firstly I study the Glorious Qur'ān of Allah ﷻ, if no specific ruling be found I turn towards the Sunnah of Rasoolullah ﷺ.

If still unclear, I incline towards the statements of the Sahābāh-e-Kirām ﷺ. Should these be various, I select the one most appropriate...however, I never go beyond their judgements...nevertheless, if still unsure I consider the judgements of (our predecessors): Ibrāheem Nakha'ee, Sh'ābee, Ibn Seereen, Hasan al-Basree, 'Attā' ibn Abee Rabah, Sa'eed bin Musayyeb, ﷺ etc. Because these personalities had made judgements, like them I too make Ijtihaad.'

Understand well, the Hanafee School of Fiqh is not the opinion of one person, rather the findings of a *Majlis-e-Shurā* (Consultative Board) which consisted of 40 outstandingly pious 'Ulamā's. Some of these brilliant Scholars were: Aboo Yousuf, Zufar bin Hazeel, Dāwood Ta'i, Asad bin 'Amr, Yousuf bin Khalid (the Shaykh of Imam Shafi'ee ﷺ), Yahyā bin Zakariyyā. Imām Asad bin 'Amr ﷺ relates,

'Whenever a masalah was presented in the service of the Great Imām; a discussion would take place with various opinions being given. Thereafter he would select the most in-depth and appropriate view; in this way each masalah would be debated upon for 3 days...before being decreed and written down.'

Incorrect Reports & Jealousy

A bdullah Ibne Mubārak ♔relates, 'When I visited Imām Awzā'ee ♔ in Syria, he asked, 'Who is this *bidatee* (deviated) person by the name of Aboo Haneefah?' Distressed, I returned to my lodgings and for 3 days researched the *masā'eels* of (my Ustadh) preparing a document wherein were related the 'Decrees of No'maan.' Thereafter, I returned to Imām Awzā'ee ♔ (who was both Mu'azzin and Imām of his Masjid) and presented the kitab. After reading, he asked, 'O Abdullah! Who is this No'maan?' I replied, 'A Shaykh of Iraq... whom I have met.' Imām Awzā'ee ♔ was so impressed with the *masā'eel's* he replied, 'O Abdullah! This person appears to be a very high Scholar, return to him and learn yet more 'Ilm!' 'Abdullah ibn Mubārak ♔ replied, 'Shaykh! This is the very same Aboo Haneefah whom you had advised me not to meet!''

From this and similar incidents we are able to comprehend the consequence of hearsay and second-hand reports. Whenever a person excels others (especially in the Deeni arena); just as there are people who admire, encourage, applaud and appreciate the work being extracted from this person by Allah ﷻ, there are always a few others, who because of personal failings and jealousy resort to *gheebat* and character assassination in an evil attempt to 'pour water over the efforts of others.' Relates the Great Imām ♔,

> *'If people wish to be jealous of me they may do so, because even before me people have always begrudged the Ahl-e-Fadhl. This attitude of ours too will remain, because within us, the majority have perished drowned in jealousy.'*

Abstention from 'Gheebat

'That Imām in whose heart gigantic 'uloom is present, worldly mountains appear as mere pebbles in his presence!'

Nowadays, *'gheebat* (backbiting) is a rampant and fashionable habit, which exists at all strata's of our *muaasharat* (society). The elite as well as laity are drowned in this abominable vice and the media serve to further inflame this malady. Imām Aboo Haneefah ﷺ totally opposed and frowned upon *'gheebat* thanking Allah ﷻ....

'Alhamdulillah! Allah ﷻ has saved my tongue from the impurity of this misfortune.'

Once an associate commented, 'Shaykh! Some people say a lot of bad things about you, yet we do not hear any comments from you about them?' Imām Aboo Haneefah ﷺ replied,

'This is indeed the Fadhl (Favour) of Allah ﷻ; He blesses whomsoever He wishes...'

Once a person mentioned to Imām Sufyān Thāwree ﷺ, 'I have never heard Imām Aboo Haneefah ﷺ making *'gheebat* about anybody?' He replied,

'Aboo Haneefah is not so stupid as to go and destroy his own ā'amāle sālihāh (good deeds) by indulging in 'gheebat.'

The Great Imām ﷺ once informed a confidante,

'If I were to make 'gheebat about anybody, it would be about my mother, for then the nemat (reward of my good deeds) would remain within the household.'

Abstention from Futility

*O*nce a person requested, 'In acquiring Fiqh, which acts serve as *mu'een* (aids)?' Imām Aboo Haneefah ﷺ replied, 'Attentiveness and freedom from unnecessary thoughts.' The person probed, 'How is attentiveness achieved?' 'Reduce relationships and associations.' 'How is this possible?' The Great Imām ﷺ replied, 'A person should take necessary things and forgo the unnecessary.' Another person asked, 'How did you benefit from *'Ilm* of Fiqh?' The Imām ﷺ replied,

> *'In propagating and teaching 'Ilm, I have never resorted to stinginess and in acquiring 'Ilm I never adopted laziness, indifference, evasion, objections or aversion.'* (p80, ibid.)

Dawood Ta'i ﷺ relates,

> *'I stayed for 20 years in the company of Imām Aboo Haneefah ﷺ and never once observed him stretching his legs or without his head covered, whether in public or private! Once I asked him, 'Shaykh! If you were to occasionally stretch your legs in private, what harm is there?'*

The Great Imām ﷺ replied, 'To maintain *adab* (respect for Allah ﷻ) in private is greater in rank than in public.' Once a person intending for Hajj visited Imām Aboo Haneefah ﷺ and requested some advise regarding which du'aa to recite when observing the Ka'bah on the first occasion (when du'aa's are assured acceptance). The Great Imām ﷺ replied, '...Make du'aa to become *mustajābat da'wat* (a person whose du'aa's are always accepted). If this du'aa is accepted, no du'aa will remain which will not be accepted.'

Abstention from Doubtful

*O*nce a stolen lamb inadvertently became attached to the flocks of sheep belonging to the herdsmen of Kufa. It was impossible to trace the stolen animal and return it to its owner; therefore the possibility existed of meat from this animal being sold in the bazaars of Kufa. Imām Aboo Haneefah ﷺ made inquiries, 'How long does a lamb live?' 'For 7 years.' Accordingly, he abstained from eating mutton for 7 years in Kufa!

Hafs bin 'Ghiyath ﷺ was a partner in the Great Imām's cloth business. Once he was sent on a trade errand wherein Imām Aboo Haneefah ﷺ clearly and repeatedly pointed out a small defect in a roll of cloth - something to be brought to any prospective purchasers attention. However, at the time of sale, Hafs ﷺ genuinely forgot to highlight this defect. The sale and business venture was completed and he returned to present the Great Imām with a profit of 30,000 dinars. Immediately, he queried, whether the defect had been shown to the customer. When Hafs bin 'Ghiyath ﷺ admitted to his error, Imām Aboo Haneefah ﷺ dismissed him as his business partner and donated the entire 30,000 dinars to charity in order to be fully saved from the possibility of employing doubtful income.

Once the Great Imām observed a soldier eating some meat and throwing the leftovers into the river of Kufa. Imām Aboo Haneefah ﷺ inquired from experienced fishermen the lifespan of freshwater fish. For this period of time he refrained from eating fish on the assumption the soldier had misappropriated the meat!

Legendary Patience

A bdu'l-Razzāq ☀ relates, 'I have never witnessed a more patient or tolerant person than the Great Imām ☀. Once he was sitting with students and associates in the Masjid-An-Khayf when a visitor from Basra posed a question. Imām Aboo Haneefah ☀ gave a lengthy and detailed reply, upon which the visitor commented, 'Yes, but Imām Hasan Basree's ☀ opinion is so-and-so.' The Great Imām ☀ replied, 'Imām Hasan ☀ appears to have erred.' Immediately, another person arose and shouted out, 'O the son of a whore! How dare you suggest that Hasan has made a mistake!' Many of those present turned red at this insulting remark and were rolling up their sleeves to manhandle this person out of the Masjid...when the Great Imām ☀ silenced everybody. Thereafter he lowered his head and with great dignity replied,

> *'Yes, Imām Hasan has erred and 'Abdullah bin Mas'ûd has related correctly...in the manner he had heard from Nabee ☀.'*
> (p130, Episodes...)

Whenever anybody behaved in an uncouth or uncivilized manner, the Great Imām ☀ always responded with dignity, big-heartedness and magnanimity. Once, a young man started shouting and swearing at the Imām ☀ whilst he was teaching in the Masjid. Unable to ruffle the Great Imām ☀ in public, the young man followed all the way home...in expectation of entangling him in a slanging match. However, the Great Imām ☀ calmly continued walking with his head lowered listening to the abuse being directed at him. Arriving home, he stood at the doorway of his house and to the surprise and amazement of the abuser commented, 'Well brother, we have arrived at my house, before I enter if you have anything further to add I am perfectly willing to wait and let you say it to your heart's content.' On another occasion, a wretched person harbouring ill-will, hatred and jealousy arrived and slapped the Great Imām ﷺ. With great tolerance and dignity, he replied,

> '*Brother, I too am capable of slapping you but will not do so. I could complain to the Khaleefh, but will not do so. At Tahajjud time, I could complain to Allah ﷻ but will not do so. Rather, if on the Day of Qiyāmah I achieve success and my plea is accepted I shall not place a step into Jannah without you!*'   (p169, Episodes…)

Shaykh Maseehullah Khan ﷺ related, 'Once a person followed Imām Aboo Haneefah ﷺ home from the masjid after Zuhr Salāh and deliberately waited until the Great Imām ﷺ had climbed the several flights of stairs to his apartment and laid down to rest. He began to bang the door loudly; the Great Imām ﷺ opened his upstairs window... 'I wish to ask a mas'alah?' The Imām ﷺ dressed and walked all the way down to open the door, 'O dear, I forgot what I was going to ask!' Calmly, Imām Aboo Haneefah ﷺ exchanged greetings and made his way back up to sleep. When he had settled, there was another violent knock, again he opened the window... 'I have remembered!' Once more, the Great Imām ﷺ dressed and walked all the way down to open the door. 'Tell me Shaykh, what is the taste of faeces?' Despite the absurdity of the question, Imām Aboo Haneefah ﷺ kept his composure and replied, 'Well, fresh stool is somewhat 'sweet' compared to dry faeces.' The visitor remarked, 'How do you know? It would appear you must have tasted manure!' Unperturbed, the Imām ❀ replied, 'We are able to make this deduction after observing the behaviour of flies: they congregate and sit upon fresh manure, yet keep well away from dried dung.' Immediately, this person fell at the feet of the Imām ❀ and apologised saying, 'Shaykh, forgive me, I had adopted such rudeness and ill-manners to test whether indeed, as is mentioned and well-known, you are the most tolerant and forgiving person living in all of Arabia.'

Another incident; living next door to the Great Imām ❀ was a shoemaker who worked during the day; drinking wine and singing when he arrived home in the evening. The sound of his bellowing would reach the Imām ❀ as he prayed throughout the night. Once, the singing stopped for a few nights and the Great Imām inquired from people of the neighbourhood as to what had happened. They informed him that the shoemaker had been arrested and thrown in jail. Immediately, Imām Aboo Haneefah ❀ proceeded to visit the Chief Police Officer, who received him with surprise, respect, courtesy and true delight at this rare honour. The Imām requested his neighbours release, whereupon the Chief immediately waived the charge and set him free. As the Imām ❀ was returning home, the shoemaker followed meekly behind...when the Imām ❀ remarked, 'O young man! I have let you down.' The shoemaker replied, 'Never! You have been very considerate and protective, may Allah grant you the best of rewards for having aided and interceded on behalf of a neighbour.' Thereafter, he repented and never ever drank alcohol again. He became a regular attendant to the *Majlis* of the Imām...and went on to become a great Faqeeh!'   (p375, Tazkiratul...)

Abstention from Adulation

haykh Ashraf 'Ali Thānwi ﷺ relates, 'During the time of 'Abbasid rule, a king had proclaimed a deed of gift which needed to be countersigned. The king ordered this document be sent to all the 'ulamā...accordingly, all signed without any hesitation. However, when the deed was brought into the *khidmat* of the Great Imām ﷺ, he commented,

> 'For the affidavit to be valid, the witness needs to be present. Until I physically hear the proposal and acceptance of the parties I cannot countersign and for this, two options are possible: either they arrive here and propose in front of me, or I travel there. As I am in no need of going there, it is appropriate they come here.'

When the king was informed of this reply, he summoned the Qādhi and inquired whether this was a true *mas'alah*. When the Qādhi confirmed this principle, the king spoke, 'Then why did you countersign?' The Judge replied, 'Out of your fear.' Immediately the king dismissed him saying, 'You people are not worthy of being Qādhi, Imām Aboo Haneefah (ﷺ) is the only person fit for this post...' Accordingly, he dispatched a request to the Great Imām ﷺ to become the Chief Qādhi but, Imām Aboo Haneefah ﷺ openly refused because of the warnings sounded in ahadeeth regarding rulership saying, 'I will not be able to uphold the *huqooqs* (rights) of this post. Yes, should it be certain that in my refusal, Muslims would suffer *zulm* (oppression), then it would be compulsory for me to accept the post.' It appears in hadeeth:

> 'Whomsoever has been appointed a Qādhi is as if been slaughtered without a knife.'   (V. 30, p166, Khair...)

Love for Acting upon Hadeeth

Imām 'Amr bin Hushaym ☙ relates, 'Once I visited the Great Imām ☙ in the masjid at 'Asr time. He prayed and stayed in the masjid from 'Asr up to 'Esha Salāh, after which he took me home and we ate together. Thereafter, he arranged for my bedding and as I laid down to sleep he retired to a corner and prayed Salāh the whole night.

At Fajr time, he awoke me and placed a jug of water for my *wudhu*. We proceeded to the masjid and prayed Fajar Salāh, after which he remained sitting in his place engaged in *zikr...* when suddenly a snake fell from the masjid rafters upon him. Immediately, without the slightest panic, the Great Imām ☙ placed his feet and pinned the snake's head to the ground and continued to sit with great composure reciting the praises and glories of Allah ﷻ! When the sun had risen, he recited:

> *'All praises are for Allah ﷻ Who has arisen the sun from its place. O Allah! Grant us its goodness and the blessings of those items upon which shine its rays.'*

He then ordered the snake be killed: whilst he continued to sit with serenity, tranquillity and reverence engaged in *zikr*. After he had performed *ishraq salāh,* he related a Hadeeth:

> *'Whomsoever, after praying Fajr Salāh until sunrise does not mention with his tongue anything except the Zikr of Allah Ta'ālā, is similar to a Mujāhid-fee-Sabeelillah (the person who strives in the Path of Allah).'* (p67, Episodes...)

From countless such episodes, it is possible to gauge the enthusiasm, determination and bravery of the Great Imām to follow every Hadeeth of our Nabee ☙.

Meeting with Imām Bāqar ﷺ

*I*mām Aboo Haneefah ﷺ once met Imām Bāqar ﷺ in Madeenah Munnawwarah. The latter had received false reports of the Great Imām ﷺ and was thus suspicious of him. He therefore inquired, 'Are you the very same Aboo Haneefah who has changed my Grandfather's Deen (by adopting and preferring *qiyas* as an *usool* over clear cut Qur'ānic and Hadeeth Injunctions)?' With great respect and dignity the Great Imām ﷺ replied, 'Shaykh, please be seated so that I may convey the correct principles in your company.' Thereafter, Imām Aboo Haneefah ﷺ sat down with respect akin to a *taalib-'ilm* sitting in front of his teacher.

Imām Aboo Haneefah ﷺ: *Shaykh! Inform us, who is weaker, the woman or man?*

Imām Bāqar ﷺ: *Women.*

Imām Aboo Haneefah ﷺ: *Inform us, what share is there for women and men?*

Imām Bāqar ﷺ: *Men receive two shares, whilst ladies receive one.*

Imām Aboo Haneefah ﷺ: *Shaykh, had I adopted qiyas as has been incorrectly related to you, then because of the weakness of women I would have decreed two shares for them. Shaykh! Inform us, which is afdhal (higher in rank), salāh or saum?*

Imām Bāqar ﷺ: *Salāh is afdhal.*

Imām Aboo Haneefah ﷺ: *Shaykh, had I adopted qiyas, then I would have decreed that women were to make qadha (repeat) the salāh missed during the days of haidh (menstruation) rather than saum because salāh is more afdhal than saum.*

Imām Aboo Haneefah 🌸: *Inform us, which is greater in impurity, manee (semen) or urine?*

Imām Bāqar 🌸: *Urine.*

Imām Aboo Haneefah 🌸: *Shaykh, had I adopted qiyās, then I would have decreed it wājib (compulsory) to make ghusl (bathe) after urinating and to make only wudhu fardh after discharge of manee...but I have not done so!*

Upon this, Imām Bāqar 🌸 arose from his place and acknowledging the integrity of the Great Imām 🌸 kissed him upon his forehead.   (p164, Episodes...)

Great Imām in the Lap of our Prophet 🌸

Shaykh Bu 'Ali 🌸 relates, 'I was once sleeping near the grave of Bilāl al-Habashi 🌸 in Damascus, when I observed a dream wherein I was in Makkah Mukarramah where Nabee 🌸 entered through *Bab Ibne Shaybah* affectionately carrying a venerably aged person in his 🌸 lap. Judging my amazement and wonder, Nabee 🌸 replied,

'*This is Aboo Haneefah, Imām of the Muslims and a resident of your country ('Iraq).*'

Remember, it appears in Hadeeth that Nabee 🌸 commented:

'*Whomsoever has observed me in a dream has indeed witnessed me; for Shaytān is unable to appear in my form.*'

(Bukhāree quoted p165, Episodes...)

Yahyā Ibne Ma'een 🌸 commented:

'*Aboo Haneefah 🌸 was a very reliable narrator. I haven't heard any of the muhadditheen commenting negatively regarding his reliability.*'   (p10, Sunnat &...)

Abundance of Isti'ghfār & Tilāwat

*W*henever the Great Imām ﷺ was faced with any difficult *mas'alah* for which a solution was not apparent, he would address his students, 'The reason for not being able to deduce and solve this *mas'alah* is my sins.' He would then commence *Isti'ghfār* (recitation of repentance). Often on such occasions, he would arise from the *majlis*, perform *wudhu* and two rakahs *salāh-ut-taubah* and thereafter recite *isti'ghfār* in abundance. Through the blessings of this act, Allah ﷻ would inspire the solution to the *mas'alah*, upon which the Great Imām ﷺ would exclaim with joy:

'I made rujû' (inclined) towards the Court of Allah ﷻ and repented for my sins: consequently, Allah ﷻ showered His Fadhl (favours) and Tawajju (Attention) thus clarifying the mas'alah.'

Some other reports relate that on such occasions, the Great Imām ﷺ would engage in *tilaawat* of the Glorious Qur'ān and complete forty khatams! The *masā'eel* would then be solved. When the Great Imām's illustrious student Fudhayl bin 'Eyādh ﷺ was informed of this, he shrieked, cried and made du'aa for his mentor in abundance.

Respect for Ustadh

The Great Imām ﷺ cherished so much respect and esteem in his heart for his *Ustadh's* and Shuyookh, that he never slept or rested with his feet pointing towards his mentors house. Whereas, there was a difference of seven streets between his house and the residence of Hammād ﷺ.   (p130, ibid.)

Intellectual Brilliance

A Roman philosopher once arrived at the Caliph's Court in Baghdad and boasted, 'I have come with three such questions that no Muslim Scholar from amongst the entire Ummah will be able to answer them!'

Agitated and worried, the Caliph quickly summoned leading 'Ulamā and Fuqahā. Imām Aboo Haneefah ﷺ too was requested to attend and arrived. The Roman philosopher requested a *mimbar* and alighting it addressed the scholars of Islām by posing three questions:

1) *Inform us, who existed before Allah ﷻ?*

2) *Inform us, in which direction is the Rukh of Allah ﷻ?*

3) *Finally, inform us, what is Allah ﷻ doing at this precise moment?*

The whole audience remained silent and perplexed...the questions appeared difficult and just at the moment it appeared the Muslim Scholars would be humiliated, the Great Imām ﷺ stepped forward and spoke:

'You asked questions from the mimbar, therefore you should let me answer from the mimbar so that the whole audience may hear with ease...'

Accordingly, the Roman philosopher stepped down and Imām Aboo Haneefah ﷺ took his place and spoke:

1) *Count numbers (after the Roman had counted to ten)...now, count backwards. The philosopher counted 10, 9, 8...2,1. When he had reached one, the Great Imām ﷺ told him to continue backwards, to which the Roman replied, 'there is no*

number smaller than one.' Imām Aboo Haneefah 🌸 commented, 'When there exists nothing before wāhid majāzee (hypothetical one), how may it be possible for anything to exist before Wāhid Haqeeqi (Allah ﷻ), accordingly Allah ﷻ is One and there existed nothing before Him.

2) *For the next question, the Great Imām 🌸 ordered a lamp to be lit and then asked, 'Tell me, in which direction is the light illuminating?' The Roman replied, 'In all directions.' Imām Aboo Haneefah 🌸 commented, 'A lamp is a created entity the light of which even you philosophers accept radiates in all direction, therefore what right do creation have to fix a particular direction for the Rukh of the Creator? Nevertheless, Allah's ﷻ Rukh faces all direction.*

3) *(Finally, in answer to your question as to what is Allah ﷻ doing at this moment?) At present, Allah ﷻ has lowered you from the mimbar and granted me the honour of sitting in your place.'*

The Roman philosopher was silenced and quickly retreated from view.   (p329, Tazkiratul…)

Despite being blessed with such intellectual brilliance and talent, he was the epitome of humility and respect for others. Such consideration, love, respect and esteem stemmed from the heart of the Great Imām 🌸. The day his son started his lessons of the Glorious Qur'ān and recited *Bismillah*, he presented 5,000 dirhams to the Ustadh. Similarly, when he finished *Surah Fatehah*, he gifted another 5,000 dirhams saying, 'By oath of Allah! If I possessed greater wealth, I would have presented it out of respect for the Glorious Qur'ān.'

The Great Imām's Benevolence

*C*here was a wealthy nobleman in Kufa, whose circumstances suddenly deteriorated whereby he was reduced to poverty. However, being of honourable character, he refrained from asking others and survived as best as possible. One day, his young daughter observing a street vendor selling fresh fruit came running home and pleaded with her mother for some money to buy just one item...but the poor lady had no money. Her husband, this nobleman, overheard this crying and plea of his daughter and being reduced to tears, he decided to approach Imām Aboo Haneefah ⚘ and seek his assistance.

He visited *Majlis-al-Barakatah* (council of the Great Imām - well renown for his generosity) and sat down. However, he who had never asked anybody in his life was, even today, unable to open his mouth because of shame...and departed. The Great Imām had observed him and intuitively concluded that this person was in some need but unable to ask because of his honour and dignity. Immediately, he followed this nobleman home and from a discrete distance noted his address. Later on that very night, the Great Imām arrived at this house with a bag of 500 *dirhams* hidden up his sleeve. He knocked at the door...when the person arrived to open... quickly, Imām Aboo Haneefah ⚘ left the bag inside and disappeared into the darkness saying, 'Observe, there is a bag at your doorstep for you.' When the person opened the bag, there was a piece of paper with a message written:

'Aboo Haneefah arrived with this money for you. It is from a halāl source. Please spend it on your needs.' (p91, Episodes...)

Honest & Astute Trader

slām has always encouraged trade, business and entrepreneurship. As Shaykh Ashraf 'Ali Thānwi ﷺ advised, there is *'barakat* (blessings) *in harkat* (endeavour).' Despite his 'Ilmi preoccupation, the Great Imām was blessed with outstanding business skills. His trading activity of manufacturing, buying and selling a type of cloth known as *'Kaz'* may be summarised into three distinguishable areas:

1) **Manufacturing:** The Great Imām had a manufacturing plant in Kufa which prepared this special material. Some reports suggest this material was prepared from a mixture of cotton, wool and thread from silk. It was a high quality fabric, much in demand in Arabia (at the time) and renown for its strength and resistance to wear. It was available in various colours and was widely employed by the Sahābāh and Tābi'een.

2) **Warehousing & Distribution:** Also located in Kufa was a warehouse depot, wherein this and other types of material were stocked. The Great Imām had installed a system of field agents, caravan's and salespersons to market this merchandise.

3) **Retail:** *Kaz* was widely available throughout the region and because of the quality, demand was high. Nevertheless, an unique feature of the Great Imām's retail outlets was the courteous, warm, fair and polite manner in which customers were treated. Whenever a customer arrived and inquired into the price of material, the price quoted would form the selling price. The Great Imām abhorred the custom of mentioning one price to entice the client and then resorting to bargaining to secure the sale.

Khidmat (Service) to Ahl-e-'Ilm

Imām Aboo Haneefah 🌸 had the custom of annually investing a large amount of merchandise in a trade caravan from Kufa to Baghdad and vice-versa. Whatever profit was obtained - and usually it was substantial - he gifted to the 'Ulamā, Mashā'ikh and the needy of Kufa saying:

> *'Spend it upon your necessities and needs praising and thanking only Allah 🌸 and no one else. Why? Because I have not gifted anything from my wealth: rather out of your blessings, it is Allah Ta'ālā's Fadhl upon me and the profits of money invested in your name.'*

Whenever the Great Imām 🌸 purchased anything for his children, he would buy an identical item for the 'Ulamā, Talabaa' and Mashā'ikh. When he had a set of clothes tailored for himself, he also arranged clothes for the 'Ulamā. Similarly, when harvest time arrived, whatever fruit he purchased for his family, he would send identical fruits for the Mashā'ikh. Moreover, the items he did gift to the *Ahl-e-'Ilm* was always of the highest standard and quality. The Great Imām would regularly inquire (discreetly) into the welfare, condition and needs of his associates, friends and students. Should any of them (or their family members) be ill, he would make *'iyaadah* and when anybody passed-away he would participate in their Janāzāh. In brief, he would assist whenever and however possible. He also had the custom, every *Jumu'ah*, of inviting all his students and associates to meals. He would have various dishes prepared and ask his students to sit down, with himself moving aside and leaving, 'You will not be able to enjoy or eat freely if I am present...'

Khair-Khwāhee (Goodwill)

*O*ne distinguishing feature of the Hanafee School of Fiqh is the Great Imām's relentless efforts to save a fellow Muslim from *kufr* (disbelieve). Should there be ninety-nine 'signs' of *kufr* in a Muslim and only one feature of Imān be visible, precedence will be given to this one quality. Once a person arrived and complained,

'Shaykh! What is your opinion of a person who professes to be a Muslim yet claims:

1) *Not to desire Jannah.*

2) *Neither is he scared of the Fire of Jahannam.*

3) *He openly eats maitah (carrion).*

4) *He prays salāh but does not perform ruku or sujood.*

5) *He testifies without having witnessed.*

6) *He prefers fitnah (strife) and detests haqq (truth).*

7) *He flees far from Rahmat.*

8) *He testifies to the statements of the Yahood and Nasārā!'*

*S*haykh 'Abdu'l-Qayyum Haqqanee *dāmat barakātuhum* relates, 'If this question were to be posed today, Heaven knows how many *Fatwās* of *kufr* we would immediately issue before the list were even read out! However, this was the Great Imām Aboo Haneefah 🌸, who instantly discerned that the questioner had an axe to grind with the person whose qualities he had described. Turning towards his students, the Great Imām inquired, 'What do you say of such a person?' They all replied, 'Such a person is amongst the worst of creation!' Imām Aboo Haneefah 🌸 chuckled and commented:

'*If I was to tell you that this person is a Mu'min and a high ranking Walee, you will...render helpless those Angels upon your shoulders who write deeds which are harmful, because in my opinion,*

1) The desire for Allah ﷻ is dominant in him and; when Allah ﷻ is his matloob (desired object), what need is there for such a person to desire Jannah?

2) He is afraid of the Fire of Allah ﷻ rather than the Fire of Jahannam.

3) He eats fish (which technically is also a form of maitah).

4) He performs Salah-ul-Janāzāh wherein is no ruku or sujood.

5) He testifies to Tawheed (the Oneness of Allah ﷻ) and Risālat (Prophethood), i.e. he recites the Kaleemah-Shahādah, whereas he has neither observed Allah ﷻ or Rasoolullah ﷺ.

6) It appears in the Glorious Qur'ān, 'Your wealth and your children are only a fitnah (trial)...' (64:15) By nature, they are beloved to man. Moreover, whilst death is haqq (a reality), because of enthusiasm for ibaadah and in order to amass more good deeds, to detest and abhor it is commendable

7) Rain is a Rahmat of Allah ﷻ from which he flees in order not to get drenched.

8) He testifies to (the Ayah of the Glorious Qur'ān), 'The Jews said that the Christians follow nothing (i.e. are not on the right religion); and the Christians said that the Jews follow nothing (i.e. are not on the right religion)...' (2:113)

Both the questioner and those listening were amazed and stunned at these replies of the Great Imām!

(p327, Tazkiratul No'man & p113 Episodes…)

Far-Sightedness

*T*he famous Tābiʻee, Imām ʻĀmash ﷺ (61-148AH/684-771CE) is considered amongst the leading *Muhadditheen* capable of relating 4,000 Hadeeth from memory. His appearance was not very handsome (ʻĀmash refers to a dim-eyed), in complete contrast to his wife, who was outstanding in beauty and somewhat proud of it. She detested her husband; always looking for an argument and excuse to be separated from him. One night, their bouts of wrangling reached such heights that she refused to speak henceforth; Imām ʻĀmash ﷺ lost his temper and blurted out, 'If you do not speak by morning, you are divorced!' After calming down, he realized his folly and the plight of his young children should their mother continue to refuse to speak with him that night. He pleaded and cajoled with her, but to no avail. In desperation, he sought the opinion and advice of elders but nobody could show a solution. Finally, he visited Imām Aboo Haneefah ﷺ who suggested a strategy, 'Not to fear, keep calm, we shall arrange for the Azān this morning to be recited before *Subah Sādiq.*' Thereafter, the Great Imām ﷺ personally approached the Muazzin of the local Masjid and persuaded him to recite one Azān before *Subah Sādiq.* Now, the wife of Imām ʻĀmash ﷺ had packed her bags and was just waiting for the Fajr Azān...as soon as she heard *'Allahu Akbar!'* she exclaimed in delight. 'All thanks to Allah! Now I am separated and free from this old-man!' Imām ʻĀmash ﷺ replied, 'All thanks to Allah ﷻ, that the Muazzin, through the ingenuity of Imām Aboo Haneefah, recited the Azān before *Subah Sādiq* thus preventing our marriage from breaking up!'

Summons to Baghdad

hen Qādhi Ibn Abee Layla, the *Chief Qādhi* of Kufa passed-away in 146 AH (766 CE), the Caliph Mansûr 'Abbasee summoned the four leading scholars of Kufa: Aboo Haneefah, Sufyān Thāwree, Mus'ar bin Kadam and Shurayk to select a replacement. Whilst all four were sitting in the Masjid after Fajr, the police arrived and escorted them to the Caliph in Baghdad. As they left Kufa, the Great Imām predicted, 'Regarding our group, I have a hunch: I will make an excuse and become free; Mus'ar will claim insanity; Sufyān Thāwree will escape but Shurayk will become entangled.' As the group reached the outskirts of Baghdad, Sufyān Thāwree 🏵 requested to answer the call of nature. He took refuge behind a river embankment, whilst a policeman stood on the other side of the wall and awaited. Just then, a barge carrying timber was cruising past when Sufyān Thāwree called-out, 'Please let me come as they are going to kill me.' This was no lie, for Nabee 🏵 has related, 'Whomsoever is appointed a Qādhi is as if been slaughtered without a knife.' Tossing the sailors a few dirhams, they gladly hoisted and concealed Sufyān Thāwree underneath their cargo. By the time the policeman finally became suspicious, the boat had disappeared from view.

The three remaining 'Alims were escorted into the court of the Caliph Mansûr. Immediately upon entry, Mus'ar bin Kadam began acting the 'clown' by boisterously addressing the Caliph, 'Stretch forth your hand so I may make bay'h to you! How are you? How are your wives, children, servants and animals?' The Caliph ordered Mus'ar to be evicted from the court, 'This man's an idiot and lunatic!' He then ordered the Great Imām to accept the post of Qādhi, which he boldly refused. The Caliph took oath, 'You *will* become the Qādhi!' Whereupon, the Great Imām also took oath, 'I will *never* become Qādhi!' When this blunt and highly charged exchange had taken place three times, a wazir Rabee Hajib tried to pressurize the Great Imām, 'Do you not observe how Ameerul Mu'mineen has taken oath?' Undaunted, the Great Imām ﷺ replied, 'Do you not observe how Ameerul Mu'mineen is more able to discharge the *kaffarah* (compensation) for oaths than I am?' Caliph Mansûr ordered the Great Imām to be imprisoned and thereafter baited, 'Are you now willing to accept what we desire, i.e. for you to become Qādhi?' Calmly, the Great Imām ﷺ replied,

> *'May Allah ﷻ make the Ameerul Mu'mineen pious. O Ameerul Mu'mineen! Fear Allah ﷻ and do not enjoin in your amānah those who do not fear Allah ﷻ. By oath of Allah! When I do not have any assurance upon myself in the state of tranquillity, how may I remain safe in the state of anger?'*

Mansûr blurted out, 'You are lying, you are perfectly capable of becoming a Qādhi!' Upon this, the Great Imām replied,

> *'O Ameerul Mu'mineen! You contradict yourself: for if I am truthful, I have already informed you that I do not have the ability to become a Qādhi; and if I am a liar (as you suggest), how may it be possible for you to appoint a liar to the post of Qādhi? Moreover, I am (of Persian origin), how will the Ahl-e-'Arab ever accept the fact that a descendent of a Persian slave presides as Qadhi over them?'*

The Great Imām's Shahādat

Caliph Mansûr ordered the Great Imām to be locked-up in jail and appointed Shurayk as the next Qadhi. Whilst in jail, at regular intervals, the Caliph offered him the opportunity to reconsider and accept the post: which he refused. Exasperated, Mansûr ordered the Great Imām be brought out of jail, flogged 10 lashes in public every day and be paraded throughout the bazaar. His food and drink were rationed. For ten days, these acts of cruel, barbaric oppression and injustice were enacted on this Great Scholar.

Finally, the Great Imām lifted his hands and cried of his weakness to Allah 🕮. The message of his imminent death arrived. Five days later, a bowl was presented by the jailers, 'drink this!' When he continued to refuse saying, 'I know what is inside and will not co-operate in my death!' The cruel prison guards manhandled the Great Imām onto the floor and forced the poison into his mouth. When Imām Aboo Haneefah 🕮 felt the effects of the poison, he immediately fell in *sujood* and passed-away in this position at the ripe age of 70 years.

'Verily, to Allah we belong and unto Him is our return.'

Aboo Hurayrah 🕮 has related a statement of our Nabee 🕮,

'Of all positions, the servant is closest to his Creator in the state of sujood.' (Muslim, p436, ibid.)

Imām Abul Mu'ayyid Khwarzami 🕮 relates,

'Imām Aboo Haneefah's 🕮 madhab ranks akin to the full moon in comparison to stars. With taqwā, the Great Imām acquired 'Uloom in Khairun Qurun and without doubt his madhab stands undisputed.' (p248, ibid.)

Why was the Great Imām Murdered?

In reality, the Caliph had summoned the Great Imām to Baghdad knowing full well that he would refuse the post of Qadhi. Why did he murder him? Imām Aboo Haneefah ﷺ was immensely popular and respected amongst the whole spectrum of society: scholars, wealthy and lay people all looked up to him. He was also a successful businessman and wealthy.

Mansûr detested this popularity, whilst enemies and enviers of the Great Imām ﷺ had falsely attributed charges of collaboration and support for Ibrāheem bin 'Abdullah ﷺ - the Grandson of the Family of Nabee ﷺ who had initiated an uprising against the tyranny of the Caliph in Kufa.

Tajheez & Takhfeen (Bathing & Shroud)

Immediately upon his death, the body of the Great Imām ﷺ was brought out of prison and bathed by Hasan bin 'Ammarah ﷺ - the Qadhi of Baghdad who commented:

'May Allah ﷺ Shower His Rahmat upon you! You fasted continuously for THIRTY years and did not sleep at night for FORTY years! You are the greatest Faqeeh amongst us; the greatest 'āabid (pious worshipper); the greatest tāriq-ud-dunya (renouncer of the world) and the greatest compiler of goodness. Now, with virtues galore we lower you into your grave. You have left your successors in perplexity: for your ittiba' (following) is very difficult; and the Qurr'ā (expert scholars of the Glorious Qur'ān) will be ashamed of not being able to emulate you!'   (p437, ibid.)

Abul Rajā' ﷺ, who also participated in bathing the Janāzāh commented, 'At the time of ghusl, I noticed how frail the

Great Imām's body had become due to abundance of 'Ibaadah.' Hardly had the bathing and shrouding been completed, that people from all over Baghdad flocked to pay their respects...it was as if somebody had announced the Great Imām's death from the Heavens. Over 50,000 people participated in the first Janāzāh Salāh...five more salāh were repeated and, such was the congregation of people from all over 'Iraq, that Janāzāh Salāh was prayed at the graveside of the Great Imām for the next 20 days! In accordance with the express wishes of the Great Imām, he was buried in the eastern side of *Muqabarah-e-Khaizran,* a private piece of land not forcefully acquired by the Caliph. Later, adjacent to this grave, when a Madrasah was built by Aboo Sa'ad Khwarzami 🕸, many famous scholars visited the site. Amongst them some notable comments were made:

> *'You are all aware that 'Ilm was awaiting in suspense, when the dweller of this grave arrived and systematically compiled it...The grave of Imām Aboo Haneefah 🕸 is a beautiful resplendent and vibrant garden from the orchards of Jannat. From beneath it arise springs and fountains of 'Uloom and rare extraordinary pearls of goodness. May limitless peace shower upon it from the Creator of the Universe until there remain stars to shine.'*
>
> *For 3 nights after death of the Great Imām 🕸, crying of the jinni and a voice from the unseen was heard by some Awliya, 'The faqeeh has departed: from amongst you, now there is no faqeeh. You should fear Allah and become saleh. No'maan has passed-away, who will now bring alive 'Ibaadah of the night when it is covered with pitch darkness?'*
>
> *(p439-440, ibid.)*

The Tabe Tābi'een

$\mathcal{S}$haykh Muheebullah Nadwee ﷺ relates, 'Whilst during the time of the *Tābi'een* systematic compilation of 'Ilm had commenced, nevertheless it was not categorized into fields, *tafseer, hadeeth, fiqh, history, lu'gat,* etc., were not treated as separate sciences. Neither did there exist specialists concentrating in specific arenas of study. Generally, an Imām would impart and elaborate in each field during his lectures, which the students would record privately in their notes and thereafter impart to others. Although a handful of books on individual areas were published, nevertheless it was during the time of the *Tabe Tābi'een* (c. 143 AH/766 CE) that this work of systemization truly commenced. During a relatively short period of time, Deeni 'Uloom became so codified and published that the very same books are still present today. Imām Zahbee ﷺ relates,

'From 143 AH, the Ulamā of Islām began to compile hadeeth, fiqh and tafseer as separate sciences. In Makkah, we had Ibn Jurayh ﷺ; in Madeenah, we had Imām Mālik ﷺ; in Syria, we had Imām Awzā'ee ﷺ; in Basra, we had Ibn 'Aruba and Hammad bin Salamah; in Yemen, we had Mu'amar; in Kufa, we had Sufyān Thāwree ﷺ.

All were researching and writing books; Imām Aboo Haneefah ﷺ wrote on fiqh....and a short time later...Ibn Mubārak, Aboo Yousuf, Ibn Wahab took upon themselves this noble task. Now, very rapidly, books and papers were systematically published on each individual science...The period 150 AH to 300 AH (725-925 CE) is considered the golden era of Deeni 'Uloom compilation and publications...' (V. 8, p43, Seerah Sahābāh)

The Great Imām's Students

haykh-ul-Hadeeth Zakariyyā ﷺ relates,

'Imām Aboo Haneefah ﷺ would with great diligence and caution research nasikh and mansûkh Hadeeth. He had compiled Hadeeth from every Muhhaddith of Kufa - the 'Ilmi centre of the time. Whenever any Muhhaddith visited Kufa, the Great Imām would instruct his students to inquire and research into the validity of any unknown Hadeeth which this person may have. This 'Ilmi Majlis which he had initiated and organised consisted of Muhhaddith, Fuqahah and Ahle Lugat...   (p113, Stories...)

haykh Muhammad Saleem Dhorat *dāmat barakātuhum* relates, 'The reason for emphasizing these facts is to highlight the concern, assiduousness and welfare with which the Great Imām supervised the development of not only *fiqh* but also his students. It was because of this that they reached such noble heights of piety, 'Uloom and khidmat. Once, Imām Aboo Yousuf ﷺ ~ a Faqeeh and student of the Great Imām was sitting in the company of Imām Ãmash ﷺ ~ a Muhaddith. The latter asked for a Sharee' ruling on a particular issue and received an answer from Aboo Yousuf ﷺ. Surprised and inquisitive, Imām Ãmash ﷺ asked, 'From which Hadeeth did you deduce this answer?' Aboo Yousuf ﷺ replied, 'From the very Hadeeth which you had narrated to us.' Imām Ãmash ﷺ commented, 'O Aboo Yousuf! I knew this Hadeeth even before you came into this world; however, until today, I could not understand this meaning (that you have understood).'

Majlis-e-Shûrā

oth from an academic and practical view, the Great Imām's *Majlis-e-Shûrā* (Consultative Board) was an outstanding body. Whilst it included Ulamā, Huffaz, Muhaditheen, Muffassireen, and experts in Arabic; it also contained such distinguished intellectuals as Zufar bin Hazeel. The result of this 'think-tank' was that whenever a *Masā'eel* came to these Ahl-e-Ilm and Scholars, it would be so closely scrutinized, debated and enlightened upon to fully and comprehensively unravel the problem for all time.

Once a person complained to Waqee' 🌸 that 'the Great Imām has erred in this matter!' Immediately, Waqee' replied,

> *'How is it possible for Aboo Haneefah* 🌸 *to make a mistake? When there are with him people of the calibre of Aboo Yousuf and Zufar to make Qiyas (presumptions); Huffaz of Hadeeth such as: Hafs bin 'Ghiyath; Yahyā bin Abee Za'idah; Habban; Mundil; experts in Arabic such as Qāsim bin M'an: pious Zāhids such as Dawood Ta'ee and Fudhayl bin 'Iyādh. If he had erred, surely these illustrious souls would have corrected him!'*   (V. 7, p607, Seerah...)

During the term of this *Majlis-e-Shûrā*, over 12,700 Masā'eels were discussed, researched and decreed. Nadhr bin Shumayl 🌸 remarked, 'People were blissfully unaware (and asleep in the field) of fiqh until Imām Aboo Haneefah 🌸 came and awoke them.'

A beautiful and vivid description of the Deeni Khidmat (Service) undertaken by our A'imma-e-Ahnāf (Founders of the Hanafee School of Fiqh) is recorded in *Dure Mukhtar...*

> *'Our Fuqahā relate that the 'crop' of fiqh was sown by 'Abdullah ibn Masûd ﷺ; 'Alqamah ﷺ irrigated it; Ibrāheem Nakha'ee ﷺ harvested it; Hammad ﷺ segregated it; Imām Aboo Haneefah ﷺ milled it; Imām Aboo Yousuf ﷺ kneaded it; Imām Muhammad ﷺ thereafter baked the bread...and the rest are all eaters!'*

(p43, Episodes...)

To elucidate, 'Abdullah ibn Masûd ﷺ illuminated *Ijtihaad & Istinbaate Ahqām* (interpretation, deductions and commands of fiqh); whilst 'Alqamah ﷺ supported and expanded it; Ibrāheem Nakha'ee ﷺ separated and classified its benefits. This 'Ilm of fiqh continued to advance until the Great Imām Aboo Haneefah ﷺ perfected and beautifully systemized it, whilst successive generations of Fuqahā including Imām Aboo Yousuf ﷺ and Imām Muhammad ﷺ recorded it into their writings and presented it for the benefit of this Ummah. Ibn Hazam ﷺ relates,

> *'It is the unanimous verdict of all the students of the Great Imām, that he considered even 'weak' Hadeeth better than qiyas (analogical reasoning) and ra'i (opinion).'* (p246, ibid.)

Imām Abul Mu'ayyid Khwarzami ﷺ relates,

> *'The eyes of Imām Aboo Haneefah ﷺ never experienced the pleasure of full sleep. To please Allah Ta'ālā, he based his madhab (School of Fiqh) upon firstly Kitabullah, secondly the Sunnahs of Rasoolullah ﷺ and thereafter the Ijma' (consensus) of the Ummah...'* (ibid.)

Imām Aboo Yousuf 鑑

(113-189 AH ~ 736-812CE)

$\mathcal{A}$boo Yousuf was the *kunyah* of Ya'qûb ibn Ibrāheem. He was a descendent of the famous Ansar Sahābee S'ad bin Hutbatah 鑑, upon whose head our Nabee 鑑 affectionately stroked his *mubarak* hand out of concern during the Battle of Khundak. Imām Aboo Yousuf 鑑 stated, 'Even now we are able to experience the blessings of this affectionate stroke.'

His father Ibrāheem was a poor man of Kufa, whose poverty had ruled out any possibility of Imām Aboo Yousuf 鑑 formally studying Deeni 'Uloom in his youth. Nevertheless, the newly married Aboo Yousuf's 鑑 sheer enthusiasm, *talab*, talent, memory and intelligence forced him to secretly miss work and sit in the company of Ulamā. For 9 years, he visited the *majlis* of Qadhi Muhammad bin Abee Layla 鑑, thereafter he conscientiously attended the *majlis* of Imām Aboo Haneefah 鑑.

Once, when he was sitting in the company of the Great Imām 鑑, his father Ibrāheem abruptly arrived and forcefully dragged him away complaining, 'Imām Aboo Haneefah is a wealthy person; he does not have to worry about his eating and living!' For a short time, under strict orders of his parents, he stayed away, however when he found out that the Great Imām had inquired into his absence, he again secretly returned. As the *majlis* finished and people were leaving, Imām Aboo Haneefah 鑑 motioned him to stay behind and privately handed him a bag of 100 dirhams saying, 'Employ it for your necessities and, when it finishes let me know.'

Although reports vary as to how long Imām Aboo Yousuf 🌸 stayed in the company of the Great Imām, whether it is 9, 17 or 29 years, what is certain is his total dedication. He never failed to perform a Fajr Salāh with the Great Imām or attend his *majlis* - even on 'Eid days - despite the responsibility of a family. When a child of his passed-away, he left the *Tajheez, Takhfeen & Janāzāh* to his relatives and neighbours so that he would not miss a single moment of the Great Imām's Lectures. Despite having over 60 Ustadhs (this was not uncommon in those days), he still commented:

> *'There is no more beloved dars in this world for me than the lectures of Imām Aboo Haneefah and Qadhi Ibn Abee Layla...I have not seen a better faqeeh than Imām Aboo Haneefah or a Qadhi of the calibre of Ibn Abee Layla.'* (ibid)

Once when he fell critically ill, the Great Imām visited him and commented, 'I have great expectations that you will be of immense benefit to the Muslims.' When Imām Aboo Yousuf 🌸 recovered, he decided to establish his own lectures. However, he still visited the *majlis* of the Great Imām, where he once posed an intricate question. Upon this, Imām Aboo Haneefah 🌸 commented:

> *'Subhannallah! A person who establishes his own halqah; teaching and speaking upon the Deen of Allah to a large number of students is unable to understand a question on leasehold! Beloved, understand well, whomsoever thinks that he has achieved independence of Husool-e-Taleem (tuition and guidance) should cry upon himself.'* (p63, ibid.)

Immediately, Aboo Yousuf 🌸 suspended his lectures and concentrated on acquiring firmness from the Great Imām.

A Reflection of the Great Imām

A distinguishing feature of the students of the Great Imām was their affectionate attitude towards students. Imām Aboo Yousuf ❀ always treated his students with respect, forbearance and inspired them to 'go further.' Whenever, he saw a student struggling, he would advise:

> *'Every imperfect is able to progress unto perfection: adopt sabr; place strain and exercise upon your intelligence; I have great hopes that you will slowly, slowly achieve success.'* (p67, ibid.)

This welfare and *Khair Khwāhee* which he undoubtedly inherited from the Great Imām - made him so popular a teacher, that people from far and wide flocked to learn from him. Once when he visited Basra, a large congregation gathered, with students of Hadeeth desiring he address them first; whilst students of Fiqh expected this honour. He replied, 'I have a *ta'aluq* (bond) with both groups and therefore am unable to give precedence of one over the other.' His list of students over 32 years of teaching include the famous Imām Ahmad bin Hambal ❀ who commented, 'I have acquired 'Ilm (the books of which would fill 3 bookshelves) from Aboo Yousuf ❀.' The Great Imām himself once related,

> *'These 40 members (of my Majlis-e-Shûra); 27 of them are worthy of being Judges; 20 of them are able to practise as Muftis; whilst two of them, Imām Zufar and Imām Aboo Yousuf possess such ability as to prepare Qadhi's and Mufti's and make them worthy of this post.'* (p78, ibid.)

Accordingly, Imām Aboo Yousuf ❀ accepted the post of Chief Qādhi of the Muslim Empire offered by Haroon Rasheed ❀.

An Episode of the Great Imām & Aboo Yousuf 🐝

Q**S** haykh Ashraf 'Ali Thānwi 🐝 relates, 'I have heard from reliable 'Ulamā that once the Great Imām and Imām Aboo Yousuf were on a night journey upon camels... when they fell asleep. They awoke quite late, a few minutes before the sun was due to rise. Quickly they dismounted, made *wudhu* and the Great Imām ushered his student forward to lead Fajr Salāh.

Imām Aboo Yousuf 🐝 used *ijtihad* (Deeni Judgement) to quickly perform only the *Faraa'idh* and *Wājibat* (compulsory) elements of Salāh in order to complete 2 *rakahs* before sunrise. Nevertheless, in his heart, he was dreading how the Great Imām might react to this 'short and brief' Fajr Salāh? However, his mentor commented,

> 'All Praises to Allah 🕌! Our Y'aqûb (i.e. Imām Aboo Yousuf) has become a Faqeeh.'   (Vol.25, p30, Lectures)

Imām Aboo Yousuf 🐝 is regarded as one of the first scholars to systematically write down and publish the *maslaq* of Imām Aboo Haneefah 🐝. Some of his advises to Deeni students are:

- *'Ilm is such an entity that when you give it your entire existence, then only will you acquire some portion of it. Moreover, when you do receive this portion, do not become arrogant (and carefree) but remain steadfastly in its pursuit.*

- *O people! Acquire 'Ilm only for the pleasure of Allah 🕌, do not corrupt it with any other intention. My own experience is that whenever I entered a Majlis with humility, I arose elevated. However, the Majlis I entered puffed-up with pride, I left disgraced and lowered.'*   (p140, ibid.)

Imām Muhammad Shaybanee

(132-189 AH ~ 755-812CE)

Imām Muhammad bin Hasan Shaybanee's ancestors are reported to be of Syrian origin who migrated to 'Iraq where the young Imām Muhammad was born in 132 AH. His upbringing took place in Kufa - where his nobility, talents and intelligence marked him out as a gifted and promising youngster.

At the tender age of 13 years, he entered the *majlis* of the Great Imām to pose a question: 'A non *baligh* (immature) prays 'Esha Salāh and goes to sleep and in this very night attains *buloogh* (i.e. he experiences a wet-dream), does he have to repeat the 'Esha Salāh?' Imām Aboo Haneefah replied with *isbat* (proofs). Because this question related to himself, the young Imām Muhammad immediately arose, made wudhu and repeated his salāh in a corner of the Masjid. Observing this spectacle, the Great Imām commented, 'Inshā'Allah, this boy will be a *Rasheed* (a guide towards the right path).'

A few days after this incident, he again arrived but this time requested to become a student. However, one of the fundamentals of gaining entry into the Great Imām's lecture programmes was to be a Hāfiz of the Glorious Qur'ān. Accordingly, the young Imām Muhammad was advised to become a Hāfiz and then return.

One week later he returned with his father to inform the Great Imām that he had become Hāfiz! Thereafter, he proceeded to ask such an intricate question, whereby the Great Imām inquired whether this was his own query or that related by another. When the young Muhammad replied, 'This question has arisen in my mind,' the Great Imām commented, 'You are asking questions like a mature person, therefore you may regularly attend my lectures.' For the next 4 years, until his mentors' death, Imām Muhammad ﷺ continuously stayed with him. Thereafter, he made *ruju* (inclined) towards Imām Aboo Yousuf ﷺ - the closest and most advanced student of Imām Aboo Haneefah ﷺ.

Besides expertise of the Qur'ān and Fiqh, Imām Muhammad ﷺ also inherited enthusiasm and yearning for Hadeeth from Shaykhayn (i.e. the Great Imām & Imām Aboo Yousuf). Although *Muhadditheen* were also present in Kufa, it was towards the blessed city of Madeenah and the personality of Imām Mālik ﷺ that he inclined for a further 3 years...

'I attended the Dars of Imām Mālik ﷺ for over 3 years; during this time I heard over 700 ahādeeth from him.'

(p149, Seerah)

Imām Muhammad ﷺ is probably unique in having acquired 'Uloom from such experts of Qur'ān, Hadeeth and Fiqh. Imām Mālik ﷺ commented, 'No such outstandingly intelligent student as this young man from the east ('Iraq) has ever come here before.'

Throughout this Taalib 'Ilmi phase, he was fortunate to enjoy the financial support of his father, 'I inherited 30,000 dirhams from my father: 15,000 I spent acquiring expertise in adab, lugat, and nahw. The remaining 15,000 I spent acquiring Fiqh and Hadeeth.' The result of such talab and training by distinguished teachers and parents? At the age of 20 years, he was appointed and commenced giving lectures.

Imām Muhammad's ﷺ Achievements

From the time of his graduation at 20 unto his death in 189 AH at the age of 57, Imām Muhammad ﷺ was a worthy deputy of the Great Imām and Imām Mālik ﷺ. People from all corners of the Muslim Empire flocked to derive benefit. Amongst his numerous students are Yahyā bin Saleh and Abul Hafdhul Kabeer Bukhāree ﷺ - the famous teachers of Imām Bukhāree ﷺ. However, his most distinguished student was Imām Shāfi'ee ﷺ who commented:

> *'Both from an 'Ilmi and worldly aspect, I am indebted to no one more than Imām Muhammad ﷺ...the knowledge I acquired from him I have not received from elsewhere...I wrote down this Ilm...after approximately 10 years, when I departed from him, I looked at my manuscripts; they were large enough to fill a camel's back.'*   (p167 ibid.)

Imām Muhammad ﷺ was of noble *soorat* and *seerat*. He had also inherited the Great Imām's good character, dedication and benevolence towards mankind and especially students. Imām Aboo Hafdh ﷺ relates:

> *'When anybody looked at him, it appeared he was created purely for 'Ilm. He was extremely saleh (pious), courteous, well-mannered and a refined person. His tongue never hurt anybody; affability and friendliness towards others were his prominent features.'*

These two students of the Great Imām are regarded as probably the most distinguished, prolific and influential writers of their era in Fiqh. Indeed, the publications of the *A'imma-e-Arb'aah* are almost exclusively based upon the works of Imām Muhammad 🐝. When Imām Ahmad ibn Hambal 🐝 was asked the source of his *mas'āeel*, he replied, 'From the kitabs of Imām Muhammad 🐝.' Moreover, in the second century of Islām, one of the greatest achievements in the field of Hadeeth was the compilation and publication of *Mû'attā* of Imām Mālik 🐝 of Madeenah. Imām Muhammad's 🐝 version of this kitab is unique in being so comprehensive and elaborate. His other distinguished publications include:

• *Kitab-ul-Āthār* - A book on Hadeeth and Statements of the Sahābāh & Tābi'een - especially of the Great Imām 🐝.

• *Kitab-ul-Hajj* - This is his third book on Hadeeth and although a student of Imām Mālik 🐝, in this kitab he highlights (with proofs) the differences between the Arab Ulamās' and the Hanafee Scholars.

• *Mabsut* - The most comprehensive kitab on Hanafee Fiqh by Imām Muhammad 🐝 in 6 volumes and containing over 3,000 Masā'eels. After reading this book, a kafir scholar by the name of Hakeem accepted Islām commenting,

> '*When such is the book of your Muhammad As'gar (smaller Imām) what to say of the kitab (Glorious Qur'ān) of your Muhammad Akbar (i.e. Nabee 🕌)?*'

Other books include *Al Jāme-ul-Kabeer, Al Jāme-ul-Sa'gheer, Al Seerul Sa'gheer* & *Zeeyadat*. A scholar commented,

> '*Imām Aboo Haneefah 🐝 is the leader of Ahl-e-Iraq; Imām Aboo Yousuf 🐝 is the most ardent upon Hadeeth; whilst Imām Muhammad 🐝 has elaborated the most Masā'eel; and Imām Zufar 🐝 resorted to Qiyas (judgement) abundantly.*'   (p179, ibid.)

'Abdullah ibne Mubārak 鑾

(118-181 AH ~ 741-804 CE)

bdullah ibn Mubārak 鑾 is considered the *Rose* of the Tabe Tābi'een because his whole life was a perfect reflection of the teachings of Islām. His Deeni enthusiasm, generosity, good character, aloofness from dunya and sense of responsibility made him a walking ambassador. These outstanding qualities made him an enormously popular figure, almost a living legend amongst the hearts of all Muslims throughout the vast Empire.

Once he visited Ruqqah...the entire city came out to meet him and walked behind in respect. Coincidentally, the Caliph Haroon Rasheed 鑾 was also a visitor and staying in a mansion, from the balcony of which a lady of his household observed this spectacle and inquired, 'Whose procession is this?' When the courtiers replied, 'Abdullah ibn Mubārak - an Alim from Khurasan.' Instinctively, she commented, 'In reality, he (i.e. 'Abdullah ibn Mûbārak) is the *Ameerul Mu'mineen* not Haroon Rasheed - for without the services of police and soldiers there is no crowd around the Caliph!'

Although father Mûbārak was a slave, his *taqwa*, nobility and piety were so obvious, that his master arranged his marriage with his very own daughter. 'Abdullah ibn Mûbārak 鑾 was the child of this bond, born in Merv (south of the Aral Sea) where he received basic *tāleem*. In accordance with prevalent custom, he then travelled all over the Muslim world, from place to place to acquire 'Ilm. Imām Ahmad 鑾 commented, 'In acquiring Deeni 'Ilm. there was nobody present in that era who travelled further than 'Abdullah ibn Mubārak. He travelled to far away places: Yemen, Egypt, Syria, Kufa, Basra, etc.'   (p302, Seerah...)

Unlike today, the wealth of 'Ilm was scattered, generally unwritten, throughout the Empire, because the Sahābāh themselves had travelled and settled in far away places to propagate Deen. Consequently, their students were resident in these places, therefore anybody wishing to congregate and publish this 'Uloom had to travel far and wide and meet many experts. 'Abdullah ibn Mûbārak ﷺ relates, 'I have benefited from over 4,000 Shuyookh....amongst them I have narrated from 1,000 teachers.' His most famous teacher is the Great Imām ﷺ, whom he revered:

> *'Had Allah Ta'ālā not blessed me with the patronage of Imām Aboo Haneefah ﷺ and Sufyān Thāwree ﷺ, I would have been like an ordinary person.'*   (p 308, ibid.)

> *'Imām Aboo Haneefah ﷺ was the most eminent of all jurists. I haven't seen anyone as skilled as him in the field of fiqh.'*   (p9, Sunnah &...)

Once a person from Khurasan posed a question to Sufyān Thāwree ﷺ who replied, 'You have the greatest Alim of the east and west present in 'Abdullah ibn Mubārak, why do you not ask him?' Imām Mālik ﷺ commented, 'Ibn Mubārak is the Faqeeh of Khurasan.' Although 'Abdullah ibn Mûbārak ﷺ excelled in every branch of 'Uloom, he is most revered in the remembrance and narration of Hadeeth. This student of the Great Imām is unique in being acknowledged an expert in both Fiqh *and* Hadeeth by consensus of the 'Ulamā of all schools throughout the last fourteen centuries of Islām.

Ameerul Mu'mineen of Hadeeth & Mujāhid

Due to this expertise he is titled *Ameerul Mu'mineen Fil Hadeeth*. Whenever there was a dispute amongst the scholars regarding a particular Hadeeth, the 'Ulamā would comment, 'Let us take this dispute to the *tabeeb* (doctor) of Hadeeth, only he will be able to arbitrate.'

In character, abstention, *ibaadat, zuhd, taqwā* and habits, 'Abdullah ibne Mubārak 🏵 was a living reflection of the Sahābāh. Contemporaries commented,

> *'At night he worshiped like a hermit; whilst during the day, like a lion he would be visible on the battlefield...I reflected upon the condition of the Sahābāh and besides the Company of Nabee 🏵, I did not observe Ibn Mûbārak 🏵 any lesser in application.'* (p318, Seerah...)

Like the Great Imām, he too was a successful businessman who devoted his wealth in the service of others:

> *'I spend my wealth upon those whose 'ilm, excellences, honesty, integrity I am personally aware of. Those who are fully involved in acquiring and propagating Deeni 'ilm (the Talabāh and 'Ulamā) have personal responsibilities which need to be catered and aided, otherwise 'ilm will suffer...this trade I undertake to protect myself; my honour and dignity from difficulties and disgrace; and to gain assistance in the worship of Allah 🏵 and to easily and fully discharge the huqooqs for which I am responsible.'* (p320, ibid.)

Like his mentor, he was extremely generous to the needy, fellow travellers and those in debt - on numerous occasions seeing to their needs without anybody's knowledge.

'Abdullah ibn Mubārak 🏵 had divided his year into three: in one-third he would trade; in another third he would teach; and the remaining third would be spent in either Hajj or Jihad. He was an accomplished *Mujāhid,* his bravery - especially in hand-to-hand combat was legendary and quite spectacular. There have been confirmed instances of him single-handedly dispatching elite Roman troops to Hell. His death also occurred during Jihad, at the age of 63 years in 181 AH (804 CE) in the Syrian town of Heet, thousands of miles away from his home. The Caliph Haroon al-Rasheed 🏵 declared the occasion one of mourning.

Some Pearls of Wisdom

* *If a person adopts taqwā and the Fear of Allah 🏵 in one hundred items, but fails to do so in just one area, he is not a muttaqee.*

* *I prefer and consider it more appropriate to refrain from acquiring and spending 1 dirham of doubtful wealth than spend 100 dirhams in charity.*

* *Prefer anonymity and keep far away from fame. Whomsoever possesses even one characteristic of ignorance will be termed an ignoramus.*

* *A person cannot be an Alim until the Fear of Allah 🏵 and indifference to dunya are not present in his heart.*

* *Takkabur (pride) is to consider others as inferior and to pick their faults. Ujub (vanity) is to consider whatever one possesses to be so exclusive as not to be present within others.*

* *Shareef (cultured) is he who has been blessed with Tawfeeq to obey Allah 🏵.* (p331, ibid.)

Other Students

Dawood Ta'i's ﷺ name is associated amongst the noble *Salaf-e-Sāliheen* of Islām. He was a distinguished student of the Great Imām ﷺ and had acquired expertise in 'Ilm of Hadeeth, Fiqh, Arabic, Qira'at and Tafseer. He was also a member of the famous *Majlis-e-Shûra*.

One day, the Great Imām addressed him, 'Dawood! All branches of your (knowledge) are perfect.' Dawood Ta'i ﷺ inquired, 'Is there anything outstanding?' The Great Imām replied, 'Yes! To act upon your 'Ilm still remains!' Immediately he heard this statement of his tutor, Dawood Ta'i ﷺ arose and sold his land and separated himself from dunya. He very rarely met anybody.

Fudhayl bin 'Eyādh ﷺ was born in Khurasan. He grew up to become a notorious bandit and fell in love with a girl whom he clandestinely planned to meet one night. As he was about to climb onto her balcony, he heard the following Ayah of the Glorious Qur'ān being recited by a Hāfiz nearby:

'Why? Has the time not yet arrived for the People of Imān that their hearts submit to the Remembrance of Allah?'

Immediately, he dropped all thought of meeting the girl and cried with pangs of remorse, 'O Creator! The time has indeed arrived when I take leave from the oceans of sins and seek refuge in the shadow of your Rahmat.' He wandered into a valley where he overheard a group of travellers discussing their time of departure... 'It is not wise to travel in the dark, we may be ambushed and robbed by Fudhayl and his bandits!' Overwhelmed upon hearing how his name and deeds created such fear in the hearts of people, he sincerely repented to Allah ﷻ and departed for Kufa to seek Deeni 'Ilm. His distinguished Shuyookh include Imām Āmash; Sulaiman Taymee; Mansūr bin Mutamar, Sufyān Thāwree and, of course, the Great Imām ﷺ. His spiritual rank may be estimated from such statements:

* *Whomsoever has recognised people has achieved comfort (that is, when you understand that none from creation may benefit or harm without the Will of Allah ﷻ), you will become completely oblivious to others and concentrate all your thoughts towards only Allah ﷻ.*

* *A person of fadhl & kamal (excellence) may only be a person of kamal when he does not consider himself kamil (perfect).*

* *It is totally unbefitting a hamil (bearer of the Glorious Qur'ān, i.e. the 'Ulamā, Huffāz and Talabāh) that they present any of their needs to rulers or wealthy people. Rather, a hamil's rank is such that the creation of Allah ﷻ should present their needs to him.*

* *Whenever I have disobeyed Allah ﷻ, I have noticed signs (of disobedience) in my animals, servants or wife, i.e. they too began to disobey me.*

* *To treat one's associates with politeness and cordiality accrues more thawāb than praying all-night and fasting all day.*

* *To perform any deed for acclaim by people is shirk and to abstain from any amal for the sake of another is riya. Ikhlaas (sincerity) is that Allah ﷻ saves you from both.*

* *The people of Rahman (i.e. the pious) are those who have khushu' and tawaadhu (humility). Whilst the people of dunya are those who have takabbur (arrogance) and self-conceit; who consider the laity as inferior.* (p428, ibid.)

Pearls of Wisdom
of the
Great Imām 🕮

Whenever a person visited the Great Imām 🕮 and started talking of this-that-and-the-other, he would adopt patience. Should the person fail to heed this polite signal and continue talking, the Great Imām 🕮 would interrupt by saying, 'Please stop your lecture; you should not relate those tales of people which they dislike...May Allah 🕮 Forgive those who say bad about us and may He be Merciful upon those who say good of us. Inculcate the understanding of Deen, become a Faqeeh and leave people upon their hāl (state); Allah 🕮 will then cause them to be dependent upon you.'

2) The Deen, gifts and Fadhl (favours) from Allah 🕮 are infinitely better and greater than any gift from (creation). One should build hopes and await (only His Fadhl). Whatever (creation) give, their gratitude despoils it, whilst Allah 🕮 is forever showering bounties without any difficulties, disgrace or humiliation.

3) Whomsoever seeks authority before its time: becomes disgraced and his life passes in ignominy.

4) Whomsoever enters a 'Ilmi Majlis whilst his mind is occupied and agitated (i.e. his thoughts are elsewhere), has neither recognised the status of fiqh or the Fuqaha.

5) Whenever the 'ilm of a person does not prevent and dissociate him from deeds proclaimed harām by Allah 🕮, then this person is in danger.

6) Whenever a (non-mahrām) lady arises from her place (of sitting), do not sit thereupon until this place has 'cooled.'

7) If in dunya and Ākhirah, the 'Ulamā are not the Walee (friends) of Allah 🕮, then nobody is the Walee of Allah 🕮!

8) People were inquiring and receiving Masā'eel from the Great Imām 🕮 immediately after Fajr Salāh...when somebody commented, 'Is this not the time when our Salaf engaged in recitation of Khair (the Glorious Qur'ān and zikr), considering all other talk to be makruh?' Imām Aboo Haneefah 🕮 replied, 'Which khair is greater than showing people what is halāl and what is harām? Praise the Purity and Glory of Allah 🕮: warn and scare people away from His disobedience! When we forego Amr bil Ma'āruf and Nahee 'Anill Munkar (propagate goodness and warn from disobedience) the Ummat will be destroyed.'

9) Once a person arrived with a kitab and requested, 'Please read this to me.' The Great Imām 🕮 replied, 'This is not the way to acquire 'Ilm, for Allah 🕮 has taken a vow from the 'Ulamā to, 'Present the Deen of Allah unto people clearly.' For 'Ilm there are no elite or lay people, because an 'Alim teaches people and expects only the Pleasure of Allah 🕮 in his teaching.'

10) Imām Aboo Haneefah 🕮 once commented, 'When I am walking on the road, do not ask any Deeni matter; when I am talking with people; do not ask any Deeni matter; when I am standing or sitting leaning against something, do not ask any Deeni matter; because during these occasions, a person's 'Aql (intellect) is not focussed.'

11) If you do not make an intention of acquiring Khair (Deeni

goodness) from 'Ilm, then you will be deprived of Tawfeeq.

12) *Once, the Great Imām commented, 'I am amazed at those people who talk and act upon zān (suspicions and presumptions), because Allah ﷻ has clearly disapproved of this for His Nabee ﷺ and Commanded, 'And follow not (O man, i.e., say, do or witness) that of which you have no (sure) knowledge...' (Glorious Qur'ān, 17:36)*

13) *The Great Imām often advised his students, 'Whomsoever seeks Deeni 'Ilm for the sake of acquiring dunya is deprived from the blessings of 'Ilm - which fails to penetrate and become grounded in his heart. Accordingly, such a person does not derive any great benefit from 'Ilm. However, when a person learns 'Ilm for the sake of Deen, barakat is created in his 'Ilm which becomes grounded in his heart. Now, genuine students derive benefit from him.'*

14) *Once the Great Imām advised the famous Ibrāheem bin Adham ﷺ, 'O Ibrāheem! You have been granted Tawfeeq to do good deeds; it is therefore appropriate you maintain your gaze towards 'ilm because, 'ilm is the root of ibaadah and the cause of progress.'*

15) *The similitude of a person who studies 'Ilm-e-Hadeeth but remains indifferent to 'Ilm-e-Fiqh is like an alchemist who although hoarding medicines is unaware of the diseases for which these drugs are to be used...until a doctor prescribes them. Similarly, a student of Hadeeth does not comprehend the mafhûm (application) of Hadeeth until explained by a Faqeeh.*

16) *A piece of bread, a cup of water and a set of clothes acquired with peace and dignity is an infinitely better proposition*

than any existence and bounties wherefore one has to suffer regret.

17) *Until a person is alive, he requires a good residence for honour and safety; this is good fortune. When he acquires such a house, he should make shukr of Allah ﷻ and make preparations for his residence in the Hereafter.*

18) *Whomsoever desires freedom from the Athāb (punishment) of Allah ﷻ should become oblivious to the Athāb of this dunya. Whoever's nafs (self) becomes Kareem (gracious), for such a person this dunya and all its difficulties become easy.*

19) *Do not relate your 'Ilm and Fiqh unto such a person who is not desirous of it. Do not inconvenience those sitting by you. Similarly, whomsoever interrupts your (Deeni) speech...do not repeat it to him a second time: because such a person does not love 'Ilm or Adab (manners).*

20) *Aboo Bakr Zaranjaree ﷺ read two couplets related to the Great Imām ﷺ, 'Of the good fortune of man is that when he is blessed with some rank and life of fakhr (glory), i.e. he be the recipient of the fineries and joys of this dunya, he makes shukr (grateful) and prepares deeds for the Akhirah.'*

21) *Once a Faqeeh requested the Great Imām, 'I have been summoned by the Ameerul Mu'mineen. When I go to him I shall enact Amr bil Ma'āruf and Nahee 'Anill Munkar: please relate some commands and prohibitions which I may relate?' The Great Imām replied, 'When you arrive, make salām and sit down silently. If he should ask anything and you have an answer, reply by all means otherwise say, 'O Ameerul Mu'mineen! Dunya is sought after for four reasons:* Firstly, *sharf (honour and respect). Mashā'Allah! Allah ﷻ*

has blessed you with being Shareef ibn Shareef (you are the grandson of the Uncle of Nabee ﷺ).

Secondly, kingship. Through the Fadhl of Allah ﷻ you are the ruler of Arabia and Ajam.

Thirdly, wealth. Allah ﷻ has blessed you with such wealth with is incomprehensible.

Fourthly, O Ameerul Mu'mineen! Fear Allah ﷻ and make 'amāl-e-Sāleh compulsory upon you. Save yourself from those things which He has prohibited. Consequently, you will acquire both dunya and the Ākhirah.'

22) *Once the Great Imām was informed, 'there is a large gathering of people in the masjid who reflect and debate upon Fiqh.' He inquired, 'Do they have an Ustadh (teacher)?' 'No.' The Great Imām commented, 'These people will never be able to become Faqeeh.'* (Tazkiratul Nomaan)

23) *In proclaiming Haqq, fear none and nobody...should a person introduce some bidat into Deen, openly publicize it, even though this person be prominent and command power, because in proclaiming Haqq, Allah ﷻ is your Helper and the Protector of His Deen.*

24) *Whenever the need arises to speak on some 'ilmi point, carefully ponder before speaking and only state what you are able to prove.*

25) *Never engage in a debate with people who are ignorant of the etiquettes of 'ilmi majlis or those who only wish to argue.*

26) *Should the need arise for an 'ilmi debate, then participate with courage, confidence and awe. Dispel any notion of defeat or fear, as these will weaken your resolve and tongue.*

27) *Never make disrespectful statements of your teachers, otherwise your students too will criticize you.*

28) *Always make du'aa of Maghfirat (forgiveness) for your teachers and those from whom you have benefited.*

29) *Treat your students with such concern and affection, that should anybody observe you, they consider the students to be your own children.*

30) *In fine and disputable matters of Deen, do not engage in dialogue with lay people. In all affairs, keep amānat and taqwā foremost...Always take stock of your nafs (self); take care of 'ilm; consider dunya to be the most despicable and never become contented over worldly matters for Allah ﷻ will demand a reckoning for all affairs.*

31) *Make the Zikr of Allah ﷻ in abundance...Whenever you hear the Azān, hasten towards preparing for Salāh and the Masjid. After every Salāh, endeavour to recite the Glorious Qur'ān and some Zikr for a while.*

32) *Be grateful to Allah ﷻ that He has granted Tawfeeq to stand firmly upon Deen.*

33) *Every month, make a habit of fasting a few days. Regularly visit the graveyard and always remember death.*

34) *Do not establish or maintain relationships with such people who are the slaves of their desires. However, for purposes of tableegh and da'wah it is appropriate to meet and associate with them.*

35) *Do not criticize or vilify anybody. Do not consider the masses to be inferior...rather respect them, however do not establish a relationship with them until they approach you.*

36) *Do not laugh in abundance; this deadens the heart. Whatever task you undertake, act with composure and dignity, do not act rashly.*

37) *Should anybody call you from behind, do not answer them because this method is reserved exclusively for animals. When you walk along the road, do not look hither-thither, rather lower your gaze. Visit the bazaar less.*

38) *In conversation, do not adopt sternness, futility, rudeness or loudness; rather maintain your dignity and composure.*

39) *Do not expose the secrets of people. Whomsoever makes mashwarah (consultation), then endeavour to advise them in accordance to your knowledge and experience. By doing so, the Qur'b (Proximity) of Allah ﷻ is achieved.*

40) *If you observe a fault of your associate, do not publicize it, because this too is an amānat. Save yourself from bukhl (stinginess), greed and lies.*

41) *Do not associate with ruffians. In all affairs, always bear in mind your dignity and awe. Always maintain isti'gna (contentment and aloofness) in your heart and display it in your behaviour and dealings; even if you be a pauper. Do not hanker or be avaricious of dunya.*

42) *Behave with courage and vigour in every affair, because whomsoever loses courage suffers indignation.*

43) *Never converse with non-mahram women nor associate with them; for this deadens the heart.*

Ten Outstanding Qualities of the Great Imām

Shaykh 'Abdu'l-Qayyum Haqqānee *dāmat barakātuhum* relates, 'Imrān al Muslee ☘ narrated, 'Allah ﷻ had blessed the Great Imām ☘ with ten such distinguishing qualities, that if anybody was to posses even one of these he would undoubtedly be a leader and benefactor for his community or nation. Those ten outstanding features of the Great Imām ☘ are:

1) *Piety.*
2) *Sadāqat (sincerity).*
3) *Sakhāwat (generosity).*
4) *Expertise in Fiqh.*
5) *Mildness and sincere affection towards laity.*
6) *To excel in benefiting others.*
7) *Maintaining silence.*
8) *Completely avoiding futility.*
9) *Truthfulness in speech.*
10) *Aiding the oppressed - whether friend or foe.*

When the famous 'Abdullah ibn Mubārak ☘ visited the grave of his mentor in Baghdad, tears flowed as he commented:

'O Aboo Haneefah ☘! When Imām Ibrāheem Nakh'aee ☘ died he left behind his deputy. When Hammād bin Sulaiman ☘ died, he too left behind a deputy. O Aboo Haneefah! When you passed away, you left not a single deputy on this entire earth!'   (p441, Tazkiratul...)

৪৩৫৪

Chapter Three

Imām

Mālik ﷺ

Imām of Darul Hijrah
(Madeenah Munawwarah)

(93 - 179 AH ~ 716 - 802 CE)

Ḥāfiz Zehbee ﷺ *comments, 'There are five qualities within Imām Mālik* ﷺ *which, to my knowledge, were not present in any other person:*

1) Consensus of the Muhaditheen on his 'adālat (justice), ittibae' (strict following) of the Sunnah and piety.

2) Such excellent fahm (understanding) and broad 'uloom.

3) Such long life and high sanad (pedigree).

4) Consensus of the A'imma (Scholars) on his hujjat (proofs) and the authenticity of his narration's.

5) His expertise in fiqh and fatwās.' (p79, States…)

Birth & Patronage

mām Mālik ﷺ was born in 93 AH (716 CE) in the blessed city of Madeenah Munnawwarah. His parents were Anas (whose forefathers are regarded as Sahābāh) and 'Āleetah binte Shurayk ﷺ.

During childhood, the young Mālik bin Anas ﷺ learnt *Qirāt* and Sanad of the Glorious Qur'ān from the Madanee Leader of Qurra' and undisputed authority Imām Naafi' ﷺ. His quest for further 'Uloom was not constrained by real poverty at home. He would sell wood to acquire money to purchase kitabs. Allah ﷻ blessed him with such outstanding faculty of memory that whatever he read once was preserved lifelong. Physically, he was tall and well built, fair skinned with a long nose and little hair above his forehead. He was handsome in appearance, impeccably well dressed - often in white and well perfumed.

Nafee' bin Kaûs ﷺ

In Madeenah Munnawwarah, after the death of the famous Sahābee and Muhaddith 'Abdullah ibn 'Umar ﷺ, his 'Ilmi successor was Nafee' bin Kaûs ﷺ (d. 117 AH/740 CE). An one time slave, his rise over 30 years under the patronage of his master Ibn 'Umar ﷺ is accredited as being the symbol and epitome of Islāmic benevolence, equality and justice. Moreover, Nafee' ﷺ directly benefited from other high-ranking Sahābāh such as: Aboo Hurayrah ﷺ; Aboo Sa'eed Khudri ﷺ and *Umm al-Mumineen* 'A'ishah ﷺ. This is why Nafee' ﷺ is known as *Imām fil 'Ilm* of Madeenah.

As long as his tutor was alive, Imām Mālik ﷺ spent

approximately 12 years in his company and lectures. This is why so many narration's of Nafee's appear in Imām Mālik's 🌸 kitabs and earned the latter the honourable title, *'Mālik bin Nafee' bin Ibn 'Umar.'*

The Imām is considered amongst the Tabe' Tābieen and his Shuyookh number approximately 900 - of whom some 300 are considered as Tābieen. After the death of Nafee' bin Kaûs 🌸, Imām Mālik 🌸 succeeded him and at the tender age of just 17 years was appointed to teach and conduct his mentor's *Majlis* in Masjid-An-Nabawee. This responsibility he faithfully discharged for the next sixty-two (62) years! Whenever the occasion arrived to teach Hadeeth, he would firstly perform either *ghusl* or *wudhu*, thereafter he would dress in expensive quality clothes, groom his hair, apply perfume and only after this elaborate ritual in respect of Hadeeth emerge outside to impart 'Uloom. As long as he remained engrossed in his Hadeeth lecture, he would at regular intervals apply *itr*. Moreover, his lecture room was impeccably clean and beautifully furnished with quality carpets and cushions. The atmosphere was so dignified, momentous yet serene that leave aside any noise or distraction, no person (and the audience numbered 13,000) had the valiancy to even raise a murmur. Sufyān Thāwree 🌸 commented:

'If Imām Mālik would stop talking, all the students would lower their heads and out of veneration would not have the courage to again raise questions. Even awe respects him and he sits resplendently upon a throne of esteem, whereas, the amazing feat is, he is held in such honour despite not possessing a kingdom.' (p79, ibid.)

The 'Ālim of Madeenah

Abdullah ibn Mubārak 🌺, the distinguished student of both Imām Aboo Haneefah and Imām Mālik 🌺 relates,

'One day I was present in the lecture of Imām Mālik 🌺 whilst he was imparting Hadeeth, when a scorpion bit him, not once, but eleven times! However, despite the horrendous pain he continued to teach. At end of the lecture when all had left, I asked, 'Shaykh! Why did the colour of your complexion change and why were you shivering during the lecture?' He replied, 'A scorpion bit me on eleven occasions...but because of the adab for Hadeeth-e-Nabawee, I did not arise. Now find it and kill it.'

(p76, Episodes)

Khalaf bin 'Umar 🌺 relates,

'I was sitting in the company of Imām Mālik 🌺, when Qāree Ibn Katheer 🌺 of Madeenah appeared and delivered a letter to him. After reading, the Imām placed it underneath his prayer mat. When he arose to leave, I too followed, whereupon he ordered me to sit down and extracting the letter instructed me to read it. Herein was related a dream wherein people are gathered around Nabee 🌺 and requesting something from him. He 🌺 replied, 'I have buried an enormous treasure underneath this mimbar and instructed Mālik to distribute it to you, therefore, you should go to Mālik.' The people departed saying, 'Pray, will Mālik distribute?' Somebody replied, 'Whatever Mālik has been instructed, of a surety, he will enact.'   (p78, States...)

It is related in Tirmizee on the authority of Aboo Hurayrah ☙ that Nabee ☙ prophesised,

'An era is very near wherein people will travel from afar on camels to seek 'Uloom, however besides the 'Ālim of Madeenah' they will not find a greater scholar anywhere.'

(p81, States of....)

Pious 'Ulamā (e.g. Sufyān bin 'Uyaynah) have concluded that this Hadeeth applies to Imām Mālik ☙.

Even in old-age Imām Mālik ☙ refused to travel mounted upon an animal or wearing shoes anywhere in Madeenah upon the blessed footprints of Nabee ☙. Imām Shāfi'ee ☙ relates, 'Once I saw an Arabian horse and some donkeys tied at the entrance to Imām Mālik's ☙ house and commented, 'they are of beautiful quality.' He replied, 'I gift all of them to you.' Imām Shāfi'ee ☙ suggested, 'Shaykh, at least keep one as conveyance for your self?' He replied, 'I feel ashamed to tarnish and trod the footprints of Nabee ☙ with the hoofs of an animal upon which I may be mounted.'   (p80, ibid.)

Once Caliph Haroon al-Rasheed inquired, 'Do you have a house?' When Imām Mālik ☙ replied, 'No,' The Caliph presented 3,000 gold coins and suggested, 'Buy a house.' When the Caliph was about to depart from the *Majlis*, he commented,

'It would be very nice if you were to come with us, because it is my wish that people should derive maximum benefit and become hāmil (bearers) of (your kitab) Mu'attā in the same way that 'Uthmān ☙ made people hāmil of the Glorious Qur'ān.'

Imām Mālik ﷺ replied,

'This is not necessary, because after the death of Nabee ﷺ the Sahābāh migrated and settled in various countries and now every city has an 'Alim. Regarding my accompanying you, well this too is not possible, because Nabee ﷺ stated, 'Al-Madeenah would be better for them if they were aware.' Regarding the gold coins, they are present, you may retake them, for if you are thereby trying to separate me from Madeenah, then this is also not possible: (p80, ibid.)

'Darul Habeeb (Madeenah) befits one's affection,

and with joy and relish do we make its mention.'

On another occasion when Caliph Haroon al-Rasheed was visiting Madeenah Munnawwarah and became aware that Imām Mālik ﷺ was teaching *Mu'attā* to people, he dispatched his *wazir* Jafar to the Imām's *Majlis* with *salāms* and a summons to attend and read *Mu'attā* to the Caliph. The Imām replied, 'Return my *salāms* and inform him, 'Ilm does not attend to you, one has to go in search of it.' Just as the *wazir* returned and was relating this message, the Imām too arrived, made salām and sat down. The Caliph commented, 'I had sent a message to you which you have failed to heed?' The Imām proceeded to relate the statement by Zayd ﷺ,

'Once upon an occasion of Nuzool-e-Wahee, the blessed thigh of Nabee ﷺ was upon my thigh. Only one small Ayah of the Glorious Qur'ān was revealed, however its weight almost reduced my thigh to pieces!' Imām Mālik ﷺ continued, 'Now ponder; one huroof of the Glorious Qur'ān, which Angel Jibra'eel ﷺ sojourned a distance equal to 40,000 years travel to bring, is it not compulsory

upon me to respect and make reverence of it? Remember, Allah ﷻ has granted you kingship and integrity, now if you should be the first person to denigrate the worth of this 'Ilm, the very real danger exist of Allah ﷻ destroying your honour and worth!'

Immediately, the Caliph descended from his throne and sat down in front of the Imām ﷺ...who motioned him to sit adjacent to him on the pillow. Thereafter, the Caliph requested the Imām to recite his *Mu'attā*...whereupon the Imām ﷺ replied, 'I have given up reciting it loudly for some time now.' The Caliph commented, 'Well in that case order all those present to leave so that I may personally recite it to you?' The Imām replied, 'One feature of 'Ilm is that should laity be deprived of it on account of the elite, then even the elite will fail to benefit from 'Ilm.' Thereafter, the Imām ﷺ requested an associate present to read and addressed the Caliph, 'O Ameerul Mumineen! It is the custom of the Ahl-e-Ilm of this City (Madeenah), that they prefer humility in the acquisition of 'Ilm.' Upon this, the Caliph moved from his pillow and sat in front like a student. Despite this awe and authority, Imām Mālik's ﷺ outstanding humility maybe gauged from a narration by 'Abdul Rahmān bin Mahdee ﷺ,

'We were present in the company of Imām Mālik ﷺ when a person appeared and spoke, 'I have travelled six months to ascertain a masā'eel.' This person thereafter presented his query upon which the Imām of Darul Hijrah replied, 'I am not aware.' Stunned, the traveller spoke in despair, 'Well, what shall I say to my people?' The Imām ﷺ replied, 'Tell them Mālik admitted to his lack of knowledge.'

(p79, States...)

Acknowledgement by Scholars

Famous Scholars have acknowledged and applauded the Imām's virtues and excellences:

1) Mus'ab Zubeeree ﷺ comments, 'Imām Mālik ﷺ was a firm, reliable 'Alim/Faqeeh who was extremely fearful of Allah ﷻ.'

2) Yahyā bin Ma'een ﷺ and Yahyā ibne Sa'eed Qattān ﷺ - who were experts of Hadeeth comment, 'Imām Mālik ﷺ is Ameerul Mu'mineen fil Hadeeth.'

3) 'Abdur Rahmān bin Mahdee ﷺ comments, 'Upon the surface of the earth, there is no more trustful person of Hadeeth-e-Nabawee than Imām Mālik ﷺ.

4) He also stated, 'Sufyān Thāwree ﷺ was Imām of Hadeeth but not Imām of Sunnah, whilst Imām Awzā'ee ﷺ was Imām of Sunnah but not Imām of Hadeeth, whereas Imām Mālik ﷺ was Imām of both Hadeeth and Sunnah!'

5) The Great Imām Aboo Haneefah ﷺ commented, 'I have not observed anyone who replies correctly with greater speed than Imām Mālik ﷺ.'

6) Imām Shāfi'ee ﷺ relates, 'After the Tābi'een, Imām Mālik ﷺ was for creation a proof from Allah ﷻ...'

7) A person inquired, 'If one wishes to memorize Hadeeth, whose (books) should one study?' Imām Ahmad ﷺ replied, 'Imām Mālik's!'

8) A person inquired, 'Whose Sanad (chain of narration) is the most reliable?' Imām Bukhāree ﷺ replied, 'Imām Mālik's!'

9) Imām Nasā'ee ﷺ comments, 'In my estimation, after the Tābi'een, there is no more wiser, pious, capable or cautious person (especially in narrating Hadeeth) than Imām Mālik.'

(p81, States...)

The Suffering & Death of Imām Mālik ﷺ

Somebody complained to Jāfar bin Sulaiman - the then notorious governor of Madeenah, that Imām Mālik ﷺ did not consider it appropriate to make *bay'h* (swear allegiance of loyalty) to such leaders. Infuriated, the governor summoned the Imām ﷺ and inflicted eighty lashes; moreover, his hands were so severely pulled whereby both shoulders became dislocated, in a despicable and inhuman attempt to prevent him from further writing.

However, when word of this torture became known, the Imām's popularity and fame only increased. When Caliph Mansur heard of this excess during his visit to Madeenah, he offered to penalize the governor, but the big-hearted Imām ﷺ replied, 'Wallah! When the lashes were striking my back, I accepted and made them halāl on account of the proximity of Nabee ﷺ.'   (p81, ibid.)

When the Imām ﷺ was ninety (90) years of age, he fell seriously ill for three weeks and on the 14th. Rabi-ul-Awwal 179 AH left this worldly abode. He was bathed by Ibn Keenanah ﷺ and Ibn Zubayr ﷺ. The Ameer of Madeenah 'Abdul 'Azeez bin Muhammad ﷺ led the Janāzāh Salāh. He is buried in Jannat-ul-Baqee' in Madeenah. The news of his death created great sorrow throughout the Muslim world. When word reached Imām Muhammad bin Hasan Shaybanee ﷺ in Baghdad during his lecture, he commented:

> *'Verily, to Allah we belong and unto Him is our return. What a great tragedy...for Mālik bin Anas has passed away...the Ameerul Mu'mineen of Hadeeth has died.'*

                                                    (p140, A'imma...)

MU'ATTĀ

'Upon the entire surface of earth, after the Glorious Qur'ān there is no kitab greater and more correct than Mu'attā Mālik.'

(Imām Shafi'ee 🌼)

Ⓘ mām Mālik 🌼 wrote many kitabs, the most famous of which is *Mu'attā* - which after the Glorious Qur'ān was the second book in the *kutub* (libraries) of Islām to be systematically arranged, codified and published. 'Allamāh Aboo Bakr ibn Arabee 🌼 comments:

'Mu'attā is undoubtedly a first and foundationary kitab; whilst Bukhāree in this aspect is a subsequent publication. Moreover, the authors' of the kitabs Muslim and Tirmizee have based their works on these previous two kitabs.' (p82, ibid.)

Although published in Madeenah, the exact date of *Mu'attā's* publication is not known; it is presumed to have been prepared between 149-150AH (c. 770 CE). The word *Mu'attā* has been translated as, 'to prepare; to knead; to soften and ease.' Why? Aboo Hātim 🌼 replies, 'Imām Mālik 🌼 had systemized this kitab for the benefit and ease of people, this is why it is known as *Mu'attā Mālik.'* Imām Mālik 🌼 relates,

'After preparing this kitab I presented it to 70 Faqeehs from amongst the Fuqaha of Madeenah. All agreed with me, this is why I have named it Mu'attā.' (p83, ibid.)

Shāh Waleehullah 🌼 and Shāh 'Abdul-Azeez 🌼 have formulated five categories for the kitabs of Hadeeth and have placed *Mu'attā* amongst the first. This is also the consensus of the majority of 'Ulamā. 'Allamāh Zurqānee 🌼 comments in the commentary of *Mu'attā*, 'After Imām Mālik ﷺ had written this kitab, some contemporary 'Ulamā's of the time also began to compile Hadeeth in this same manner. When people informed the Imām of this development, he commented, 'Only Ikhlaas and good intention remains.' This prophesy was witnessed, with the rival works of such people as Ibn Abee Zab having disappeared into oblivion.

Number of Narration's

'Ateeq Zubayree ﷺ relates, 'From approximately 10,000 Hadeeth did Imām Mālik ﷺ compile *Mu'attā*. Over a lengthy period of time, he narrowed this selection down to 1720, of which 700 are with *sanad.*. This is why Yahyā ibn Sa'eed Qattān ﷺ commented, 'The 'Uloom of people increases whereas that of Mālik has decreased (out of caution).'

Over 1,000 people (from all walks of life) had studied this kitab directly from the Imām. The Ahl-e-Ilm of both the east and west have copiously referred to *Mu'attā*. This is also why so many different editions (up to 30) have been published of this 16 volume publication. Fātimah binte Imām Mālik ﷺ had learnt *Mu'attā* by heart. When her father delivered *dars,* she used to remain secluded behind the doorway and listen to recitation by students. Whenever anybody erred, she would lightly knock upon the door and, Imām Mālik ﷺ would immediately understand and redress the mistake. Sometimes, the Imām's wayward son Yahyā would uncouthly stroll into the Masjid, whereupon the Imām would address his students,

'The teacher of adab (manners) is Allah, observe, this is my son whilst over there (listening attentively behind purdah) is my daughter!'   (p111, A'imma...)

Later in life, Yahyā bin Imām Mālik's ﷺ carefree attitude disappeared; he proceeded to become an expert upon *Mu'attā* and a leading scholar of repute. It is through him that Allah ﷻ spread *Mu'attā* throughout Yemen, before his migration to Egypt to teach Hadeeth.

Aboo Muhammad Yahyā bin Yahyā Andalusee ﷺ

Amongst the many illustrious students of Imām Mālik ﷺ, the name of Aboo Muhammad Yahyā bin Yahyā Andalusee ﷺ (d. 234 AH) glitters. He had *walked* all the way from Spain to Madeenah (some 3,500 miles of hostile environment) to learn Hadeeth from the Imām!

One day, an elephant had arrived in Madeenah...all the locals and students flocked to observe this rare spectacle. However, the young Yahyā Andalusee ﷺ remained seated in his place. To please him, the Imām commented, 'You too go and have a look at the elephant.' His golden student replied,

'I left my hometown to come and look at you and acquire 'Ilm and Adab, not to observe an elephant.'   (p.114)

Overjoyed and heartened with this reply, Imām Mālik ﷺ commented, 'Aāqeel (intelligent) of the People of Andalus!'

The result of such dedication by a student and du'aa's from his teacher? When Yahyā Andalusee ﷺ returned to Spain, he became the centre of Deeni 'Uloom and virtues. It was through him that Allah ﷻ spread *Mu'attā* and Māliki Fiqh throughout the Spanish peninsula and north-east Africa. His edition of *Mu'attā* is very famous, acknowledged and referred to by the Ahl-e-Ilm. In this noble behaviour is a great lesson for all students of Deen.

Caution in Fiqh & Fatāwā

Imām Mālik ﷺ commented,

'*It is a very serious matter and one of great concern to me that I shall be questioned about halāl and harām. I have observed such 'Ulamā and Fuqaha in my city Madeenah, for whom death was a better choice then passing a Fatwa. Whereas, nowadays I am witnessing some who wish and desire to pass judgement and decrees in Fiqh & Fatwa. If they were to fully understand the repercussions of this responsibility (tomorrow on Qiyāmah), of a surety, they would abstain. Sayyidina 'Umar & 'Ali ﷺ were senior Sahābāh, yet whenever a Masā'eel was brought to their attention, they would gather and consult with the Sahābāh before decreeing a verdict. Nowadays, to pass a Fatwa appears to have become a matter of pride...this is why people are taught 'Ilm to only this extent and why they have deprived themselves from the reality of 'Ilm. It was never the method of our aslaf (pious predecessors) to simply pronounce, 'this is halāl' or 'this is harām,' for they used to say, 'I consider this to be makruh (reprehensible)' or 'I regard this to be desirable,' because halāl and harām are those concepts which Allah ﷺ and His Rasool ﷺ have shown to be halāl or harām.*'

(p117, A'imma...)

When Imām Mālik ﷺ was about to die, those nearby observed him crying and inquired. He replied,

'*Who else is there more befitting than me to cry? Wallah! It is my wish that I would rather be whipped for every Masā'eel for which I gave a fatwa based upon my opinion in lieu of salvation from possible past errors. Would that I had never passed fatwa's based upon my opinion.*' (p118, ibid.)

Character

mām Mālik 🕮 would spend the first night of every month in worship...as if he was welcoming the new month with *ibaadah*. His daughter Fātimah 🕮 narrated, 'Every night, the Imām would complete his *wazeefah* (nafl acts), he also spent the entire night of *Jumu'ah* in *ibaadah*.' All these nafl deeds were performed in privacy to avoid any fame.

Although his family house was located in 'Valley 'Aqeeq' just outside Madeenah, he had rented the house of 'Abdullah ibn Mas'ûd 🕮 inside Madeenah in order to be associated with this great *Muhaddith*. It is also related in kitabs, that out of respect for Nabee 🕮, the Imām had reduced his intake of food, whereby he only needed to answer the call of nature every three days and, that too he would travel outside Madeenah to perform!

He was famous for his intelligence from childhood. Whenever his teacher Rabee' 🕮 observed him coming, he would comment, 'The 'aqeel has arrived.' The Imām had impeccable manners and he never ever associated with ignoramuses and uncultured fools. After acquiring 'ilm, Yahyā Andalusee 🕮 stayed for a further one year with the Imām in order to acquire *adāb*. He comments, 'I stayed so as to learn the virtues and manners of the Imām because they are a reflection of the akhlaaq of the Sahābāh and Tābeein and this is why the Imām is named 'Aqeel.' (p126, ibid.)

Whenever questioned about his condition, he always displayed contentment, happiness and resignation upon the choice of Allah 🕮 in order to avoid degrading Deeni 'Ilm.

Selflessness of Imām Mālik

$\mathcal{S}$haykh 'Abdul-Qayyum Haqqanee *dāmat barakātuhum* relates, 'Although Imām Aboo Haneefah 🌟 was 15 years older than Imām Mālik 🌟 and despite differing in opinion both were full of genuine respect towards each other. Sometimes, both would spend the entire night in discussing 'Ilm. Imām Mālik 🌟 was an avid reader of the Great Imām's kitabs. Once when both were walking towards Masjid-An-Nabawee, Imām Mālik 🌟 took hold of Imām Aboo Haneefah's 🌟 hand and ushered him into the Masjid before entering.

This selflessness amongst our *Salaf* may be gauged from an incident wherein the Abbasee Caliph Aboo J'āfar Mansur - an antagonist of the Great Imām 🌟 arrived in Madeenah during the time of Hajj. In every way possible, he tried to flatter and cajole Imām Mālik 🌟 in a despicable attempt to remove the esteem and respect of Hanafee Fiqh and replace it with a national code supposedly based on the statements of Imām Mālik 🌟. However, the Imām was too astute and noble to fall for Caliph Mansur's strategy and without the slightest fear addressed the Caliph with great wisdom:

> '*Your excellency! Scholars of every locality have chosen the words of hadeeth and statements of 'Ulamā; accordingly leave them upon their choice.*' (p256, Episodes...)

Consequently, the hopes of Caliph Mansur's to lessen the grip of Hanafee Fiqh upon Iraq and other localities of the Muslim Empire were nullified and dashed.

Imām Mālik's Pearls of Wisdom

*C*he statements of pious elders reflect their experience and wisdom, moreover they contain very beneficial knowledge for others. Should one be fortunate to understand and act upon these pearls of wisdom, a great *inqillab* (betterment) takes place. Many such statements of Imām Mālik 🌸 are available in kitabs:

1) *'There are various categories of Ahl-e-Ilm:*

   i) The 'Alim who acts upon his 'Ilm is described by Allah 🌸 as,

   '...It is only those who have knowledge amongst His slaves that fear Allah...' (Glorious Qur'ān, 35:28)

   ii) The 'Alim who acquires 'ilm but fails to impart it to others is described by Allah 🌸 as,

   'Verily, those who conceal the clear proofs, evidences and the guidance, which We have sent down, after We have made it clear for the people in the Book, they are the ones cursed by Allah and cursed by the cursers.' (Glorious Qur'ān, 2:159)

   iii) The 'Alim who acquires 'ilm, imparts it to other's but fails to act upon it himself is described by Allah 🌸 as,

   'Or, do you think that most of them hear or understand? They are only like cattle - nay, they are even further astray from the Path.' (Glorious Qur'ān, 25:44)

2) *Proximity to bātil (deviation) brings destruction because bātil is far from truth.*

3) *Dunya which is acquired after harming one's Deen or honour is devoid of goodness, no matter how great the gain.*

4) *I have become aware that whatever the Ambiya* صلى الله عليه وسلم *will be questioned about, the very same questions will be posed to the 'Ulamā.*

5) *The similitude of hypocrites in Masjids is like birds trapped in a cage; as soon as the door is opened, birds fly away.*

6) *'Ilm of Deen is not acquired by much talking, rather it is a Nur (Heavenly Light) which Allah ﷻ imbues into a person's heart. The acquisition of 'Ilm is strenuous, accordingly just observe what one needs to do from morn till evening to achieve it. Therefore adopt these measures.*

7) *Once the Imām asked an associate, 'What do people say about me?' The associate replied, 'Friends praise; whilst enemies criticize.' The Imām replied, 'This is the condition of people; friends and enemies are both present; may Allah ﷻ save us from the verbal vulgarity of people.'*

8) *The final body of this Ummah is able to achieve success by adopting the same mode (the Sunnah) as the original body employed.*

9) *Sins originate from pride, jealousy and stinginess.*

10) *You may amuse yourself, but do not amuse or toy with one's Deen.*

11) *Before acquiring 'ilm, acquire hilm (forbearance).*

12) *Whomsoever adopts truthfulness in all his affairs, will until old-age benefit from his intelligence and not fall pray to nonsense or become senile like others.*

13) *The Adab of Allah ﷻ is in the Glorious Qur'ān; that of His Rasool ﷺ is in Sunnah and Ahadeeth; and the Adab of the Sāliheen is in Fiqh.*

quired about *'ilm-e-bātin (spiritual knowledge).*
ss *the Imām replied, 'Only that 'Alim is aware*
.. *knowledge who is aware of Zāhiree (external)*
'ilm and this 'ilm is bestowed when Nur is created in the heart. Therefore adopt Deen in entirety; and woe betide of befalling into gossip and hearsay. Adopt that which is beneficial and forgo the person who is unaware.

15) *Whomsoever desires to enlighten his heart; be saved from the tribulations of death; acquire protection from the harshness on the Day of Qiyāmah; should ensure one's internal deeds are superior to the external deeds.*

16) *Whenever a quarrelsome person came to argue, the Imām separated himself saying, 'I adopt the proofs from my Creator whilst you are drowned in doubts; therefore debate with a person of a similar temperament to yourself.'* (p121-137, A'imma)

The Enlarged & Revised

Ashraf's Advice Upon the

DEATH

of a Muslim

A Comprehensive & Essential Manual of
'What to do & What Not to do'

Based Upon the Teachings of

Shaykh Ashraf 'Ali Thānwi, Shaykh Muhammad Saleem Dhorat
Shaykh-ul-Hadeeth Zakariyyā, Shaykh Dr. 'Abdul 'Hai 'Ārifee,
Shaykh Abrārul Haqq, Shaykh Mufti Taqee Uthmānee, Shaykh Maseehullah

Ashraf's Amānat©.

PO Box 12, Dewsbury, W. Yorkshire, UK, WF12 9YX,
Tel: (01924) 488929 ~ email:info@ashrafsamanat.org

Chapter Four

IMĀM

SHĀFI'EE

(150—204 AH ~ 773—827 CE)

Nasir-ul-Hadeeth

(Aid, Protector & Defender of Hadeeth)

N abee 🌸 made this du'aa:

'O Allah! Give guidance to the Quraysh; whereby their 'Alim will fill the surface of the earth with 'Ilm.

O Allah! In the way, you drowned them (the Quraysh) in Athab (Punishment); confer upon them In'ām and forgiveness (Your Favours).' (p178, A'imma...)

A llamah Ibn Hajar 🌸 comments,

'This statement refers to such a Qurayshee scholar, whose 'Ilm will circumvent the entire earth and whose teachings will be well publicized. Besides Imām Shāfi'ee 🌸 we do not know of any other (Makkan) scholar who fits the above description and prophesy.' (Vol. 9, p326, Seerah...)

Birth & Lineage

Imām Muhammad bin Idrees Shāfi'ee ﷺ was born in 150 AH in the town of Ghazah (some reports say 'Asqallan) in Palestine. Amongst his forefathers was Shafaa' bin Saib ﷺ... who despite being the flag-bearer of the Quraysh became a Muslim after the Battle of Badr. According to 'Umar ﷺ, Shafaa's physical appearance closely resembled that of our beloved Nabee ﷺ.

Father Idrees ﷺ died around the time of Imām Shāfi'ee's ﷺ birth, it was therefore his mother Fatimah binte 'Abdullah ﷺ who migrated to Makkah with her two year-old son. During her pregnancy, she had observed a dream, wherein a star emerged from her stomach, landed in Egypt and illuminated every town of that country.

Despite poverty, Imām Shāfi'ee ﷺ spent his youth in two activities: acquiring Deeni 'Ilm and archery. In both, he excelled. The best part of day *and* night was involved in learning and studying whilst during free-time he had mastered horse riding and could strike bulls-eye with 10-out-of-10 arrows! Imām Shāfi'ee ﷺ recalls his *Taalib-Ilmi* phase:

> *'...although I did not have sufficient funds to pay for a Muallim's fee's, nevertheless, events transpired whereby my teacher was prepared to teach me for free. Whatever lesson he imparted to children, I would immediately learn by heart and during his absence teach it to the other students. My Muallim was so delighted at this arrangement that he happily taught me for free...thereafter I learnt Hadeeth narration from my Uncle and Khalid Zanjee. Whatever*

Hadeeth or Masā'eel I heard from the 'Ulamā's Majlis, I immediately learnt by heart. Moreover, because mother did not have enough money to buy writing paper, I would collect pieces of papyrus, date leaves and bones to be able to write on. By the age of 7 years I had memorized the entire Qur'ān in such a way as to be able to comprehend its meaning...by the age of 10 years I had memorized Mu'attā of Imām Mālik (in nine nights)!' (p143-4, A'imma...)

Hijrah to Madeenah & Student of Imām Mālik

Allah ﷻ had created enthusiasm in this young boy to protect His Deen of Islām. The young Imām would often plead to his mother, 'O Respected Mother! Grant me permission to travel from Makkah to acquire Ilm?' His mother would start crying, whereupon Imām Shāfi'ee ﷺ often concluded, 'Because father is not here, my mother probably does not wish to be left all alone in old-age.'

One day, he implored, 'Dear Mother! If you continue to cry like this, how will your son ever be able to come out of the depths of ignorance and acquire 'Ilm...grant me permission to leave for a short while please?' His mother replied, 'Darling! Whenever, you mention *Talab-ul-Ilm,* tears appear in my eyes, not because of the worry of being left alone when you have gone, but because I do not have the money to finance your journey!' The young Imām replied, 'Dear Mother! Do not worry about money for the journey, for this is Allah's responsibility. You bid me farewell and make du'aa for me!' With his mother's blessings, he approached the Ameer of Makkah and requested a reference to take to Madeenah.

Arriving in Madeenah, he proceeded to the Valley of Ateeq

and awaited upon the door of Imām Mālik 🌸. When finally he emerged, the young Shāfi'ee 🌸, 13 years of age pleaded, 'I am a student of Deen and these are my circumstances...' Upon hearing of his plight, the Imām stared at him for a while, asked his name and then commented:

> '*Muhammad! Fear Allah 🌸 and save yourself from sins, because in the future you shall achieve great rank. Come tomorrow and bring somebody who is able to recite Mu'attā for you.*'
>
> (p145, A'imma)

The young Shāfi'ee 🌸 informed the Imām that he had memorized *Mu'attā* and now became a regular reciter of this kitab in the *Majlis* of his mentor. He often stated:

> '*Mālik is a shining star amongst the 'Ulamā...There is no more correct kitab on the surface of this earth than Mu'attā...If Mālik and Sufyān bin 'Uyaynah were not present, then 'Ilm would have vanished from Arabia...*'
>
> (p156, ibid.)

Shaykh Muhammad Saleem Dhorat *dāmat barakātuhum* continues, 'The young Shāfi'ee 🌸 stayed and toiled here for many years, acquiring *rusûkh* (firmness and expertise) and becoming Imām Mālik's 🌸 *manzur-e-nazar* (golden favourite). However, the young Shafi'ee had such thirst for Deeni knowledge, that after taking permission from the Imām he departs for Baghdad (Iraq) and the patronage of Imām Muhammad ibnul Hasan Shaybānee 🌸 - a student of Imām-e-Azam Aboo Haneefah 🌸. He stayed here for many years, acquiring expertise in *Fiqh*. Even after being acknowledged a leader in this field, he does not forget his teachers:

The Golden Student of Imām Muhammad ﷺ

'The knowledge which I have acquired from Imām Muhammad ﷺ, I have not received from elsewhere...I wrote down this Ilm...after approximately 10 years, when I departed from Imām Muhammad ﷺ, I looked at my manuscripts; they were large enough to fill a camel's back. If it was not for Imām Muhammad ﷺ, my (knowledge & tongue) would not be as ample...When I listen to his recitation of the Glorious Qur'ān it appears as if the Qur'ān descended from his tongue...Whenever I questioned any scholar, except for Imām Muhammad ﷺ, signs of displeasure were visible upon their face...' (p148, ibid.)

Imām Muhammad ﷺ too was full of admiration and affection for his golden student. On numerous occasions, he advised him to stay further and aided him financially. Qadhi ʿEyāz ﷺ narrates:

'Imām Shāfiʿee ﷺ studied Muʾattā from Imām Mālik ﷺ in such a manner as to acquire his teacher's pleasure; thereafter he travelled to ʿIraq and stayed with Imām Muhammad ﷺ. With him he discussed and debated the Fiqh of Ahl-e-Madeenah and wrote down the kitabs of Imām Muhammad ﷺ....' (p150, ibid.)

In reality, it was only after studying in Baghdad that Imām Shāfiʿee's ﷺ ʿilmi rank became well-known. He visited Baghdad twice (some reports say 3 times, with the first visit being in 184 AH). On his visit in 195 AH (818 CE) he stayed 2 years; whilst on the final occasion in 198 AH he stayed for 6 months.

Other Famous Teachers...

Qari Ism'aeel bin Qastanteen Makki 🌸 (d. 190 AH)

This final student of Ibn Katheer 🌸 was the teacher from whom the young Shāfi'ee 🌸 of seven years learnt *Tajweed* & *Hifz* of the Glorious Qur'ān.

Uncle Muhammad bin 'Ali bin Shafe' Makki 🌸

Imām Shāfi'ee 🌸 learnt Hadeeth from his Uncle - who was a renown Muhaddith of Makkah.

Imām Waqee' 🌸

This is the famous teacher who advised Imām Shāfi'ee 🌸,

> *'I complained to Waqee' of my weak memory; he advised me to abstain from sins; for, verily, knowledge is a Nûr from Allah; and this Nûr of Allah is not awarded to sinners.'* (p51, Taqleed...)

Muslim bin Khalid Zanjee Faqeeh Makki (d. 190 AH)

The Faqeeh of Makkah and Shaykh of Haram, Muslim bin Khalid 🌸 narrates from famous Sahābāh and Tābe'een. A very pious person who taught and gave permission to Imām Shāfi'ee 🌸 to issue Fatwa's.

Sufyān bin 'Uyaynah Makki 🌸 (d. 198 AH)

This high-ranking Muhaddith of Haram, about whom Imām Shāfi'ee 🌸 commented, 'If Mālik 🌸 and Sufyān bin 'Uyaynah 🌸 were not present, then 'Ilm would have vanished from Arabia...He was the greatest 'Alim of Hadeeth in Arabia...I have not heard anybody who could elucidate Hadeeth better... I have acquired all the Hadeeth of Ahqāms from Imām Mālik 🌸 except for 30: of these, I acquired 24 from Sufyān 🌸.'

Features of Shāfi'ee Fiqh

uring the time of Imām Shāfi'ee 🕮, Hadeeth and Fiqh were concentrated in two centres: Arabia & 'Iraq. Obviously, there were some differences in principles between the scholars of both centres. Imām Shāfi'ee 🕮 benefited from both and despite disagreeing with Imām Mālik 🕮 on certain issues, he is still considered his student. A scholar relates,

> *'The differences between Imām Shāfi'ee 🕮 and Imām Mālik 🕮 are fewer than those between Qadhi Aboo Yousuf 🕮 and Imām Aboo Haneefah 🕮.'*   (p162, Aimma...)

The main feature of Shāfi'ee Fiqh is adoption of the 'middle ground' between the scholars of Arabia & 'Iraq. It regards the Qur'ān as *hujjat*...thereafter derives *istidlal* (reasoning) from Sunnah-e-Rasool 🕮 to the extent of acting upon *Khabr-wahid* (those Hadeeth which have been related from the time of Nabee 🕮 with a minimum number of narrators). He gives precedence, like Imām Mālik 🕮 to the works of Ahl-e-Madeenah. His principles may be understood from the prerequisites he had enumerated for scholars:

'It is not permissible for Qādhi's and Mufti's to adjudicate and decree until they are qualified and proficient in Kitabullah (and its Commentary), Sunnan, Athār and the Ikhtilaaf (differences in opinion) between the 'Ulamā. In this regard they should possess: far-sightedness, correct fahm, taqwā and the willingness to consult (with other 'Ulamā) in doubtful masā'eel.'   (p162, ibid.)

Regarding the differences between the Sahābāh, the Imām 🕮 comments, 'I adopt whichever statement is in accordance with the Qur'ān, Sunnat, Ijmā' or Qiyās...'   (p163, ibid.)

'Ilm of Usool-e-Fiqh

mām Shāfi'ee's 🌼 greatest contribution is undoubtedly the development of *Usools* (principles) of Fiqh. As a concept, he was the first to formulate its foundations. Asnawee 🌼 comments:

'There is unanimous consensus that Imām Shāfi'ee 🌼 was the first author of Usool-e-Fiqh.' (V9, p321, Seerah...)

'Allamah Fakruddeen Rāzee 🌼 narrates, 'It is consensus of the Ummah, that Imām Shāfi'ee 🌼 is the founder of *Usool-e-Fiqh*, moreover it was he who devised categorizations defining reliable and weak narrations.

Nevertheless, some scholars aver that it was Imām Aboo Yousuf 🌼 who was the first to formulate Usool-e-Fiqh and that Imām Shāfi'ee 🌼 followed later by devising the principles of his own School of Jurisprudence. Imām Ahmad bin Hambal 🌼 comments:

'Imām Shāfi'ee's 🌼 worth with regards to 'Ilm is comparable to the need of sunlight for this world or the need of health for the body. Why, is it possible to have substitutes for either of these?' (p323, ibid.)

'Allamah Anwar Shāh Kashmiree 🌼 writes,

'In Fiqh, another distinctive feature of Imām Shāfi'ee 🌼 was to consider strong Ahadeeth as Hujjat [proofs] and to disregard weak Hadeeth. No other School of Fiqh acts in this way...' (An-Noorul Baaree)

Four Famous Baghdādee Students...

mām Shāfi'ee's 靐 'Ilmi activities were divided into three centres: Makkah; Baghdād and Egypt. During his time in these places, only his *majlis* prevailed. His concern, affection and dedication towards his students is legendary. Once, he addressed his student Rabee' Sulaiman Muradee 靐:

'*O Rabee! If it was in my power to feed you 'ilm, I would certainly have done so.*' (p163, ibid.)

The Imām's activities in Baghdad are known as *aqwāl-e-qadeem* (former statements), whilst his teachings in Egypt are known as *aqwāl-e-jadeed* (later Statements).

During his final visit to Baghdad, four students became his special *hamil* (bearers) and deputies, through whom the *aqwāl-e-qadeem* of Shafi'ee Fiqh was persevered and propagated.

Hasan bin Muhammad Zafranee Baghdadee

A great scholar, Imām and writer of Fiqh and Hadeeth who diligently attended the *dars* of Imām Shāfi'ee 靐. He was appointed to read-out the Imām's kitabs and about whom he commented, 'The Muhaditheen were in slumber when Imām Shāfi'ee 靐 awoke them. Moreover, whomsoever has lifted pen and ink to write Hadeeth is indebted to Imām Shāfi'ee 靐.' (ibid.)

Imām Shāfi'ee 靐 conferred upon **Hasan bin Muhammad** 靐 (d259 AH) the title, 'the leader of Zafran.'

Imām Ahmad bin Hambal Baghdadee (d. 266 AH)

The golden student of Imām Shāfi'ee 靐 whose life is considered in detail in chapter five.

Aboo Thûr Ibrāheem bin Khalid Baghdadee

Aboo Thûr 🕮 (d.240 AH) was a prolific writer upon the publications of Imām Shāfi'ee 🕮, even though he differed regarding certain *masā'eels* which resulted in him forming a separate *maslak* (school of thought). Many scholars from Azerbaijan and Armenia followed his Fiqhee Maslak.

Husain bin 'Ali Karabasee Baghdadee (d. 245 AH)

An one time very close friend of Imām Ahmad bin Hambal 🕮 who is considered amongst the leading scholars of Baghdad. He too wrote extensively upon the works of Imām Shāfi'ee 🕮 and became an exponent of his *maslak.*

Hijrah to Misr (Egypt) & Ibn 'Abdul Hakeem

In 200 AH, Imām Shāfi'ee 🕮 migrated for the final time, on this occasion to Egypt saying:

> *'Brother, my nafs is very eager to travel to Egypt even though there is great difficulty in this journey. Wallah! I am unaware, whether I travel there for peace and independence or to enter my grave.'* (p159, ibid.)

His sole intention for journeying to Egypt was to establish and propagate *Fiqh,* 'Inshā'Allah, I shall visit Egypt and place such Fiqhee concepts in front of them that they will be constrained to forgo other Schools of Jurisprudence.' (v9, p313, Seerah…)

During his four year stay in Egypt, he completely transformed *Misri Fiqh.* Many Misri 'Ulamā's, when they became aware of Shāfi'ee Fiqh changed allegiance. 'Abdullah bin 'Abdul Hakeem 🕮 was a famous scholar of Egypt and Imām of Māliki Fiqh. He acted as host to Imām Shāfi'ee 🕮, aiding financially and lending Māliki Fiqh kitabs.

Six Famous Misree [Egyptian] Students...

'Abdullah bin 'Abdul Hakeem 🕮 assigned both his sons' into the *khidmat* of the Imām. Both, especially Muhammad 🕮 narrated Hadeeth and wrote kitabs of the Imām and became his favourite student. Six other students are also considered leading exponents of the Imām's later statements:

Ismā'eel bin Yahyā Maznee Misree 🕮 (d. 264 AH)

It is related about Aboo Ibraaheem Ismā'eel bin Yahyā Maznee Misree 🕮 that, 'He was an Imām of Shafi'ee fiqh, fatwa & traditions.' Imām Shāfi'ee 🕮 commented, 'Maznee is the protector and defender of my *maslak.*' He was an extremely pious, abstentious and brilliant scholar, who despite possessing such 'uloom never hesitated to quote the work of a contemporary 'Alim. He performed the *Tajheez, Takhfeen & Ghusl* (bathing & shrouding) of the Imām. He died in Ramadhān and is buried near Mount Muqattam, near to Imām Shāfi'ee's 🕮 grave.   (p168, ibid.)

Rabee' bin Sulaiman Jazee Misree 🕮 (d. 256 AH)

Aboo Muhammad Rabee' bin Sulaiman bin Dawood Jazee 🕮, a student of Imām Shāfi'ee 🕮, who has quoted Fiqh extensively from 'Abdullah bin 'Abdul Hakeem 🕮. A very pious person from whose works later scholars of the calibre of Aboo Dawood, Nasa'ee and Tahawee have referred.

Rabee' bin Sulaiman Muradee Misree 🕮 (d. 270 AH)

The final student of Imām Shāfi'ee 🕮 about whom he commented, 'Rabee is my narrator...the way in which Rabee has acquired abundant 'ilm from me, nobody else has done so.' He is titled *Al-Mua'zzin.*

Harmala bin Yahya Misree (d. 244 AH)

Aboo 'Abdullah Harmalah bin Yahya ۩ is considered amongst the inner circle of Imām Shāfi'ee's ۩ lecture group. He studied eight kitabs directly from his mentor and has related another 70 kitabs. He was a Hāfiz of Hadeeth from whom Imām Muslim ۩ has quoted extensively.

Younus bin 'Abdul Alee Misree (d. 264 AH)

About his tutor Imām Shāfi'ee ۩, Younus bin 'Abdul Alee Misree ۩ stated:

'If the whole Ummah were to get together, Imām Shāfi'ee's ۩ intelligence would be sufficient for them.'   (p170, ibid.)

Despite being poor, he was a very pious and Allah-Fearing 'Alim whose du'aa's were regularly sought. He was also a student of Sufyān bin 'Uyaynah ۩ and Waleed bin Muslim ۩. Many leading *Muhadditheen* have narrated from him. It is said, 'Younus Misree is an Arkan of Islām.'

Yousuf bin Yahya Bultee (d. 231 AH)

Amongst the close associates of Imām Shāfi'ee ۩, he too was very pious. He was arrested in Egypt, transferred and imprisoned in Baghdad for his orthodox views. Whilst in prison, on Jumu'ah, when the Azan was heard, he would bathe and don fresh clothes before proceeding towards the closed gates of the jail. Unable to leave, he would utter, 'O Allah! I have answered Your Call, however these people are holding me back.'   (p171, ibid.)

These 10 leading Baghdadee & Misree students were the leading proponents of Shafi'ee Fiqh and instrumental in its spread throughout the world.

Wisdom & Intelligence

mām Shāfi'ee ﷺ was an extremely intelligent, understanding and wise person. Aboo 'Ubaydah ﷺ relates, 'We have not witnessed a more intelligent or more perfect human.' Haroon bin Sa'eed 'Ali ﷺ comments, 'If Shafi'ee wished to (hypothetically) prove these stone columns to be of timber, he would be able to do so.'

Younus bin 'Abdul Alee Misree ﷺ stated,

'Shāfi'ee used to converse with people in accordance to their intelligence. Whenever anybody requested something, and he did not possess anything, his face would become woeful out of shame.'

He was always a happy and contented 'Alim, forever magnanimous towards his associates and students. He often stated, 'Whomsoever does not lower (humble) himself, will never be respected.'

Once, Imām Shāfi'ee ﷺ, Yahyā ibne Ma'een ﷺ and Imām Ahmad bin Hambal ﷺ travelled to Makkah and stayed in the same place. At night, Imām Shāfi'ee ﷺ and Yahyā ibne Ma'een ﷺ rested, whilst Imām Ahmad bin Hambal ﷺ spent the entire night in naf'l salāh. In the morning, Imām Shāfi'ee ﷺ commented, 'Last night, I solved 200 *masā'eel's* for the benefit of Muslims.' Yahyā ibne Ma'een ﷺ asked, 'How?' Imām Shāfi'ee ﷺ replied, 'I have purified the Hadeeth of Nabee ﷺ from 200 false narrators.' When Imām Ahmad ﷺ was asked how he had passed the night, he replied, 'I recited one *khatm* of the Glorious Qur'ān in naf'l salāh.'

'Ibaadah & Taqwā

Rabee' relates that Imām Shāfi'ee ﷺ used to complete one *khatm* of the Glorious Qur'ān *every* night. Whilst during the blessed month of Ramadhān, during every night and day, he would complete two *khatms*. Some reports imply he completed 70 *khatms* inside salāh during this month.

Bahar bin Nasar ﷺ reports, 'Whenever we visited the young Shāfi'ee ﷺ and listened to his beautiful recitation of the Glorious Qur'ān, we would be overcome with crying.' Observing this spectacle, the Imām would stop his recitation. Husain bin 'Ali Karabasee Baghdadee ﷺ relates,

'I have spent many nights in the company of Imām Shāfi'ee ﷺ; he would spend half the night in naf'l (salāh) reciting up to 100 Ayah's. After every Ayah, he would make du'aa for all Muslims and upon every Ayah of Punishment, he would seek Allah's Protection.' (p179, ibid.)

Imām Shāfi'ee ﷺ narrated, 'In a dream I was fortunate to make *Salām and Musāfahah* (handshake) with Sayyidina 'Ali ﷺ, thereafter he removed his ring and placed it upon my finger. When I related this dream to my Uncle, he interpreted it as, *'Musāfahah* with Sayyidina 'Ali ﷺ symbolizes safety from *Athāb* (punishment), whilst the ring implies that to wherever his name, jurisdiction and authority reached, unto there will your name (and thereby Fiqh) reach.' (p176, ibid.)

The Charge of Shiah Overtures

The aftermath of the murder's of 'Uthmān ﷺ and 'Ali ﷺ were still present during the time of Imām Shāfi'ee ﷺ and had divided the Ummah into two quite visible groups. Each was on the lookout to associate leading personalities into their camp. Consequently, Imām Shāfiʿee 🌺 too did not escape this categorization, with certain narrow-minded people accusing him of Shiah overtures because of his close relationship and affection for the Ahl-e-Bayt and Hashimites. Imām Shāfiʿee's 🌺 commendable respect for the descendants of Nabee 🌺 maybe gauged from his refusal to address any *majlis* where scholars of Ahl-e-Bayt were also present. When people began to object to this reverence and accused him of being a Shiah, he replied:

'Why? Did Rasoolullah 🌺 not comment, 'None from amongst you maybe a perfect Mu'min, until I am dearer to him than his father, sons and all others.'

Moreover, Rasoolullah 🌺 also advised that pious people are His friends and associates, therefore the command is to have affection for the pious and relatives. Accordingly, why should I not respect and revere the pious relatives of Rasoolullah 🌺? Thereafter, he recited the couplet:

'If affection and love for the Ahl-e-Bayt implies Shiʿism,

then O mankind & jinni, bear witness that I am a Shiah.'

When this charge was brought to the notice of Imām Ahmad bin Hambal 🌺, he commented,

'What nonsense! By Allah, I have strong conviction of only goodness about Imām Shāfiʿee 🌺. Remember, whenever, Allah 🌺 grants any 'Alim a greater rank than that to any of his contemporaries and peers...they become jealous and enviously accuse him of unfounded and false charges. What a despicable trait amongst the Ahl-e-Ilm!'

(Vol. 9, p329, Seerah…)

Acknowledgement by Scholars 🌸

Nabee 🌸 made this du'aa:

'O Allah! Give guidance to the Quraysh; whereby their 'Alim will fill the surface of the earth with 'Ilm.

O Allah! In the way, you drowned them (the Quraysh) in Athab (Punishment); confer upon them In'ām (Your Bounties) and forgiveness (Your Favours).' (p178, Aimma…)

Aboo Na'eem Abdul Malik 🌸 states, 'In this Hadeeth, 'Alim Quraysh' implies Imām Shāfi'ee 🌸. Imām Ahmad bin Hambal 🌸 commented,

'During the beginning of every century, Allah 🌸 sends such an 'Alim of Deen who propagates the Sunnah to people; he represents dafa' (negation of evil) from Rasoolullah 🌸. We have witnessed 'Umar bin 'Abdul Azeez 🌸 at start of the first century, and at beginning of the second century, Imām Shāfi'ee 🌸 carried out this khidmat (service).' (p178, ibid.)

Bilal 🌸 comments, 'Shāfi'ee has opened the lock of 'Ilm.' Maznee 🌸 narrates,

'I have not observed a more handsome person than Shāfi'ee. Both cheeks were fair and light, whenever he stroked his beard it was no more than a fistful. He used to apply (natural) henna, it'r and halāl perfumes. The column which he used to lean against whilst teaching, would also be scented. His temperament was exquisite and refined, he was very careful and particular regarding his diet and clothing. He used to apply loban (frankincense) to preserve and increase his quwwat-e-hāfizāh (faculty of memory).' (p181, ibid.)

Publications & Pearls

mām Shāfiʿee ﷺ was a prolific author. Hāfiz Ibn Hajar ﷺ reports the Imām to have written over 150 titles. Jahiz commented:

'I have read the kitabs of Shāfiʿee. They are polished emeralds. I have not observed a better author.' (p183, ibid.)

During his *Qawle Qadeem* (Baghdadee Phase), his most famous publication was *Kitabul Hujjat.* Three famous *Jadeed* (later Egyptian) kitabs are:

1) **Kitabul Umm** (c. 200 AH) ~ This 15 volume publication on Shafiʿee Fiqh has been narrated by Rabee' bin Sulaiman Al-Muradee ﷺ and commences with Kitab-ut-Taharah (Book of Purity).

2) **Al-Risalatah** ~ This kitab discusses *usools* (principles) of Fiqh; outlining the prerequisites of *istidlāl* (proofs and reasoning) from the Glorious Qur'ān, Sunnah, Ijm'ā and Qiyas. This kitab was compiled upon the specific request of Imām ʿAbdur Rahman Ibn Mahdee ﷺ.

3) **Masnad-e-Shafi'ee** ~ Compiled by Aboo Jafar Muhammad ﷺ, this is a collection of Hadeeth (with chain of narrators) which the Imām used to relate to his students.

mām Shāfiʿee ﷺ commented...

'One's temperament is akin to soil; whilst its seed is ʿilm. Now, ʿilm is only acquired by talab (quest). When one's temperament is receptive and fit, only then will the harvest of ʿilm blossom; reaping and cascading its meaning and purpose.' (p183, ibid.)

Death in Egypt

Imām Shāfi'ee ﷺ fell ill at the home of his host, 'Abdullah bin 'Abdul Hakeem ﷺ and died on the night of Jumu'ah in Rajab/Shaban, 204 AH (827 CE) at the age of 54 years. He was bathed and shrouded by his two sons, Abul Hasan Muhammad ﷺ and 'Uthmān ﷺ. The Ameer of Egypt led the Janāzāh Salāh and the Imām is buried near Mount Muqattam. Rabee' ﷺ narrates, 'Upon returning from burial we observed the new moon of Sh'aban. That night, I observed the Imām in a dream and inquired, 'How did Allah treat you?' The Imām replied, 'Allah Ta'ālā granted and seated me upon a chair of Nûr.'

(p184, ibid.)

After his death, as the students were seated around the Imām's place of *dars,* a bedouin arrived and inquired, 'Where is the sun and moon of this gathering?' Upon being informed of the Imām's death, he burst into tears and commented, 'May Allah ﷻ have Mercy and Forgive him. With great skill, he used to enrich his lectures with proofs; with broad and in-depth reasoning, he used to enlighten his critics; he would wash away unhappiness from the faces of the abashed. Moreover, with Ijtihad he opened the closed doors of Masā'eel.' Rabee' bin Sulaiman ﷺ concludes, 'During his four year stay in Egypt, the Imām had published over 1,500 pages of findings; authored the 2,000 page *Kitabul Umm,* in addition, he wrote *Kitabul Sunnan* and carried out various other Deeni activities.'

(p315, Seerah...)

৪৩০৪৫৩

Chapter Five

Imām

Ahmad Ibn

Hambal ﷺ

(164—241 AH ~ 787—864 CE)

Imām-us-Sunnat & Nasir-ud-Deen

Ali bin Al-Madanee ﷺ (the famous teacher of Imām Bukhāree ﷺ) commented,

'Allah ﷻ has chosen two people to protect and propagate His Deen besides whom a third example is difficult to find: Aboo Bakr Siddeeq ﷺ upon the occasion of irtidad (when certain Arab tribes threatened to renege after the death of Nabee ﷺ); and Ahmad bin Hambal ﷺ upon the occasion of Fitnah Khalq-e-Qur'ān...'

(Vol 1, p101, Dawat...)

Birth & Lineage

Imām Aboo 'Abdullah Ahmad bin Muhammad bin Hambal ﷺ was born in Rabi'ul Awwal 164 AH, in Baghdad. He heralded from the Arabic Clan of Shayban, who were renown for their courage, patience, steadfastness and resolution. His grandfather Hambal bin Hilal had migrated from Basrah to Khurasan where he was appointed a governor.

The Imām's mother Safiyah binte Maymoonah binte 'Abdul Malik Shaybanee ﷺ migrated back from Merv to Baghdad whilst she was pregnant. Before the birth of Imām Ahmad ibn Hambal ﷺ, his father Muhammad died shortly upon the family's arrival in Baghdad.

With great diligence, affection, care, discipline, foresight and prudence did Safiyah ﷺ nurture her child. She arranged his *t'aleem* at a local Maktab, where his piety, promise and talents were visible even at this tender age. Aboo 'Afeef ﷺ, a contemporary relates, 'Ahmad bin Hambal ﷺ was with us in the Maktab. Despite being much younger than us, we senior students were acquainted with his piety.' During childhood, he became Hāfiz of the Glorious Qur'ān and a leading scholar prophesied, 'If this youngster lives, he will become a hujjat for the people of his era.' (Vol. 1, p87, History...)

After this Maktab T'aleem phase, at the young age of 16 years, the Imām commenced study of Hadeeth under the tutorship of Qādhi Aboo Yousuf ﷺ, the golden deputy of Imām Aboo Haneefah ﷺ, 'I learnt Hadeeth firstly from Imām Aboo Yousuf...' Thereafter, for four years he studied under the leading Muhadditheen of Baghdad such as Imām of Hadeeth

Hushaym ibne Basheer ﷺ (d. 182 AH). His enthusiasm for the 'Uloom of Hadeeth maybe gauged from his desire to depart from home for lessons well before Fajar Salāh, whereupon his mother would grab hold of his *kurta* and affectionately remonstrate, 'At least wait until the Azān has been called and some light appears.' After benefiting from the scholars of Baghdad, the Imām, despite being impoverished, travelled to Kufa, Basrah, Madeenah, Yemen and acquired 'Uloom from the Muhadditheens of these localities. Ahmad bin Ibrāheem Durqee ﷺ relates:

> *'When the Imām arrived in Makkah, extreme fatigue was visible upon his body; I asked, 'Aboo 'Abdullah! You have tolerated great hardships on this journey...?' He commented, 'These difficulties pail into naught against the 'ilmi and Deeni benefits that we have derived from Abdur Razak ﷺ. From him, I have narrated Hadeeth related by al-Zahree, 'an-Salam, 'an-Abdullah, 'an-Ubaydah, Sa'eed bin Al-Musayyeb, an-Abee Hurayrah.'* (p193, A'imma)

At times, during strenuous journeys to acquire Hadeeth, he had to resort to manual labour in order to pay necessary expenses. Whilst studying in Makkah under Sufyān bin 'Uyaynah ﷺ, his belongings were stolen. His immediate concern? To find out whether his Hadeeth manuscripts had also been taken! The result of such devotion, dedication, effort, selflessness and outstanding memory was that Allah ﷻ blessed him with Hifz of over 10,000 Hadeeth!

However, despite this expertise, experience and excellence, he became the student of Imām Shāfi'ee ﷺ and commented, 'I learnt the *usools* of Ijthihad from him.'

Golden Student of Imām Shāfi'ee

mām Ahmad bin Hambal 🌸 met Imām Shāfi'ee 🌸 for the first time whilst visiting Arabia in 187 AH. Thereafter, when Imām Shāfi'ee 🌸 arrived in Baghdad (in 195 & 198 AH), he derived full benefit from him. Ibn Khulkan 🌸 relates:

> *'Ahmad bin Hambal 🌸 is amongst the close associates and students of Imām Shāfi'ee 🌸; whom at the time of his final departure commented: 'I depart from Baghdad in such a state as not to leave a greater Muttaqee or Faqeeh' than Ahmad bin Hambal.'*   (p198, ibid.)

Imām Ahmad bin Hambal 🌸 commented, 'Only after sitting in the *majlis* of Shāfi'ee 🌸 did I understand and comprehend *nasikh* and *mansukh* Hadeeth.' One should remember, the Imām was an accomplished and well-respected scholar before he met Imām Shāfi'ee 🌸, nevertheless he never hesitated to respect and study from him. Yahyā bin Ma'een 🌸 once observed the Imām following the conveyance of Imām Shāfi'ee 🌸. Yahyā addressed the Imām's son, 'Is your father not ashamed in following the conveyance of Shāfi'ee?' When 'Abdullah related this comment to his father, the Imām replied, 'Inform Yahyā bin Ma'een that if he was to walk on the other side, he would acquire 'Ilm.' On another occasion, a scholar upon observing the Imām running towards *dars* with shoes in hand stopped him, 'O Aboo Abdullah! For how much longer will you behave like a Tālib-'Ilm? Do you not feel ashamed running with these children?' The Imām merely replied, 'until death!' and left.

With Ink-Pot to the Grave

When Imām Ahmad bin Hambal's ☼ 'ilmi fame and popularity was at its peak, when his name was being mentioned with reverence throughout the Islāmic World, a person observed him walking with kitab clung to his chest and an ink-pot in his left hand. The observer commented, 'O Aboo 'Abdullah! You have reached such high stations of 'Uloom, you are *Imām-ul-Muslimeen*, yet you still going for further studies?' The Imām replied, 'With Ink-Pot to the Grave!' The result of such devotion and dedication was that his numerous *Ustadh's* (and even their family members) respected and held him in esteem. Once during the *dars* of Ibn 'Ūlayah ☼, a student mentioned something, whereupon all those attending started laughing. Furious, Ibn 'Ūlayah ☼ commented, 'Ahmad ibn Hambal is present here and you people have the audacity to laugh?' Similarly, during his *dars,* Yazeed bin Haroon ☼ made a light-hearted, though inappropriate remark. Ahmad ibn Hambal ☼ discretely coughed to display his disapproval. Yazeed asked his audience, 'Who?' The students pointed towards the young Imām, whereupon Yazeed commented, 'Had I known that Ahmad bin Hambal was present, I would not have made a jocular remark.' From his student days, the Imām was very particular about acting upon every hadeeth...

'I have acted upon whichever Hadeeth I have written; to the extent that when I became aware of the Hadeeth wherein Rasool ☼ performed cupping and remunerated Aboo Taybbah the barber, one dinar, then I too had a cupping operation and paid the barber one dinar.' (p196, ibid.)

Teaching Career & Ifta'a

ven in teaching Hadeeth and passing Fiqh decree's, Imām Ahmad bin Hambal 🕮 enacted the Sunnah of Nabee 🕮 by only teaching formally at the age of 40 years in 204 AH. This despite his immense 'Uloom, qualifications, recognition and popularity at a much younger age. Nûh bin Habeeb Qûlsee 🕮 relates,

> *'In 198 AH, I observed Ahmad bin Hambal leaning against the minaret of Masjid-e-Khaif teaching Hadeeth and fiqh to students and rules of Hajj to others. Prior to this, I had not met him...after the crowd dispersed I proceeded to meet and make salām...hence onward we became close friends.'*   (p202, ibid.)

From this observation, it is quite obvious that despite his attempts to remain aloof, the young Imām had attained the rank of a Shaykh in the eyes of his elders and contemporaries. Qutaybah bin Sa'eed 🕮 commented:

> *'The highest ranking 'Alim of our times is (Abdullah) Ibn Mubārak, after him this youngster...Ahmad bin Hambal.'*

Similarly, a person posed a question to Aboo Mashar 🕮, 'Is there anybody to your knowledge who is able to safeguard the Ummat's Deeni affairs in this era?' He replied,

> *'Besides the young man inhabiting the eastern quarters of Baghdad (i.e. Ahmad bin Hambal), I do not know of any such person.'*   (p203, ibid.)

Wakee' Ibne Jarrāh & Hafs bin Ghiyāth 🕮 often commented:

> *'An 'Alim such as the young Ahmad bin Hambal has not been observed in Kufa before.'*   (p204, ibid.)

Despite his rank and acceptance amongst the Ahl-e-Ilm, this young Saleh scholar refused to formally commence lectures before the age of 40 years. Whilst his *ustadh's* were alive, he would, out of humility, even decline to narrate Hadeeth he had heard from them and refer the questioner to his elders. Ibn Jawzee 🌺 has confirmed that Imām Ahmad bin Hambal 🌺 systematically began to teach Hadeeth when he attained 40 years. When he did so, with great sincerity, affection, caution and self-assessment, he completely transformed and rejuvenated the science of Deeni 'Uloom. People from all strata's of society, the learned and laity, the rich and poor, especially the latter flocked to his *majlis*. Hasan bin Isma'eel 🌺 relates:

> *'A minimum of over 5,000 people would gather in the majlis of Ahmad bin Hambal. Of these, over 500 scribes would write down the Hadeeth he related...with the other's attentively acquiring Ādāb and 'Adat.'* (p206, ibid.)

Despite his amazing memory, out of caution, he never related Hadeeth without referring to a kitab. 'Ali bin Madanee 🌺 commented:

> *'Amongst our Asatizah (teachers), there was no greater Hāfiz of Hadeeth than Ahmad bin Hambal 🌺. However, he still chose to relate Hadeeth from a kitab. This is a great example and precedence for us.'* (p210, ibid.)

Nevertheless, the Imām still preferred to both memorize and write Hadeeth, thereby avoiding even the remote possibility of erring. He even prohibited his students from writing in very fine fonts, as it made future reference difficult. At all times, he was conscious of the welfare of Deeni 'Ilm and his students.

Character

haykh Abul Hasan 'Ali Nadwee ﷺ relates, 'The *dars* and *Majlis* of the Imām were dignified, composed and serious affairs. Any matter or approach inappropriate to the status of hadeeth was not tolerated...

> *'An associate of the Imām narrates, 'The respect which the Imām conferred to the poor I have not observed elsewhere. He always inclined towards the needy and, displayed aloofness towards the affluent...he was the model of dignity, forbearance, calmness, humility, wisdom....all these noble qualities radiated from his face. When he sat for his dars-majlis after 'Asr, until somebody questioned, he maintained silence.'*   (p89, Dawat..)

The Imām's life, like that of the other A'imma was one of abstinence, *tawwakul* and contentment. His poverty was self-imposed for he never accepted the gifts offered by rulers or the affluent saying,

> *'This wealth is halāl, hajj is acceptable from it, I abstain from it out of caution rather than from considering it to be harām.'*   (p90, ibid.)

He dressed very simply and detested clothes which created a false awe. Muhammad bin 'Abbas ﷺ relates, 'My father had observed Imām Ahmad bin Hambal ﷺ. He was extremely handsome of medium stature. He used to employ natural henna, wear a turban, white clothes and a shawl.' He lived upon the income from his own ancestral farmlands and efforts. Moreover, despite his straitened circumstances, he was extremely generous and big-hearted. Once, a person shouted abuse at him and shortly thereafter came to apologize. The Imām replied, 'I forgave you the moment this incident took place and before a step had been taken.' Sometimes, he used to say, 'What possible benefit is there for you, if a Muslim is apprehended in athāb (punishment) because of you.' Despite these noble characteristics, he never displayed the least vanity. His humility and wish to remain discreet maybe gauged from the fact, that despite being an Arab - a fashionable feature of the time, he refrained from mentioning it. His associate Yahyā Ibne Ma'een 🕮 narrates:

> *'I have not observed a person like Ahmad, for I stayed with him for forty years; never once did he pompously mention or hint at his virtues and excellences.'* (p90, ibid.)

It has always been the way of our *Salaf-e-Saliheen* to practice 'ilm and 'amal. From childhood, the Imām was a devout worshipper. His son 'Abdullah relates,

> *'Even at the age of approximately 80 years, my father used to daily pray 150 naf'l rakahs every day and at least a seventh part of the Qur'ān. He would sleep for a short time after 'Isha Salāh and then pray throughout the night.'*

The Imām stayed for a few days with Ibrāheem bin Hanee 🕮,

> *'I have not observed a greater 'ābid, zāhid and mujāhid than Aboo 'Abdullah. He would fast during the day, make haste with iftaar and then pray a few rakahs after 'Isha before quickly retiring to sleep for a while. He would arise, make wudhu and pray until Fajar...'* (ibid.)

Allah 🕮 had blessed the Imām with such dignity, that even rulers and the military became overawed and were forced to respect him. An associate relates,

'I have visited the deputy of Baghdad and many such people in authority, however, I have not observed a more awe-inspiring personality. Once, I proceeded to debate a matter with him, when his presence totally overpowered and reduced me to shivers. All the sulahāh and scholars of his era respected him.'   (p92, Dawat...)

The famous Muhaddith Ibraaheem al-Harbee ﷺ narrates:

'I have observed Ahmad bin Hambal; it appeared as if Allah ﷻ had bestowed every kind of knowledge of the past and future endowed to humanity in his bosom. Whatever he wished to talk about, he could divulge and, withhold in his heart that which he desired.'   (p92, ibid.)

Imām Ahmad ﷺ was acknowledged by the 'Ulamā of his era as *Imam-ul-Hadeeth*. His authority and standing maybe gauged from statements of peers...

'Whenever you observe somebody cherishing affection for Ahmad bin Hambal, then understand him to be a follower of the Sunnah...Whenever you hear somebody reviling or criticizing Ahmad bin Hambal, then consider such a person's Islām as mashkuk (doubtful).'   (p101, ibid.)

Amongst his numerous famous students are Imām Bukhāree ﷺ and Aboo Dāwood ﷺ. The latter narrates, 'The majlis of Imām Ahmad were majlises of the Akhirah, wherein no worldly mention was ever made.'   (p72, Muhaditheen)

The Imām is reported to have performed five Hajj in his lifetime, of which 3 were on foot from Baghdad. During one Hajj, his total expenses were a mere 30 dirhams!

Fitnah of Khalq-e-Qur'ān (c. 220AH)

From the beginning, Iraq was infamous for strife and dissension. Before the formation of Baghdad, the towns of Kufa and Basrah were also the centres of anti-Islāmic groups, activities and propaganda. As Baghdad developed, almost all the notoriety of the two towns was wrapped together and dumped into it. During the time of Imām Ahmad bin Hambal ﷺ, the movements of *Mu'tazilaism, Jahmiyah, Qādareeyah, Jabareeyah*, etc., all reared their ugly heads in an attempt to distance the Ummah from *Kitabullah, Sunnah* and our *Aslaf.* Before the time of Caliph Mamûn 'Abbasee (b. 170 AH), these groups lacked the courage to publicly proclaim their beliefs and views. However, in 218 AH, Qadhi Ahmad bin Abee Dawûd Mu'tazalee convinced Caliph Mamûn and initiated the fitnah of Khalq-e-Qur'ān. Basically, this was an attempt by the over-philosophical Caliph to hoist upon the entire *Ummah* the false belief that the Glorious Qur'ān, unlike Allah ﷻ, was not *qadeem* (original) but a *makhlûq* (creation) and *hadith* (recent), the purpose of which was merely to proclaim exclusive *Tawheed.*

Caliph Mamûn decreed this belief compulsory and ordered his police and governors to cajole the Ahl-e-Ilm of their localities to vouchsafe and testify to this view. Any opposition or dissension would mean imprisonment and a summons before the Caliph. Accordingly, the Chief of Police for Baghdad, summoned all the leading 'Ulamā's of the city and attempted to pressurise the scholars into approving and rubber-stamping this belief. When they voiced their opposition, Caliph Mamûn ordered the execution of two scholars: Bashar bin Al-Waleed

🌸 and Ibrāheem ibn Al-Mahdee 🌸. Of the remaining 30 scholars, all except two capitulated: Imām Ahmad bin Hambal 🌸 and Muhammad bin Nuh 🌸. These two were summoned to the Caliph, however, during the journey Muhammad bin Nuh 🌸 passed away and was shrouded and buried by the Imām who was recalled to Baghdad, in chains, as news arrived of Mamûn's sudden death.

The new Caliph Mu'atasam wickedly followed his predecessor's footsteps and placed the Imām under 'house-arrest.' Thereafter, he was imprisoned in jail for approximately eighteen months. During this period, Caliph Mu'atasam would regularly summon the Imām to his court and arrange for a debate on *Khalq-e-Qur'ān*. Unable to break the Imām's resolve, he descended unto having him very severely flogged in public. One day, a bedouin came up to the Imām and advised, 'O Ahmad! If you are killed in this stand of haqq, you will become a shaheed. Should you survive, you will live a very praiseworthy and famous existence.' The Imām was greatly strengthened by this advise as Aboo Hatim Razee has commented, 'The prophesy of this bedouin became true. After this trial, Allah 🌸 greatly elevated the rank of the Imām. Both laity and the elite held him in esteem.' The Imām recalled,

> *'In jail, my biggest worry and fear was the flogging. Despite the horrendous conditions and fear of being tortured and executed, I accepted my lot in jail (he used to lead the inmates in Salāh and teach Hadeeth). At times, the floggings were unbearable, however, an inmate consoled me, 'There is no need to fear this either: after two strokes, one is unable to feel where the whip is striking you.'* (p237, Aimma)

Nevertheless, the tyrant Mu'atasam spared no efforts, even during the Ramadhan of 220 AH, in inflicting horrendous pain upon the fasting Imām, whose body was now covered with dried blood and bruises. Fearing his death may lead to an uprising, the Caliph finally decided to free the Imām. Through *tawfeeq* from Allah ﷻ, the Imām single-handedly stood up to this movement, thereby safeguarding the Ummah. Despite the horrific and life-scarring injuries suffered, he forgave every one of his persecutors by publicly reciting the Ayah...

'...but whosoever forgives and makes reconciliation, his reward is with Allah...'   (Glorious Qur'ān, 42:40)

Thereafter, he recalled the *tafseer* (commentary) of Hasan Basree ﷺ upon this Ayah:

'On the Day of Qiyāmah, all the Ummahs will be summoned before Allah Ta'ālā and an announcement will be made: 'Whomsoever has a claim for which Allah Ta'ālā is responsible should stand up.' On this occasion, only that person will arise who practised 'Afw (forgiveness) and pardon.' Accordingly, of those who have died, I forgive him who assaulted and injured me. Indeed, what harm is there for a person, through whose pardon, Allah Ta'ālā relieves another from athab?'   (p239, ibid.)

After the death of Mu'atasam in 227 AH, Waasiq became the next Caliph. Wary of the fate that had befallen his predecessors who had propagated *Khalq-e-Qur'ān* and opposed the Imām, the Caliph merely ordered Ahmad Ibne Hambal ﷺ not to stay in Baghdad in an attempt to curtail his popularity. Accordingly, until the death of Waasiq, the Imām lived in various towns and secretly imparted the teachings of Hadeeth.

The End of Khalq-e-Qur'ān

$\mathcal{A}$ fter the death of Waasiq in 232 AH, Mutawakkal became the next Caliph. He encouraged and supported the 'Ulamā, Fuqaha and Muhaditheen in outlawing this movement of *fitnah*. He financially aided the scholars to publicly launch a verbal and intellectual crusade against such deviated sects and impart correct teachings of Hadeeth. All this was undoubtedly due to the resolute steadfastness of the Imām throughout trials which encompassed the rule of four separate Caliphs. Where others had buckled, compromised and appeased, alone he had stood firm. Scholars and the laity now lauded titles: *Imām-ul-Muhaditheen, Nasir-ud-Deen*, etc. Commentators like 'Ali bin Madanee 🏵 have even claimed:

> *'After Rasoolullah 🏵, nobody like Ahmad bin Hambal 🏵 is visible who has so resolutely defended Deen.'* When probed, *'Not even Aboo Bakr Siddeeq 🏵?'* Ibn Madanee replied, *'Not even Aboo Bakr Siddeeq 🏵, because he had the support of the Muhajireen 🏵 and Ansar 🏵, whilst Ahmad bin Hambal 🏵 was all alone.'* (p240, ibid.)

Rabee' bin Sulaiman 🏵 relates,

> *'During his stay in Egypt, Imām Shafi'ee 🏵 dispatched me to Baghdad with a sealed letter to Ahmad bin Hambal 🏵 and instructed me to bring a reply. Upon reaching Baghdad, I met the Imām after Fajar Salāh and conveyed the message, 'Your brother Shafi'ee sends this letter from Egypt.' Upon opening and reading the letter, tears appeared in the eyes of Ahmad bin Hambal 🏵. Rabee inquired to be informed, 'Shafi'ee writes that in a dream*

he has observed Rasoolullah ﷺ, *who instructed, 'Write my Salāms to Aboo 'Abdullah and inform him that, quite soon, you will become entangled in a trial wherein you will be enticed to support Khalq-e-Qur'ān. Do not reply to its votaries for Allah* ﷻ *will elevate your station until Qiyāmah.'* (p241, ibid.)

Upon hearing this glad-tiding, Rabee' ؓ commented, 'Mubarak!' Thereafter, Ahmad bin Hambal ؓ forwarded a reply to his tutor Imām Shafi'ee ؓ and gifted his kurta to Rabee. Upon his return to Egypt, Imām Shafi'ee ؓ inquired, 'What has Ahmad given you?' Rabee replied, 'His kurta.' Imām Shafi'ee ؓ commanded, 'Submerge it in water and let me have this water, for I wish to derive blessings from it.'

Reluctance to Accept Authority

When Imām Shafi'ee ؓ was residing in Baghdad, the then Caliph Haroon Rasheed ؓ had requested, 'A Qādhi is required in Yemen, if you are aware of somebody suitable from amongst your associates, inform me.' The next day, Imām Shafi'ee ؓ arrived at his *halqah-e-dars* and spoke to his student Ahmad bin Hambal, 'The Caliph has spoken to me about the post of Qādhi in Yemen...I prefer and would like to delegate you for this post?' Ahmad bin Hambal ؓ replied, 'I wish to stay in your company and acquire 'ilm, whilst you are advising me to accept a post of authority to please Royalty?' Hearing such a noble reply, Imām Shafi'ee ؓ adopted silence. Similarly, on another occasion, the Caliph Ameen, an admirer of Imām Shafi'ee ؓ, requested, 'I am in need of such a person who is Ameen (truthful) and a staunch follower of Sunnah.' The Imām replied, 'Ahmad ibn Hambal.'

Family & Publications

mām Ahmad bin Hambal ﷺ married 'Aishah binte Fadhl ﷺ when he was 40 years old. A son Saleh ﷺ was born in 203 AH who became a scholar, Muhaddith and the Qādhi of Isfahan, where he died in 265 AH.

After the death of his first wife, the Imām married Rayhanah from whom 'Abdullah ﷺ was born. He has narrated the most from his father and passed away in 209 AH. The Imām's other children are: Zaynab, Hasan, Husain, Hasan, Muhammad and Sa'eed. In addition, the Imām left thousands of spiritual followers who have propagated Deen throughout the world.

Imām Ahmad bin Hambal ﷺ was not very enthusiastic about compiling kitabs and discouraged the writing of his *masā'eels* and *fatawas.* Nevertheless, his works are based upon Ahadeeth and *āthar* and his students and associates faithfully recorded, systemised and published his works. His famous publications include: Kitab-ul-Musnad; Kitab-ul-Tafseer (containing over 120,000 Ahadeeth); Kitab-us-Salāh; Kitab-us-Sunnah; Kitab-un-Nasikh & Mansukh, etc.

The epic *Kitab-ul-Musnad* is based upon 30,000 Ahadeeth, which are not categorised in the manner of Bukhāree but appear under the name of their first narrator. The Imām advised his son 'Abdullah ﷺ:

> *'Ensure you preserve 'Masnad,' for this kitab will become both Imām and Muqtadee for Muslims. They contain... over 300 Ahadeeth which are Thalatheeyat, i.e. those Ahadeeth in whose chain of transmission, there are only three narrators.'*   (p244, ibid.)

Imām Ahmad's Pearls of Wisdom

* *We do not waste time discussing any mutual differences between the Sahābāh ﷺ; we leave and hand over their affairs to Allah ﷻ.*

* *That person is indeed fortunate for whom Allah ﷻ has decreed anonymity.*

* *Should a person posses 100 good qualities, yet be fond of alcohol, then this one evil will destroy and override all virtues.*

* *Do not acquire 'ilm from such a person who hankers and exchanges dunya in lieu of 'ilm.*

* *Aboo Hatim Razee ﷺ inquired, 'How did you survive the sword of Waasiq and the punishment of Mu'atazam?' The Imām replied, 'Aboo Hatim! If truth is placed upon a wound, it immediately heals.'*

* *Once a person, observing the Imām ﷺ sitting despondently inquired, 'Nephew, why are you so sad?' The Imām ﷺ replied, 'Uncle, happiness is for that person whose good name Allah ﷻ maintains in this world.'*

* *Once somebody was mentioning the worth of dunya when the Imām ﷺ commented, 'A small portion of dunya is sufficient whilst a greater portion is inappropriate.'*

* *Whomsoever respects and venerates the Muhaditheen will be elevated in the sight of Rasoolullah ﷺ. Moreover, whomsoever ridicules them becomes disgraced, because the Muhaditheen are the Abdal and Ahbar of Rasoolullah ﷺ. If the Muhaditheen are not Abdal, then which people are Abdal?*

* *Clearly and emphatically inform the Ahl-e-Bidah, there is no relationship between us and you.* (p247, ibid.)

Death

mām Ahmad bin Hambal ﷺ died early on a Friday in Rabi-ul-Awwal, 241 AH at the age of 77 years. He had been ill for nine days, during which time, people had flocked to visit him.

The doctors had diagnosed that constant worry and concern had affected his physique and well-being. His sons relate that scars of flogging were still visible upon the Imām's back at the time of his death. A great commotion took place in Baghdad and surrounding areas as news spread of the Imām's death. After Jumu'ah Salāh, an estimated 800,000 men and 60,000 ladies performed his *Janāzāh Salāh*, with rows formed throughout the city: through streets, bazaars and even on boats upon the River Tigris. Throughout the following week, people flocked to the Martyrs Cemetery, near the Harb Gate in Baghdad and prayed *Janāzāh Salāh* next to the Imām's grave.

Even non-muslims mourned his passing away just as they had expressed their admiration of him during his life. Once a Christian doctor arrived to meet him and commented:

'For many years, I had a yearning to meet you, for your life is not only a khair and blessing for Islām, but it is barakah for the whole of creation. All my friends and acquaintances are happy with you.' (p91, Dawat...)

After the doctor had departed, an associate commented, 'It appears, du'aa's are being made for you throughout the Islāmic world.' The humble Imām replied:

'Brother, when one truly realises his own worth, then whatever another may say, one is not deceived.' (ibid.)

Features of Hambalee Fiqh

mām Ahmad bin Hambal 🙵 commented:

'When we relate Hadeeth of Rasoolullah 🙵 regarding halāl, harām, sunnan and ahqāms, then in relating such Hadeeth we are extremely particular about their sanad and narrators. However, in relating those Hadeeth which refer to fadhail 'amal (virtues) or those that do not decree commands, we adopt mildness with regards to sanad and narrators.'

(p247, ibid.)

Shaykh-ul-Islām Abul Wafa 'Ali bin 'Aqeel Baghdadee 🙵 (d. 513 AH) was asked why the Hambalee 'Ulamā, unlike the scholars of the other Schools of Fiqh, had lagged in propagating their own maslak? He replied,

'The Hambalee are munkashif and stern, because of which they associate less with people. They refrain from visiting the higher echelons of society; haqeeqat pasandee (high principles) are dominant within them; rather then adopting āra' (opinions) they prefer narrations. In order to save themselves from taweel (elucidation) they act upon external meanings. 'Amāle Saalihah (good deeds) predominates over them, this is why they refrain from intellectual concepts. They adopt the farû'at (externals) of religious doctrines: accepting ayahs and ahadeeth on face value without interpretation. As a consequence, the charge of tasbeeyah has been levelled against them...In reality, the Hambalees themselves have committed zulm upon the Hambalee maslak. The students' of Aboo Haneefah and Shafi'ee successfully accepted the posts of qadhi's and authority, because of which they had the opportunity to teach and lecture, however, few if any of

Imām Ahmad bin Hambal's students, after acquiring 'Ilm, took part in affairs of the state or laity with any relish. This is why their 'Ilmi chain became interrupted and dispersed. It may be concluded that amongst the students of Imām Ahmad bin Hambal ﷺ: the concept of fiqh was overwhelming amongst the young; whilst zuhd and taqwā were dominant features of the Mashaikh.' (p226, ibid.)

There has always been fewer followers of Hambalee Fiqh than the other *madhabs* because of a number of factors. One should appreciate, the Imām appeared in the 3rd. Century AH, by which time, the teachings of the other *A'imma* were well established. Moreover, only in the 4th. Century AH, did Hambalee followers spread further than Baghdad, towards Syria and even then sparingly, never dominating.

'People say, 'The followers of Imām Ahmad are few; and whomsoever is small in numbers is always held in contempt.' Upon this we reply, 'Wait a moment, you have misunderstood. Why, do you not observe how the Sharfaa' (nobles) are always few in number? If we are few, what is the harm? For our neighbours (the other maslaks) are large in numbers...' (p121, Fiqhee Mathahib...)

It was not until the 7th. century, that Hambalee fiqh made any in-roads into Egypt. During the 8th. Century AH, Imām Ibn Taymeeyah & Imām Ibn Qayyum propagated this school. Thereafter, during the 12th. Century AH, Shaykh Muhammad bin Abdul Wahhab established this *maslak* in Arabia. Finally, in the 14th. Century AH, the founder of present-day Saudi Arabia, King Abdul-Azeez ibn Saud (1880-1953 CE) adopted this as the School of Fiqh of the state and it has continued until today.

Maktûb (Reply) of Imām Ahmad

During the time of Imām Ahmad bin Hambal ﷺ, when fitnahs had become prevalent amongst the Ummah, a scholar Abul Hasan Musadded Basree (d. 228 AH) wrote to the Imām and requested, 'During these turbulent times, please write the Sunnahs of Nabee ﷺ.' When this letter reached Imām Ahmad ﷺ, he cried and commented, 'Verily, unto Allah we belong and unto Him is our return! This Basree scholar had spent time and money in talab 'ilm, yet the condition of his 'ilm is such, that he is unable to even recall the Sunnahs of Nabee ﷺ...' Thereafter, he wrote this reply:

All praises are for Allah ﷻ Who has established the Ahl-e-Ilm in every era to safeguard Deen. They invite the deviated towards hidayah (guidance); save them from destruction and by means of Kitabullah and the Sunnah of Nabee ﷺ revive the (spiritually) dead.

The Ahl-e-Ilm have revived many a victim of Iblees; guided many a deviated: their efforts and labour have been extremely beneficial for the cause of Muslims. They have defended and purified the Deen of Allah ﷻ from the schemes, excesses and plots of enemies who had amplified fitnah and had attempted to distort Kitabullah. The deviated people had slandered Allah ﷻ and conjured many incorrect concepts; they had commented upon the Glorious Qur'ān without proper 'Ilm.

We seek Allah's Protection from every deviation and fitnah. Allah ﷻ shower His Salām and Rahmat upon His Nabee ﷺ.

May Allah ﷻ grant all of us Tawfeeq to acquire His Ridha (Pleasure) and may He Protect us all from His Wrath. May He guide us unto the path of those who fear Him and who posses His Ma'arifat. I exhort myself, you and Muslims to compulsory adopt taqwā and the Sunnah of Rasool ﷺ. You are aware of the dreadful consequences of opposing and the beautiful reward for those who follow. The following statement of Rasoolullah ﷺ has reached us:

'Allah Ta'ālā will grant Jannat to a person who with rigour follows a Sunnah.'   (p249, ibid.)

After Kitabullah is the rank of Ahadeeth and Sunnahs of Rasoolullah ﷺ. Thereafter, the statements and judgements of the Sahābāh and Tābi'een. There is undoubtedly salvation in accepting the statement's of the Messenger ﷺ and, this reality has been transmitted from the upper ranks of the Ahl-e-Ilm.

Imān is a combination of statements and deeds; wherein progress and shortfalls take place. If you perform good deeds, Imān will increase; but should you sin, it will weaken... Remember, besides shirk or the denial of any farāidh, nothing else is able to extricate one from Islām. Should a person forgo any farāidh because of apathy, then his affairs are with Allah ﷻ; should He wish, He may punish or forgive...

Our 'Ulamā are unanimous that the Shiah's hold the view that 'Ali ؓ is greater in rank, Imān and Islām than Aboo Bakr ؓ and 'Umar ؓ...Whomsoever, holds this view, is beyond the fold of Islām. Allah ﷻ states in the Glorious Qur'ān:

'Muhammad is the Messenger of Allah. and those who are with him are...'   (48:29)

Herein, the rank of Aboo Bakr ⚘ above 'Ali ⚘ (and the whole Ummah) is very clear. Nabee ⚘ stated:

'If I were to make somebody a bosom friend, it would be Aboo Bakr. However, Allah has made me His friend.' (p251)

Whomever considers 'Ali ⚘ to have accepted Islām before Aboo Bakr ⚘ is in error. Why? Because at the time of their acceptance, Aboo Bakr ⚘ was 35 years old; whilst 'Ali ⚘ was 7 years of age: even Sharee' ahqāms and farāidh were not obligatory upon him at this age...These four (Aboo Bakr ⚘, 'Umar ⚘, 'Uthmān ⚘ and 'Ali ⚘) are the Khulafaah-e-Rāshideen Mahdiyyeen and are amongst the ten Asharah Mubassharah - those noble souls about whom Nabee ⚘ gave glad tidings of Jannah. The remaining six are: Talhah ⚘; Zubayr ⚘; S'ad ⚘; Sa'eed ⚘; 'Abdur Rahman bin 'Auf ⚘; Aboo 'Ubaydah bin Jarrah ⚘...

It is necessary for all Muslims to believe that fate; whether good or bad is from Allah ⚘, who has created Jannah before He created man and decreed who will enter therein. Its nemats are real...similarly, Allah ⚘ has created Hell; its inmates and punishment are real. People will be granted leave from Jahannam through the intercession of Nabee ⚘. Firmly believe that (Jannatees) will be granted the vision of Allah ⚘...

We should make du'aa of khair for all Muslims and not arise in rebellion against Muslim rulers...Pray salāh behind every (Muslim) Imām, whether he be pious or otherwise...May Allah ⚘ grant me and you the knowledge of Sunnah, the Tawfeeq to acquire His Pleasure and death upon Islām.'

(p248-254, ibid.)

ഇന്ദ

Ijmā of the 'Ulamā

haykh Muhammad Saleem Dhorat *dāmat barakātuhum* relates, 'Everybody is aware of the extraordinary *quwwat-e-hāfizah* (faculty of memory) of our *Muhadditheen* - whose task was to remember and preserve Ahadeeth. However, to the *Fuqahā*, whose responsibility was to deduce *masā'eels*, Allah ﷻ bestowed unique *fah'm* (the ability to comprehend and understand). Once a person entered the *majlis* of the Muhaddith Imām Āmash ﷺ and raised a query. He reflected upon his wealth of Hadeeth...but could not answer, so he maintained silence. However, his gaze fell upon Imām Aboo Haneefah ﷺ who was also sitting in the *majlis*. Turning towards him, 'O No'maan! Say something regarding this query.' Imām Aboo Haneefah ﷺ proceeded to clarify the matter, upon which Imām Āmash ﷺ commented, 'O No'maan! From which Hadeeth did you derive this answer?' He replied, 'From the very Hadeeth you narrated to us!' Imām Āmash ﷺ commented,

> *'We (Muhadditheen) are akin to pharmacists who search, collect and horde ingredients; you people (the Fuqahā) are doctors and hakeems. It is you, who are able to prescribe and formulate these medicines for the benefit of the Ummah. We are unable to prescribe.'*

After Bukhāree and Muslim Shareef, the third highest-ranking kitab of Hadeeth is by Imām Tirmizee ﷺ. In his writings, whilst relating the *masā'eel* on *ghusl-e-mayyit*...he adds, 'This is what the Fuqahā have said and these are the people who have most understood the meaning of Hadeeth.' This is the advance level of the Fuqahā's *faqāhat* (perception and understanding) not present in the *Muhadditheen*. Fiqh - the science of deducing *Masā'eel* from the Glorious Qur'ān, Hadeeth and Sharee' *Usools* (Principles) is an obligatory duty on the Ummah; without which the Ummah is unable to act with *'Kamā Haqqo-hû'* (duly and justly) upon the Sharee'ah. This is why we are so indebted to the *Fuqahā-e-Ezām* for their untiring endeavours - without which today we would undoubtedly be wandering in darkness.

Understand well, it is the unanimous verdict of all the pious 'Ulamā of the Ummah - throughout the fourteen centuries of Islām - that Imām-e-Azam Aboo Haneefah ﷺ, Imām Mālik ﷺ, Imām Shāfi'ee ﷺ, Imām Ahmad ibn Hambal ﷺ were all *Mujtahids* who possessed the ability to *istimbāt* (deduce) *Masā'eel* from the Glorious Qur'ān and Hadeeth. If they were not *Mujtahids* or had lacked 'Uloom of the Qur'ān, Hadeeth and the Sharee'ah, great 'Ulamā's from the time of the Tābieen to the present would not have acknowledged them nor would they have referred to them in their books.

Study the books upon the commentary of Hadeeth by Allamāh Hāfiz Ibn Hajar Asqalāni ﷺ and Allamāh 'Ayni ﷺ (who wrote the commentary on Bukhāree). Their kitabs are replete with reference to the statements of the Great Imām ﷺ, Imām Mālik ﷺ, Imām Shāfi'ee ﷺ, Imām Ahmad ibn Hambal ﷺ...is this then not sufficient proof that these later scholars considered them as great 'Ulamās and Mujtahids? Upon every reference (in their books) to these *Fuqahā-e-Ezām,* they wrote 'ﷺ' after their names. Pick up any kitab of the *Mutaakhireen* (later authorities of the Sharee'ah), wherever they have discussed Fiqh, they have referred, with reverence, to these four

Mujtahideen. This is sufficient proof of their acceptance by the general body of the 'Ulamā.

The rank of the Great Imām 🌸 is so high that the name of his students speak volume of his greatness: Imām Aboo Yousuf 🌸; Imām Muhammad Al-Hasan Shaybanee 🌸; Imām Zufar 🌸; Yahya bin Sa'eed Qattan 🌸; 'Abdullah ibn Mubārak 🌸; Imām 'Abd'ul-Razāk 🌸 - all great Fuqahā and 'Ulamā who sat at the feet of the Great Imām and acquired 'Ilm. Thereafter, their students include such illustrious souls as Imām Bukhāree 🌸; Imām Muslim 🌸; Imām Aboo Dāwood 🌸; Ali ibn Madanee 🌸; Imām Tirmizee 🌸, Imām Ibn Majah 🌸, Imām Nasa'ee 🌸. This then is the *maqām* (rank) of the Great Imām 🌸.

We are indebted to the *A'imma-e-Mujtahideen,* it is therefore compulsory upon the Ummah to maintain its bond with these Fuqahā. Only in this way will our Deen be preserved; otherwise slowly, slowly, such dubious statements will begin to emerge from our lips: 'These *A'imma* did not have 'Uloom of the Qur'ān or 'these *A'imma* did not have 'Uloom of Hadeeth,' or 'Imām Aboo Haneefah 🌸 knew no more than a few Hadeeth,' or 'Imām Aboo Haneefah 🌸 was a bidatee,' (Allah Forbid). When a person raises objections and casts aspersions on the *A'imma,* automatically esteem in his heart for the Sahābāh will decline. We should be alert to the cunning schemes of our enemies to detach us from these illustrious Fuqahā. Why? Because should the Ummat become separated from the Fuqahā, they will be gradually detached from the Sahābāh and consequently Nabee 🌸 and Allah 🌸! When this is the consequence, then there is no hope of Divine Aid or Assistance, both in dunya or the Ākhirah.'

Chapter Six

The Sharee' Reality

of

Taqleed

An Abridged Study of the Urdu Kitāb 'Taqleed Kee Shara'ee Haytheeyat' by

Shaykh-ul-Islām

Mufti Taqee 'Uthmānee

dāmat barakātuhum

*T*here are two forms of taqleed. Firstly, where no specific Imām or mujtahid is chosen (mu'ayin): wherein one Alim from a maslak is chosen for one matter and another Alim from another maslak is chosen for another matter. This is known as Taqleed-e-Āam or Taqleed-e-Mutlaq or Taqleed-e-Ghair Shakhs.*

In the second concept, one chooses to make taqleed of a specific Mujtahid 'Alim. In all affairs, his judgement is accepted and acted upon. This Ta'yin (fixation of a maslak) is known as Taqleed-e-Shakhs.

May Allah ﷻ grant our Fuqahā the best rewards. Observing the deterioration in our condition, they have decreed that nowadays only Taqleed-e-Shakhs (wherein one maslak is mu'ayin - fixed lifelong) is permissible.'

The Reality of Taqleed

Q⌐haykh Mufti Taqee 'Uthmānee narrates, 'No Muslim is able to deny that the original *da'wah* of Deen is submission to only Allah ﷻ. Moreover, obedience of Nabee ﷺ is made compulsory because his ﷺ statements and actions had related and translated the *ahqāms* (Commands) of Allah ﷻ. What is halāl? What is harām? In all affairs, we obey only Allah ﷻ and His Rasool ﷺ. Whomsoever, advocates following any other than Allah ﷻ and His Rasool ﷺ undoubtedly removes himself from the Fold of Islām. Accordingly, it is incumbent upon every Muslim to obey all the *ahqāms* of the Glorious Qur'ān and the Sunnah.

Within the Glorious Qur'ān and Sunnah, there are those *ahqāms,* which even laity is able to easily comprehend; these contain no *ijmāl* (abstract), *ibhām* (ambiguous) or *ta'ārruz* (conflict). These are clear-cut and obvious commands, which any right-minded person is able to understand. For example, it appears in the Glorious Qur'ān, '*...do not backbite one another.*' (49:12) As this command is clear, everybody will be able to comprehend it. Similarly, where Nabee ﷺ has stated:

'*No Arab has fadheelat (greatness) over a non-Arab.*' (p8)

This statement too is crystal-clear. However, there are some commands of the Glorious Qur'ān and Sunnat where *ijmāl* (abstraction) or *ibhām* (ambiguity) is visible and some, which appear to contradict other Ayahs or Hadeeth. For example, it appears in the Glorious Qur'ān:

'*And the divorced women shall keep themselves waiting for three periods...*' (2:228)

Herein, mention is made of the word *Qurû* to refer to *iddat* (the period in waiting) for a divorcee. However, in Arabic, this word *Qurû'* is employed to refer to monthly *haidh* (menstruation periods) as well as *tuhur* (period of purity). Should the first concept be applied, then the divorcees' *iddat* will be the passing of 3 menstruation periods. But, should the second meaning be applied, it will imply the passing of three periods of purity. Now, which meaning do we accept? Similarly, Nabee ﷺ commented,

> *'Whomsoever does not forgo the trade of batāee (the division of crop between the cultivator and landlord), should hear the announcement of war from Allah and His Rasool ﷺ.'*
> (p9, Taqleed...)

In this Hadeeth, the prohibition of *batāee* is related, yet, there are many forms and variations of this practice - about which this Hadeeth is silent. Are all forms of *batāee* harām? Or, are certain forms halāl whilst other types are harām? A degree of *ijmāl* appears to be present in this Hadeeth, which give rise to the above questions. Another example; Nabee ﷺ commented,

> *'Whomsoever (follows) an Imām (in salāh); then the Imām's Qirrat (recitation of Qur'ān) will become (the followers) Qirrat also.'*
> (p9, ibid.)

Here, it appears that during salāh, when the Imām recites *Qirrat*, the *muqtadee* (follower) should maintain silence. However, in another hadeeth, it is stated:

> *'Whomsoever fails to recite Surah Al-Fatihah, his salāh is not accepted.'*
> (p9, ibid.)

In this hadeeth, it appears as if it is compulsory for every person to recite *Surah Al-Fatihah*. Yet, when we view both hadeeth together, the question arises; do we give precedence to the first hadeeth and conclude that the second hadeeth applies to only an Imām and *munfarid* (the lone performer of salāh), whilst the *muqtadee* (follower) is absolved? Or, do we give preference to the second hadeeth and say by *Qirrat* is implied any other Surah besides *Surah Al-Fatihah,* and assume the latter is exempted?

Dear reader, you will appreciate the many difficulties present in deducing (*mustanbit*) such *masā'eel* from the Qur'ān and Hadeeth. Consequently, two options are available to us: either we choose to rely on our own *fahm* (understanding) and *baseerat* (faculty of insight) to grasp and act upon our decree. The alternative when confronted by such matters is to study what our illustrious *Salaf* (pious predecessors) decreed in the Light of the Qur'ān and Hadeeth. These lofty personalities of *Qurûn-e-Ûla* (early epoch of Islām) - accepted as experts of the Qur'ān and Hadeeth with greater *fahm* and *baseerat* - should be acknowledged and their findings acted upon.

If any unbiased right-minded person reflects, one must conclude the first option to be fraught with great danger and eventual failure. The second course, is to take prudent refuge in the greater *'ilm, fahm, zakawat* (sagacity), *hifz* (memory), *deen* and *deeyanat* (trustworthiness), *taqwa* & piety of the 'Ulamā of *qurûn-e-ula.* Remember, these scholars had greater affinity and proximity to the era wherein the Qur'ān and Hadeeth were revealed. They experienced the atmosphere of revelation, whilst we have arrived fourteen centuries later. The prevailing customs, norms and values of the era of revelation are extremely difficult for us to comprehend. Without such contextual insight and awareness, it is very difficult to fully understand. Accordingly, if we accept the verdict of one of our *Salaf-e-Saliheen*, then we have made *taqleed* of a scholar. This is the reality of *taqleed* and if I have been successful in my explanation, it will be clear that we make *taqleed* of a Imām or *Mujtahid* only on those occasions wherein there is some form of difficulty in comprehending a specific command of the Qur'ān and Hadeeth; irrespective of whether on such an occasion more than one meaning may be deduced; whether there is some *ijmāl* or various proofs. Accordingly, there is no *taqleed* of any Imām or *Mujtahid* on any clear-cut commands of the Qur'ān and Hadeeth. 'Allamah Khateeb Baghdadee 🌸 narrates:

> *'There are two forms of Sharee' ahqāms. Firstly, those which are undoubtedly pillars of Deen: for example; the five daily Salāh; Zakat, Saum of Ramadhān; Hajj; forbiddance of zina, alcohol and other such prohibitions, etc. In such matters, the question of taqleed does not arise, because all people are aware of these commands...The second category refers to those matters wherein without fikr, nazar and istidlal correct 'ilm is not possible; for example, the indirect masā'eels related to 'ibaadah, mu'amalaat, nikah, etc. In such matters, taqleed is commendable because Allah 🌸 has stated, '...Ask the people of Zikr if you do not know.' (21:7)*
>
> *Remember, if every person had to compulsory pursue the systematic acquisition of Deeni 'Uloom, all affairs of our worldly existence would be in turmoil. Who would tend to agriculture, business and industry? This is why such a command has not been ordained.'*   (p13, Taqleed...)

Dear reader, you will be aware of the system of law which operates in your country. It is well documented in statute books. However, how many people in the country will be able to self-study these books? Leave aside laity; from amongst the highly educated professionals within society, how many would dare to contest a point of law? When these professionals need to raise some statute, they hire a qualified and competent lawyer and act in accordance to his advise. On such occasions, does any right-minded person conclude the employment of a lawyer to be an acknowledgement by the client of the formers right to *make* laws? Of course not, this is precisely the ethos of *taqleed*. To understand the *ahqāms* from Qur'ān and Hadeeth, we make *ruju* (incline) and place *i'timad* (trust) upon the A'*imma-e-Mujtahideen*. Accordingly, those who make *taqleed* should not be castigated as those people who, instead of following the Qur'ān and Hadeeth, obey the A'*imma-e-Mujtahideen*.

The Two Forms of Taqleed: Āam & Ta'yin

Moreover, there are two forms of *taqleed*. Firstly, where no specific Imām or *mujtahid* is chosen (mu'ayin); wherein one Alim from a *maslak* is chosen for one matter, whilst another Alim from another *maslak* is chosen for another matter. This is known as *Taqleed-e-Āam* or *Taqleed-e-Mutlaq* or *Taqleed-e-Ghair Shakhs*.

In the second concept, one chooses to make *taqleed* of a specific *Mujtahid* '*Aalim*. In all affairs, his judgement is accepted and acted upon. This *ta'yin* (fixation of a *maslak*) is known as *Taqleed-e-Shakhs*.

Khwāhish Parastee - Fulfillers of Desires

May Allah ﷻ grant our *Salaf-e-Saliheen* and Fuqahā the best rewards. Observing the deterioration in our condition, they have decreed that now only *Taqleed-e-Shakhs* (wherein one maslak is *mu'ayin* - fixed lifelong) is permissible. Why? What great upheaval amongst Muslims has justified this decree? Before answering this question, let us briefly consider the harms of *khwāhish parastee* (fulfilment of desires) - the epidemic disease which sometimes leads man unto kufr. This is precisely why, upon numerous occasions, the Glorious Qur'ān has warned us of the dangers of *khwāhish parastee...*

'Is he who is on a clear proof from his Lord, like those for whom their evil deeds that they do are beautified for them, while they follow their own lusts (evil desires)? (47:14)

One form of *khwāhish parastee* is that a person who commits wrong accepts his action to be evil - and is trapped in this villainy because of the wickedness of his own *nafs* (self). In such a case, there is hope of this person receiving *tawfeeq* to become repentant and make *taubah* for his sins. Although wrong, this behaviour is nowhere as reprehensible as the other more lethal form of *khwāhish parastee*, wherein a person reaches such a low ebb of fulfilling his *nafsanee* desires: that he considers his evil to be permissible and regards *halāl* to be *harām*. Such a person makes the *Sharee'ah* a plaything. This second deadly form is greater in evil and more dangerous than the first type.

Our Fuqahā had comprehended the daily fall in standards of piety, taqwa and caution. Under such circumstances, should the doors of *Taqleed-e-Mutlaq* be left open, many people will destroy themselves or allow others to do so. For example, in summer, a person begins to bleed (without injury), according to Imām Aboo Haneefah ﷺ; his *wudhu* is broken, whilst Imām Shāfi'ee ﷺ considers his *wudhu* to be intact. Obviously, such a person will choose the latter's ruling on this occasion and pray salāh without a fresh wudhu. However, if shortly hereafter, this very same person was to fondle a lady, according to Imām Shāfi'ee ﷺ, his *wudhu* will break, whereas with Imām Aboo Haneefah ﷺ, his wudhu is intact. This person's desires will incline him towards the easy option on both occasions; whichever Imām's decree is to his fancy, he will adopt. Whatever ruling is burdensome and against his desires, he will forgo. Moreover, his *nafs* will soothe and dupe his conscience into considering his choice, on both occasions, to be justified and in order. Such a person very quickly becomes a victim of *khwāhish parastee*.

'Allamah Ibn Taymeeyah ﷺ & Taqleed

This flirting from *madhab* to *madhab*, merely to appease one's desires has always been decreed *harām* by all. 'Allamah Ibn Taymeeyah ﷺ comments:

> *'Imām Ahmad ﷺ and other authorities have categorically stated that nobody has the right, for the sake of his nafsanee desires, to consider something as harām and then later decree it as halāl and vice-versa. For example, when he is a neighbour of somebody and wishes to claim Shuf'ah (pre-emption), he adopts the maslak of Imām Aboo Haneefah ﷺ: that the right of Shuf'ah belongs to the neighbour. However, later when one of his neighbours' claims Shuf'ah, he adopts the maslak of Imām Shāfi'ee ﷺ...*

that the neighbour does not have a right to Shuf'ah.

Another example; a person happens to be the brother of somebody dying whose grandfather is still alive. Here, he adopts the maslak wherein the brother shares in inheritance with the grandfather. However, later in life, when he becomes a grandfather and one of his grandchildren passes-away leaving a brother, he adopts the maslak wherein in the presence of the grandfather, the brother of the deceased does not become an inheritor.

Under such circumstances, the person who flirts from madhab to madhab, decreeing permissible as impermissible and vice-versa; merely in order to fulfil his desires, is indeed thoroughly despicable and expelled from dārh 'adālat (justice). Moreover, Imām Ahmad ﷺ and others have decreed such conduct as impermissible.'

'These type of people, on one occasion will make taqleed of an Imām who decrees a nikah as fasid (void) and on another occasion he who decrees it permissible. Such behaviour is unanimously considered impermissible, by consensus of the Ummah.' (p63, ibid.)

Although many Qur'ānic Ayah's, Hadeeth and Judgements of the 'Ulamā outline and prohibit such behaviour, here we have related only the statement of 'Allamah Ibn Taymeeyah ﷺ, because generally the modernists who do not subscribe to *Taqleed-e-Shakhs* still uphold and have confidence in Ibn Taymeeyah ﷺ whose condemnation of flirting from *madhab* to *madhab* is clear.

Understand well, during time of the Sahābāh and Tābi'een, because the fear of Allah ﷺ and *fikr* of the Ākhirah was paramount, in adopting *Taqleed-e-Mutlaq,* the danger was not present of even laity following their desires in choosing from various *mujtahids* whenever it suited their fancy. However, when the later *fuqaha* observed the steady decline in *deeyanat* and people succumbing to *nafsaniyat,* then out of caution (and extreme benevolence) they passed the *fatawa* that henceforth it is only possible and compulsory to make *Taqleed-e-Shakhs* of one of the four Great Imām's. Accordingly, Shaykh-ul-Islām 'Allamah Nawawee 🌸, the commentator of Saheeh Muslim writes:

> *'Taqleed-e-Shakhs is compulsory because if it was permissible for man to adopt and choose from whichever fiqhee madhab he wishes, then people will search and seek out ease and fulfil their nafsanee desires. Under such circumstances, people will have a licence to decide for themselves what is halāl, harām, wājib and permissible. Consequently, the principles and restrictions of Sharee' ahqāms will be torn asunder.*
>
> *Moreover, understand well, one reason why Taqleed-e-Shakhs was not obligatory in the early era was the lack of complete categorisation, documentation and widespread availability of Fiqhee Mazaheeb. (However, now that Fiqhee Mazaheeb are well known and accessible) it is incumbent upon every person to endeavour and choose one madhab and make taqleed of it with mu'ayeen.'* (p66, ibid.)

Since the time of the Sahābāh, there have been numerous *Fuqahah* and *Mujtahideen.* The Ahl-e-Ilm are aware that within each Fiqhee *madhab,* there are certain rulings, which provide ease...unavailable in other *maslaks.* Moreover, these people were not angels, within each *maslak*, a few misjudgements – acknowledged as such by scholars – are also visible. Now, should the door to *Taqleed-e-Matlak* be reopened, instantly the scenario described above by 'Allamah Nawawee 鑾 will be enacted...to the extent that people will pick, choose and extract so many such *ahqāms* as to create a new *nafsānee* and *shaytānee maslak*. Shaykh Mu'amar 鑾 relates:

> *'Should a person listen to music and commit anal intercourse (on the pretext of following) some (obscure) Madeenite; perform Mu'tah (the harām Shiah practise of taking a temporary wife) upon the statement of some (obscure) Makkan; quote somebody from Kufa to justify his crooked mansheeyat (dealings), then such a person is amongst the worst and most despicable creation of Allah 鑾.'*

Although, the above is an extreme and revolting scenario, it does highlight the danger of drifting away from *taqleed-e-shakhs*. Moreover, people will seek to satisfy their desires in even trivial issues. This is why the Fuqaha have decreed *taqleed-e-shakhs* as compulsory, '...These conditions have been imposed to stop people from seeking ease and following their nafsānee desires.' Allamah Ibn Khaldûn 鑾 comments:

> *'Taqleed of the four Great Imām's is now decreed for all localities. It is no longer permissible to make taqleed of any other Imām...one reason for this is that 'Uloom and its terminology has now expanded to such an extent that making ijtihad is now extremely difficult. The second reason is the danger of unscrupulous and unqualified people taking control of ijtihad...those whose deen and*

judgements are unreliable. Accordingly, the 'Ulamā have announced their reluctance to make ijtihad and decreed it compulsory for people to make taqleed–e-shakhs of only these four Great Imām's. Moreover, they have prohibited the practice of changing from one Imām to another, because this would amount to making Deen an object of play.' (p71, ibid.)

Remember, because of the *faidh-e-suhbat* (blessed company) of Nabee ﷺ, the *nufoos* (desires) of the Sahābāh ﷺ and the Tābi'een had become so *maghlub* (annihilated), the danger of them following their desires in any Sharee' *ahqāms* was almost non-existent. This is why they were able to practise both forms of *taqleed.*

Why is Taqleed-e-Shakhs Compulsory Nowadays?

At this point, many people question why something that was not obligatory during *khairul qurun,* should now be made compulsory? The famous Muhaddith of Delhi, Shah Waleehullah ﷺ (1703-1762 CE) replies:

'Understand well! During the first two centuries, everybody was not bound to one specific madhab...however, after the second century, the practice of following one particular madhab took hold...to the extent that very few people lacked i'timmād (confidence) upon a mu'ayeen mujtahid. This is precisely the practise that is wājib nowadays...

With regards to objections (of the ghair muqallideen), I wish to draw attention to the obligation upon the Ummah of having a group who have detailed knowledge (with authentic proofs) of Sharee' Ahqams. (Thus, people are able to inquire and ascertain Masā'eel from them). Upon this, the Ahl-e-Haqq are unanimous.

Moreover, the methods of discharging wājib are also wājib. Consequently, should there be numerous avenues of fulfilling this wājib, then adoption of any one method will fulfil the requirements of this wājib. However, should there be only one way of acting upon this wājib, then it becomes compulsory to adopt this one specific method.

For example, our aslaf (pious predecessors) did not write down Hadeeth, however, in our era it has become wājib to write Hadeeth because no other reliable method besides kitabs/written format remains in transmitting Hadeeth. Similarly, our Aalaf did not preoccupy themselves with nahw (syntax) and lugat (dialect) because Arabic was their mother tongue and they had no need for such basics. However, in our time, it has become compulsory to study the Arabic language because we are so far removed from the original Ahl-e-Arab...

Accordingly, should any (Deeni unqualified) person be in the Indian sub-continent (for example) and no Shāfi'ee, Mālikee or Hambalee Scholar nor access to books of those maslak (under supervision) be available, then it will become compulsory for such a person to make taqleed of only Imām Aboo Haneefah ﷺ. Moreover, it will be harām for him to forgo this maslak, because then he would be removing the constraints of the Sharee'ah from around his neck and become completely liberal. On the contrary, if such a person (hitherto unconnected to any maslak) were to reside in Haramain, he is at liberty to select one of the four maslaks...

Without doubt, these four madhabs are documented in detail and the Ummah for obvious reasons unanimously accepts their taqleed. These are all the more apparent when we consider the current lack of resolve and surrender to khwāhish parastee (desires) amongst people. Today, every person proudly considers his opinion as sacrosanct.' [p75, ibid.]

Now that the reality and necessity of *taqleed-e-shakhs* is apparent, one more question arises. If we accept the need to make *taqleed* of a *mu'ayin* (particular) Imām, what is so special about these four Imām's? There have been numerous other *mujtahideen* throughout history, for example, Sufyān Thāwree 🌼, Imām Awzā'ee 🌼, 'Abdullah bin Mubārak 🌼, Ishaq bin Rahwee 🌼, Imām Bukhāree 🌼, Ibn Abee Layla 🌼, Hasan bin Saleh 🌼, etc. Why is it not possible to make *taqleed* of any of these other *Mujtahids*?

Exclusiveness of the Four Great Imāms 🌼

The reply to this question is to realise the inability of being able to act upon the Fiqhee *madhahib* of these other noble personalities because their teachings were not systematically preserved. If they were available, then undoubtedly it would be permissible to choose to make *taqleed* of one of them also. However, none of their publications or scholars remain. Accordingly, the famous *muhaddith* 'Allamah Abd'ul Rauf Munadee 🌼 narrates from Hāfiz Zahbee 🌼,

'It is compulsory upon us to hold the view that Sufyān Thāwree 🌼, Sufyān bin 'Uyaynah 🌼, Imām Awzā'ee 🌼, Dawûd Zāhiree 🌼, Ishāq bin Rāhwee 🌼 and the other A'imma 🌼 were all rightly guided... Moreover, the person who himself is not a Mujtahid, it is wājib upon him to

make taqleed upon a mu'ayeen madhab...However, according to Imām-ul-Haramain, it is not possible to directly make taqleed of the Sahābāh, Tābi'een and those whose madhab is not documented and (elaborated upon by scholars)...Imām Rāzee ﷺ has quoted the consensus of the Muhaqiqeen on this issue, that laity should be prevented from making (direct) taqleed of the Sahābāh and other Akabir.'

'Allamah Nawawee ﷺ elaborates,

'Undoubtedly the Sahābāh and other Akabir of Qurun-e-Ula occupy a higher rank than the later fuqaha and mujtahideen, nevertheless they did not have the same opportunity to categorise, propagate or publicise their 'Uloom, this is why it is not permissible (or possible) for anybody to make their taqleed. The compilation of Deeni fiqh was undertaken by later fuqaha like Imām Aboo Haneefah ﷺ and Imām Mālik ﷺ; scholars who personally witnessed and experienced the teachings of the Sahābāh and Tābi'een.'   (p8, ibid.)

'Allamah Ibn Taymeeyah ﷺ writes in his *fatawa*,

'With reference to Kitab and Sunnah, there is no difference between the Great Imām's and the mujtahideen. Accordingly, Imām Mālik ﷺ, Layth bin S'ād ﷺ, Imām Awzā'ee ﷺ, Sufyān Thāwree ﷺ, all are Imām's (and mujtahideen) of their era. With regards to taqleed, the command is the same as for the others, for no Muslim is able to aver that, 'his taqleed is permissible whilst the other's is impermissible.' Nevertheless, where the scholars have forbidden taqleed, it is based upon one of two principles:

Firstly, in their opinion, no scholars remain who have complete 'ilm of the maslak (of these other mujtahideen). Moreover, there are great differences in the schools of these Imām's...and as there are no scholars of these maslaks, consequently, it is not possible to make their taqleed... Secondly, our scholars say, the mujtahideen whose maslak's no longer remain, the statements of other's against some of their teachings has attained Ijma' (consensus). Nevertheless, wherever the opinions of the later Ulamā coincide with those of the (now extinct scholars), the judgement of the former will be further strengthened.'   (p83, ibid.)

'Remember, there is great wisdom in adopting these four madhahib and, in shunning them all together there is great mufasid (evil and harm). We are able to substantiate this claim...

Synopsis of Shāh Waleehullah 🌼

1) 'In understanding the Sharee'ah, the Ummah is inevitably indebted to our *Aslaf*. However, the statements of our *Salaf* are accepted on the condition that they have reached us either by way of correct *sanad*, or through the medium of reliable and authentic kitabs. Furthermore, for acceptability, it is also necessary for these statements to be *makhdum* (elaborated upon), i.e. subsequent Ulamā have explained and illustrated, clarifying and finalising any contentious issues.

For example, sometimes, a mujtahid's statement appears to be general, however it hints towards a specific issue (which the scholars of that maslak are able to comprehend). Accordingly, it is also necessary, for such 'Ulamā to have studied these issues in-depth and provided the proofs for such findings. Moreover, until this form of research into any mujtahideen's *maslak* is not undertaken (by qualified and pious scholars), then it is not permissible to rely upon it. Accordingly, such (rigorous study and precaution) has only been undertaken, in our era, into the Schools of the four Great Imāms and no one else (except Amameeyah and Zaydeeyah, but because they are ahl-e-bidat and shiah's, it is not permissible to follow them).'

2) The authenticity of the madhab's of the four Great Imāms is further substantiated by the Hadeeth of Nabee 🌸:

'*Make ittaba (follow) the sawād-al-āzam (majority).*' (p84)

When besides these four madhab's no other true madhab remains, then on the basis of sawād-al-āzam (majority), it will become necessary and imperative to make *ittaba* of the A'imma.

3) The third criteria which Shāh Waleehullah 🌺 relates is that should permission be given to decree a fatwa upon the statement of any mujtahideen besides the four Great Imāms, then unscrupulous scholars (Ulamā-e-Soo), who are slaves of *khawahish parastee*, will align their false decrees towards some famous scholar amongst our salaf and content, 'This is substantiated by the statement of so-and-so Imām.' Obviously, this danger does not exist in the maslaks of the four Great Imāms, whose works has been thoroughly researched by countless pious 'Ulamā-e-Haqqa throughout history.

However, where such study and caution is absent, the grave danger and possibility exists of a statement by some other mujtahideen being distorted by a unscrupulous person for an ulterior reason.'   (p85, ibid)

The Various Degrees of Taqleed

haykh Mufti Taqee 'Uthmānee continues, 'We now need to study the various degrees of *taqleed*, each of which have different *ahqāms*. Failure to appreciate these differences gives rise to many misunderstandings and errors. The majority of objections raised by the *ghair-muqallideen* is because of either failure to understand these differences or to treat them lightly and as insignificant.

1) Taqleed by the 'Awām (laity)

The first degree of *taqleed* is 'Taqleed by the *'awām* (laity).' By *'awām* is implied all of the following:

a) Those people who are completely unaware of the Arabic language and Islāmic 'Uloom, irrespective of how much expertise, competence, skill and qualifications they may hold in other branches of learning.

b) Those people who understand the Arabic language and are able to read Arabic Kitabs, yet have not systematically studied *tafseer, hadeeth, fiqh* and associated Deeni 'Uloom from qualified *Asateezah* (Ulamā).

c) Those people who have gone through the motions of studying and graduating from Islāmic 'Uloom; yet have failed to acquire competence and *baseerat* (insight) in *hadeeth, fiqh* and its *usools* (principles).

With regards to *taqleed*, these three categories of people are classified as *'awām* and fall under the same *hukm* (command): they have no alternative but to make *taqleed-e-shakhs*. Why? Because they do not posses the required *isti'dād* (ability) and *salaheeyat* (capacity) to directly understand *Kitabullah* and

Sunnah. Neither do they posses the ability to differentiate, compare or prioritise the various proofs. Consequently, they have to cling unto one *mujtahid* and acquire the *masā'eels* of the Sharee'ah from him. 'Allamah Khateeb Baghdadee 🌸 relates:

> *'There now remains the question, for whom is taqleed inevitable? That 'amee (lay) person who is unaware of the methods of Ahqām-e-Sharee'ah. Accordingly, it is compulsory for him to make taqleed of an 'alim and act upon his teachings...why? Because, the lay person is unqualified and unfit to make ijtihad, consequently it is Fardh upon him to make taqleed in the same way a blind person depends upon the services of somebody with vision to ascertain the direction of the qiblah...'* (p87, ibid.)

Such people, who lack the required *isti'dād* and *salaheeyat,* need to *muta'yeen* (appoint) a *mujtahid* and thereafter follow him in all affairs with confidence. Even if such a layperson was to come across a hadeeth, which externally appears to be at odds with the statement of his Imām, even then it is compulsory to act upon his Imām's teachings. As far as the hadeeth in question is concerned, he should comprehend, 'I have failed to either understand it correctly or, the Imām will have certain proofs.' Although, such a stand may appear surprising, wherein the *maslak* is accepted and *taweel* (interpretation) is adopted for the hadeeth in question, nevertheless, for this type of *muqallid* (follower), this is the only option. If these *muqallids* were given the leeway to act upon any hadeeth which they consider to be at variance with the teachings of their Imām, it will open up the door to extremes and eventual self-destruction. Understand well, the science of making *istinbat* (deductions) of *masā'eels* from the Qur'ān and Hadeeth is so vast and delicate, that even after a lifetime of devotion and study, not all are able to achieve competence. Sometimes, the external words of a hadeeth imply one concept, whilst in the light of other proofs from the Qur'ān and Hadeeth, it appears very different. Now, if a layperson, observing only the external words of one hadeeth, begins to act upon it, the danger exists of grave mistakes.'

An Example of Incorrect Comprehension

Shaykh Mufti Taqee 'Uthmānee continues,

'A graduate friend was very fond of reading Hadeeth kitabs. He was also of the opinion, that although he was a follower of the Hanafee maslak, nevertheless, should any matter appear contrary to any hadeeth, he would forgo that aspect of the Hanafee maslak. One day, in my presence, I heard him advising an acquaintance, 'In passing wind, wudhu (ablution) does not break until the odour or sound of having passed-wind is discerned.' Immediately, I understood the cause of his misunderstanding. Upon my attempts to make him comprehend his error, he insisted he had read a hadeeth to this effect in Tirmizee and could not forgo its meaning. Eventually, when I related the meaning of the hadeeth with detail, he realised his error and confessed how he had acted thus for so many years... 'Allah knows, how many salāh's I have prayed like this, thinking until I smell or hear wind-breaking, my wudhu is intact!' The reason for this glaring mistake was that he had read two hadeeth in Jāme' Tirmizee...

'Aboo Hurayrah ⸎ relates that Rasoolullah ⸎ commented, 'Wudhu becomes wājib only when the sound or smell is noticeable.' (1)

'If anybody from amongst you is in the masjid and he discerns wind from between his buttocks, then he should not leave the masjid (to make wudhu) until he notices the noise or smell (of wind).' (2)

This graduate friend had misunderstood the external words of this hadeeth to imply that breaking of wudhu was dependent upon experiencing either the smell or noise of passing wind. Whereas, all the Fuqaha-e-Ummah are unanimous that this is not the meaning of this hadeeth. Rather, this advise of Nabee ⸎ is only for those 'over-suspicious' people who needlessly fear the breaking of wudhu. The purpose being to reassure such people, that until you are certain wind has passed (by discerning either the noise or smell) your wudhu is intact. This is further clarified by another hadeeth in Aboo Dawood, wherein Aboo Hurayrah ⸎ narrates Nabee ⸎ to have related...

'If anybody from amongst you is in salāh and he feels some movement in his backside (anus) whereby the doubt arises whether wind has passed or not, then he should not leave his place (i.e. terminate salāh) until he has (experienced) either the noise or smell.' (p91, ibid.)

It is also mentioned in Aboo Dawood wherein Abdullah bin Zayd ⸎ relates that, 'Nabee ⸎ gave this reply to a person who was the victim of awham and wasaawis (thoughts and suspicions).'

Unsupervised Self-Study of the Qur'ān & Hadeeth

There are many such Ahadeeth, should anybody besides those qualified scholars who have expertise in the Qur'ān & Hadeeth attempt to study them, then they will make fundamental mistakes and incorrect conclusions. This is precisely why the 'Ulamā have decreed that whomsoever has not systematically acquired 'Ilm-e-Deen, then it is forbidden for such a person to study the Qur'ān and Hadeeth without the supervision of an expert Ustadh.

Our *Fuqaha* have gone to the extent of saying,

> *'Should a layperson be given a wrong fatwa by a Mufti, then the sin will fall upon the latter; the layperson will be considered mazûr. However, should a layperson self study hadeeth, understand it incorrectly and act upon his error, then he is not mazûr, for it was his duty to make ruju towards a Mufti and not personally try and derive masā'eel from the Qur'ān and Hadeeth.'* (p93, ibid.)

We have already noted that *taqleed* of an Imām and Mujtahid is only made when there is the possibility of *ta'āruz* (conflict) in any *dalāeel* (proofs) of the Qur'ān and Hadeeth. Accordingly, should there be a difference between Imām Aboo Haneefah 🙏 and Imām Shāfi'ee 🙏 on any issue, understand both will have proofs for their findings. The very purpose of *taqleed* is for the *muqallid* to follow one of these four Great Imāms. Thereafter, should one come across a hadeeth upon which another *Imām* has based his *maslak,* we should still follow our own *maslak,* for it is accepted beforehand that each of the *A'imma* have authentic proofs for their teachings. Imām Aboo Yousuf 🙏 comments,

'It is fardh upon laypeople to recognise the iqtidār (authority and rank) of the fuqahā, because (laity) do not possess the salahiyat (ability) to acquire and correctly understand the 'ilm of hadeeth.' (p94, ibid.)

2) Taqleed of the Mutabahhir 'Alim

The second degree of *taqleed* is that of the *Mutabahhir 'Alim* – a scholar, who although not having reached the rank of *ijtihad*, nevertheless possesses a very high level of Islāmic 'Uloom, acquired from expert *Asātizah*. Thereafter, under the supervision of Akābir 'Ulamā, he had lectured and authored for some considerable time. Well versed and conversant with *tafseer, hadeeth, fiqh* and its *usools*, he possesses the ability to *tahqeeq* (research) *masā'eel* from the *ifādāt* (instructions and teachings) of our *aslāf*. Moreover, he should be appreciative of the approach and style of their writings, outlook and temperament, thereby fully understanding and benefiting from their works and contributions.

Shāh Waleehullah ﷺ describes the attributes of a *Mutabahhir 'Alim...*

'Mutabahhir fil Madhab is that person who is Hāfiz of the kitābs (of his Mujtahid Imām)...other prerequisites are that he should be of saheeh fahm (correct understanding); well versed with the Arabic Language and its modes; be able to categorise and prioritise (the Imām Mujtahid's various aqwāls); fully understand the meaning of the fuqaha's statements; moreover, be able to appreciate those 'ibarat's (compositions) which are absolute (and may contain attached conditions).' (p95, ibid.)

Although such a person is still a *muqallid*, nevertheless he is able to become a Mufti of his *madhab*. A perfect appraisal of such a person's role is succinctly provided by Shaykh Ashraf 'Ali Thānwee ﷺ...

'In whichever matter an 'Alim of wasee-u-nazar (comprehensive outlook); zakee-ul-fahm (outstanding intelligence); munsif mizāj (just mindedness), concludes through his own research...(on the condition he is also pious) that rajih (superior finding) is in another direction, then he should consider whether there is Sharee' daleel and permission to do this? If there is and when the possibility of fitnah or tashwish (confusion) amongst the masses is real, then to save Muslims from extreme behaviour, it is best to act upon this murajjah (preferred) finding. The proof for this is a hadeeth wherein...

'Āishāh ﷺ narrates that Nabee ﷺ commented, 'You are unaware, but your Clan the Quraysh, when they rebuilt the Ka'bah, they had reduced (it in size) from bunyad-e-Ibrāheemee (original foundations excavated by Prophet Ibrāheem ﷺ). I inquired, 'O Rasoolullah ﷺ! Then why do you not rebuild it to its original foundational (layout)?' He replied, 'If the Quraysh were not so close to (their previous) age of kufr, this is precisely what I would have done... (however), there will be needless tashwish (confusion) amongst people who will say, 'Look! (They have) demolished the Ka'bah!' This is why I am not correcting it.' (p105, Tajweed...)

Observe, despite the fact that it would have been rajih (better) to rebuild to the original bunyad-e-Ibrāheemee, nevertheless, as it was permissible according to the Sharee'ah to retain it (even though smaller); in order to avoid the possibility of fitnah and confusion, Nabee ﷺ adopted this strategy.

Similarly, once during a journey, 'Abdullah ibn Mas'ûd ﷺ prayed four rakahs fardh. Somebody inquired, 'You had objected to 'Uthmān's ﷺ decision not to perform Qasr (the musafir's performance of two rakahs instead of four) and here we observe you praying four rakahs? He replied, 'To oppose is a cause of turmoil...'

From these incidents, it is learnt that whenever 'janib marjûh' is permissible, then to adopt it is awlā (better).

However, when there is no Sharee' basis for acting upon 'janib marjûh,' or when it would involve violation of a wājib...and through qiyas, no daleel is noticeable...moreover, the original 'janib rajih' is supported by hadeeth, then without doubt it is incumbent to act upon hadeeth. In such a case, there is absolutely no scope for taqleed because the original sources of Deen are the Qur'ān and Hadeeth. Remember, the whole maqsûd (purpose) of taqleed is to practice upon Qur'ān and Hadeeth with peace and ease...

Nevertheless, when a (genuine need does arise) to forgo taqleed, remember it is still impermissible to be rude, uncultured, harbour ill-will or baseless suspicions towards a mujtahid. For example, to conclude, 'he has gone against so-and-so hadeeth.' Why? Because, it is possible he was unaware of that hadeeth or, a weak sanad of this hadeeth may have reached him or, he had considered it at variance with another Sharee' arrangement...under these circumstances he is ma'zur. Remember, for the hadeeth not to have reached him is in no way an excuse to conclude, 'his 'ilm of hadeeth is imperfect.' Why? Because, even certain senior Sahābāh – who are considered undisputed Scholars of high rank – even they were unaware of certain ahadeeth...

Similarly, it is not permissible for the muqallid of a Mujtahid to criticize somebody (who is following another Mujtahid), because such ikhtillaf (differences) have existed since the time of our aslaf. Regarding these differences, our 'Ulamā state the golden rule, 'Regard one's own madhab as zinnan sawāb (presumed correct) and muhtamil khatā (possibly misjudged); whilst other maslaks are zinnan khatā (presumed misjudged) and muhtamil sawāb (possibly correct).'

This will also dispel the notion that, 'if all the (four) maslaks are haqq, then why only follow and act upon one?' Accordingly, when there is ihtimale thawāb (the possibility of correctness) in other (maslaks), then no justification or reason remains to denigrate, belittle, mock, criticise or harbour hatred and jealousy – attributes which are harām.

Moreover, the person who opposes 'aqāid (fundamentals) or ijmā'iyat (consensus), or criticises our salaf-e-sāliheen then he becomes expelled from the Ahl-e-Sunnah-wal-Jam'āt. Why? Because, the Ahl-e-Sunnah-wal-Jam'āt are those who in 'aqāid follow the path of the Sahābāh, therefore such umûr (disrespectful behaviour) is against their 'aqāid's. Consequently, such a reviler is amongst the ahl-e-bid'at and hawa.

Similarly, the person who commits 'ghulû (excess) in taqleed by rejecting or refuting the Qur'ān and Hadeeth, both these types of people should be shunned and disputes avoided.'

(p107, ibid.)

haykh Mufti Taqee 'Uthmānee *dāmat barakātuhum* continues, 'Shaykh Ashraf 'Ali Thānwi 🌸 has, through special *tawfeeq* from Allah 🌸, outlined such a moderate and pragmatic approach to this matter, that if we were to act thereupon, so many mutual disputes of Muslims would be solved.

Bearing in mind the above mentioned prerequisites, a *Mutabahhir 'Alim* may, in some special matter, forgo the statement of his Imām, if there is a *Saheeh* (authentic) hadeeth to this effect. Nevertheless, such singular incidents of differences of opinion do not negate his still being a *muqallid* of his Imām. Many *fuqaha* of the Hanafee School of Fiqh have adopted this stand on certain issues; leaving aside the statement of Imām Aboo Haneefah 🌸 and passing a *fatawa* based upon the teaching of one of the other *A'imma*.

For example, according to Imām Aboo Haneefah 🌸, it is permissible merely in order to derive strength (and not for purpose of intoxication) to partake minute doses of alcohol beside those derived from grapes. However, the *Fuqaha-e-Hanafeeyah* have separated themselves from this statement and adopted the *jamhur* (majority view of the scholars - that *all* alcohol is prohibited). Similarly, where Imām Aboo Haneefah 🌸 has stated *mazāri'at* (farming whereby produce is divided between landowner and farmer) to be impermissible. However, the *Fuqaha-e-Hanafeeyah* disagree and have decreed it permissible to arrange a *mutanāsib* (proportion) between the farmer and land owner.

These examples are those wherein all the *mutaakhireen* (later) *fuqahah* are *muttafiq* (united) upon disagreeing with the Great

Imām 🌸 on these matters, for there are many other issues wherein individual *fuqahah* have, based upon some hadeeth, personally differed from the Great Imām 🌸. Nevertheless, these issues are very delicate, therefore the greatest caution is required and such sensitive matters are not the preview of laity. It is not for everybody to imagine themselves as within the group of *Mutabahhir 'Ulamā*.

3) Taqleed of the Mujtahid-fil-Madhab

The third degree of *taqleed* is that of the *Mujtahid-fil-Madhab*. These are the (high-ranking) 'Ulamā, who with regards to *istidlāl and istinbāt usools* (principles of reasons, proofs, deductions and selections) are staunch followers of a *Mujtahid*. However, based upon these *usools*, they have the authority and competence to directly *mustanbit* (derive) *juzwee* (minor) *masā'eels* from the Qur'ān, Sunnah and Āthār (statements) of the Sahābāh. Accordingly, such 'Ulamā's do differ with their *Mujtahid Mutlaq* on numerous *furū'ee* (peripheral) matters, nevertheless as far as *usools* are concerned, they are still regarded as *muqallids*. Famous examples of such *Mujtahid-fil-Madhab* in *Fiqh-e-Hanafee* are Imām Aboo Yousuf 🌸 and Imām Muhammad 🌸; in *Fiqh-e-Shāfi'ee*, Imām Maznee 🌸 and Imām Aboo Thûr 🌸; in *Fiqh-e-Mālikee*, Sahnoon 🌸 and Ibn-ul-Qasim 🌸 and in *Fiqh-e-Hambalee*, Ibrāheem al-Harbee 🌸 and Aboo Bakr al-Athram 🌸. 'Allamāh Ibn 'Abideen Shāmee 🌸 describes the features of such Scholars:

> *'The second degree of Fuqaha are the Mujtahid-fil-Madhab. For example, Imām Aboo Yousuf 🌸 and Imām Muhammad 🌸 - and the other close associates of Imām*

Aboo Haneefah ﷺ - *who were well-versed and qualified to derive and decree ahqāms based upon the Qur'ān, Sunnah, Ijma and Qiyas as taught by their Ustadh...'*

To summarise, with regards to *usools* (principles), a *Mujtahid-fil-Madhab* is a *muqallid*, whilst in *furû'ee* (peripheral) matters, he is a *mujtahid*.

4) Taqleed of the Mujtahid Mutlaq

The final degree of *taqleed* is that of the *Mujtahid Mutlaq* -this is such a person in whom *all* the prerequisites of *ijtihad* are present. Through his 'ilm and *fahm*, he is able to *wazā* (deduce) *Usools* from the Qur'ān and Sunnah and through these *Usools*, he is able to *mustanbit* (extract) all the *ahqāms* of the Sharee'ah from the Glorious Qur'ān. These personalities are Imām Aboo Haneefah ﷺ, Imām Shāfi'ee ﷺ, Imām Mālik ﷺ and Imām Ahmad ibn Hambal ﷺ.

Moreover, although these noble souls are *Mujtahid* in both *Usools* and *furû*, nevertheless, they too have to make *taqleed* of a sort. In whichever *masā'eel* no clear-cut answer is available from the Glorious Qur'ān or Sunnah, then these personalities try, as far as possible, to follow the statements of the Sahābāh and Tābi'een rather then make their own judgement.

1) The precedence for this approach is a letter of 'Umar ﷺ to Qādhi Shurayh ﷺ...

'Should any such matter appear before you, the answer for which is present in Kitabullah, then arbitrate accordingly and do not allow the personal ārā (whims) of people to detract you. However, should any such matter appear before you which is not present in Kitabullah, then

scrutinise the Sunnah of Rasoolullah ﷺ and act accordingly. Moreover, should any matter appear, the answer for which is neither present in the Glorious Qur'ān or Sunnat of Rasoolullah ﷺ, then search for a precedence from the consensus of the (Sahābāh) and act accordingly. But should a matter appear before you, which is not present in the Glorious Qur'ān or Sunnah and upon which a Faqeeh before you has not commented upon, then you should adopt one of the following two options: firstly, through your opinion and resolution make ijtihad. Secondly, should you wish to withdraw then do so...and for you I consider it more appropriate and better to withdraw.'

(p111, ibid.)

Ponder, a judge and mujtahid of the calibre of Qādhi Shurayh ؓ is being advised by 'Umar ؓ to only make personal *ijtihad* when no precedence is forthcoming from the statements of the *aslaf*.

2) 'Abdullah ibn Mas'ūd ؓ relates,

'Whenever 'Abdullah Ibn 'Abbas ؓ was asked any matter for which the answer was present in the Glorious Qur'ān, then he would reply accordingly. When this was not possible and a hadeeth of Nabee ﷺ was applicable, he would present the hadeeth. If this too was not possible and a statement of Aboo Bakr ؓ and 'Umar ؓ was appropriate, he would relate this. (Only), in the absence of all these would he reply and act in accordance with his ijtihad and opinion.'   (p113, ibid.)

Despite being a *Mujtahid Mutlaq*, rather than give a personal opinion based on *ijtihad*, Ibn 'Abbas ؓ tried to make *taqleed* of the Shaykhain ؓ.

3) It is related in *Sunan-e-Darmee.…*

> *'A person came and requested a masalah from Imām Sh'ābee* 🌸, *who replied, 'The statement of 'Abdullah ibn Mas'ūd* ⚶ *is so-and-so.' The person retorted, 'But I would like your opinion please?' Imām Sh'ābee* 🌸 *turned towards those present and spoke, 'Are you not surprised and amazed at this person? I have just showed him the Fatwa of 'Abdullah ibn Mas'ūd* ⚶*...and he is asking me my opinion!' My deen (to me) is more important then the fulfilment of his desire. By oath of Allah! I prefer to (be drowned) than relate my opinion in front of the statement of 'Abdullah ibn Mas'ūd* ⚶.*'*

Remember, Imām Sh'ābee 🌸 was an acknowledged *Mujtahid* and the Ustadh of Imām Aboo Haneefah 🌸, nevertheless, rather than present his *ijtihadee* opinion, he preferred and gave precedence to the *taqleed* of Ibn Mas'ūd ⚶.

4) Imām Bukhāree 🌸 has related the statement of Mujahid 🌸 in his *tafseer* of the *Qur'ānic* Ayah,

> *'O Allah! Make us such Imām's who make iqtidā' (follow) those (pious) before us, whilst our successors make iqtidā' of us.'*

Hāfez Ibn Hajar 🌸 narrates, 'The meaning here is not that we make Imāmat (leadership) of people, rather it implies, 'O Allah! In matters of halāl and harām make us their Imām, whereby they *iqtidā'* (follow) us. Ibn Abee Hatim 🌸 concludes, 'The purpose herein is that we receive such *maqbooliyat* (Divine Acceptance) whereby when we say something, people make *tasdeeq* (verify) and *qabool* (accept) our words.' (p114, ibid.)

Doubts & Objections to Taqleed

llah ﷻ says:
'O you who believe! Obey Allah and obey the Messenger (ﷺ) and those of you (Muslims) who are Ulul Amr (in authority)...'   (Glorious Qur'ān, 4:59)

Nabee ﷺ commented,
'Without doubt, Allah Ta'ālā will not lift 'ilm (from this world) by snatching it away from (the hearts) of His servants. Rather, He will remove 'ilm by recalling the 'Ulamā...(until a stage will arrive), whereby when no 'Alim remains, people will take the ignoramuses as their leaders. When such people will be questioned, then without 'ilm they will give fatwas. They themselves will be astray and will lead others astray.'   (p28, Taqleed...)

Should any unbiased person carefully study the *haqeeqat* (realities) of *taqleed* which have been related, he will realise that the *usools* present in the Glorious Qur'ān and Hadeeth clarify and answer the objections commonly labelled against *taqleed*. Nevertheless, it is appropriate to specifically answer those questions and doubts which are often heard from the tongues of those who object to *taqleed*.

1) Glorious Qur'ān and Taqleed of Ãbā & Ajdād

Allah ﷻ says:
'And when it is said to them, 'Follow those ahqāms which Allah has decreed,' they reply, 'Never! We shall follow that which we have observed our forefathers.' (Allah ﷻ relates), 'What even if your forefathers were lacking in Hidāyat (guidance) and 'aql (intelligence)?'

Understand well, this Ayah refers to the principles of 'aqaaid (beliefs), i.e. the acceptance of Tawheed: the Akhirah; Risaalat; and the need to accept such Haqq masā'eels. Moreover, the stand and claim of the mushriks in recalling and clinging on to the kufr practices of their ābā and ajdād (forefathers) is in fact their taqleed of the fundamentals of a false religion. We too agree there is no taqleed in the fundamentals and this fact is well-related and highlighted in all the kitabs of fiqh; that the question of taqleed just does not apply in 'aqaaid and the essentials of Deen. Why? These fundamental masā'eels are absolute; there is no scope for ijtihad or taqleed. Imām Bukhāree ﷺ relates...

'Istiftā (clarification) in masā'eel only applies to zañee (peripheral) ahqāms and not those 'aqlee (intellectual) ahqāms which are related to e'tiqād, because herein qat'ee (absolute) 'ilm is necessary. Accordingly, the correct madhab is that there is no taqleed in bunyadee 'aqaaids (fundamental beliefs), moreover it is necessary to accept these beliefs, such as Wujud-e-Baree–Ta'ālā (existence of Allah ﷻ) with correct istidlāl (reasoning and proofs).' (p116)

The muqallids (followers) of the Great Imāms also prohibit the form of taqleed which the above Ayah is prohibiting. 'Allamah Khateeb Baghdadee ﷺ comments:

'...Allah ﷻ has related two sabab (reasons) for forbidding the taqleed of ābā and ajdād (forefathers). Firstly, these people openly proclaim their refusal to accept the revealed ahqāms of Allah ﷻ by saying, 'we will rather follow the ways of our forefathers;' secondly, their forefathers were without correct 'aql and hidāyat.

Now the taqleed to which we are referring to is mafqud (bereft) of these two sababs (causes). No muqallid throws aside any ahqāms of Allah ﷻ and His Rasool ﷺ to make taqleed of any 'Alim. Yes, what he does, is make his Imām and Mujtahid a shārih (a commentator or means) to understanding the Qur'ān and Sunnah and, through the light of tashreeh (explanation) act upon the Qur'ān and Sunnah.

Similarly, the second sabab is also lacking, because no Ahl-e-Haqq is able to deny that the Great Imāms whose taqleed is being made, no matter how great the differences in opinion with any of them, their respect and esteem is absolutely paramount. Consequently, to allegorise their taqleed with the following of the ābā and ajdād by the mushriks is a grave injustice.' (p117, ibid.)

2) Taqleed of Ahbar (Rabbis) & Ruhban (Monks)

Some modernists relate the following Ayah of the Glorious Qur'ān in an attempt to detract people away from making *taqleed* of the A'imma-e-Mujtahideen...

'They (the Jews & Christians) took their ahbarahum (rabbis) and rûhbanuhum (monks) to be their lords besides Allah (by obeying them in matters which they made lawful or unlawful according to their own desires without being ordered by Allah)...' (Glorious Qur'ān 9:31)

We have already related that *taqleed* of a *Mujtahid* is not made on the assumption that he is the lawmaker, rather he is appointed as an *shārih* (annotator). It is fully understood and accepted that it is not his personality which is being followed, rather his *tashrihat* (explanation) are trusted to fully understand and act upon the Qur'ān and Sunnat. Upon this, Shaykh Muhammad Ismā'eel Salafee 🌸 wrote the following criticism:

> *'This is the type of fiqrah (artful glib-tongued deception) practiced by our (ahl-e-bidah) brethren: that we do not consider the ahl-e-qubur (inmates of the graves) and Saints to be mutaqil-bi-zat Allah; rather we consider them to be deputies of Allah! Moreover, the use of terms like adab (respect), waseelah (medium), shifa'at (intercession), etc, are only employed to (hoodwink) the acts of shirk (associating others with Allah).'*

(p 128, Tahreek Azaadee Fikr, quoted on p118, Taqleed…)

The reply to this objection is that, if our *ahl-e-bidah* brothers have incorrectly used (some terms), then it does not follow that whomsoever uses such technical terms is necessarily wrong and astray. 'Allamah Ibn Taymeeyah 🌸, whom nobody has accused of being amongst the *ahl-e-bidah* comments:

> *'It is wājib (compulsory) upon man to obey Allah and His Rasool 🌸; moreover, these Ulul Amr (ulamā and rulers) whose itā'at (obedience) Allah has commanded implies their tā'at (obedience) under the compulsory tā'at of Allah and His Rasool 🌸...not because the (ulul amr) are objectives in themselves.'*

(Fatawa Ibn Taymeeyah, Vol. 2, p461 quoted p118, ibid.)

'Allamah Ibn Taymeeyah 🌸 has also employed the same words; will he too be labelled as being amongst the *ahl-e-bidah*? On another occasion, he writes…

> *'This concept is binding upon every human and jinni in all conditions, state and time that they obey only Allah and*

His Rasool 🕌 - whatever (They) have decreed halāl - accept it as halāl. Whatever (They) have decreed harām - accept it as harām. Whatever (They) have decreed as Wājib - accept it as Wājib. However, because there are so many ahqāms of Allah and His Rasool 🕌 which many people do not know of, this is why, in this matter they need to make ruju' towards such an 'Ālim who is able to show them the ahqāms of Allah and His Rasool 🕌. Why? Because, such an 'Ālim is more aware of the irshādāt (Commands) and murad (objectives) of Allah and His Rasool 🕌.

Accordingly, the Imāms, whom Muslims follow, are in reality waseele (mediums) between people and Allah and His Rasool 🕌. They serve the purpose of guides and rehnuma (patrons) through whom the irshādāt (Commands) of Rasool 🕌 reaches people. Through the (Ālim's) ijtihād and istitā'at (capabilities) people understand the murad (objectives) of Rasool 🕌. Sometimes, Allah 🕌 bestows such special 'ilm and fahm (understanding) to a khas (special) Ālim which other (scholars too) do not possess.' [p121, ibid.]

Now ponder, do the followers (muqallideen) of the Great Imāms say anything in addition to what is related above by Allamah Ibn Taymeeyah 🕌? In the final analysis, one should remember the following points of *taqleed...*

1) *There is no taqleed of any Imām in the foundational 'aqāid of Deen.*

2) *There is no taqleed of any Imām in those ahqāms of the Sharee'ah which are confirmed by continuity.*

3) There is no taqleed of any Imām in those nusus (clear-cut Ayahs) of the Qur'ān & Sunnah which have no contradiction.

4) Taqleed is enacted for the sole purpose that wherever in the Qur'ān & Sunnah there is a possibility of numerous isbāt (outcomes), then in order to establish and practice upon one mua'yin (fixed) meaning, instead of resorting to self-choice, reliance is made upon the fahm of a Mujtahid.

5) No Mujtahid of the Ummah is considered sinless or free from error, the possibility of misjudgement is accepted in his ijtihad.

6) If a Mutabbahir 'Alim discerns a statement of a Mujtahid in conflict to a Saheeh (correct and authentic) Hadeeth (which is not conflicting), then it is incumbent upon him to forgo the ruling of the Mujtahid and act upon the Hadeeth.

Now if this concept of taqleed is also 'shirk' and tantamount to appointing our 'Ulamā as 'gods' (as the ghair-muqallideen claim), then which human is living in this world who is free from such 'shirk?'

One should appreciate, those people who are anti-taqleed, they also to some extent or other, are practicing taqleed. Did all of them arrive from their mothers womb as mujtahideen or qualified scholars? They too need to study and read kitabs...but from whom and whose kitabs? Moreover, the ghair-muqallideen kitabs they do study are not all furnished with proofs and, those that are, how is it possible for a layperson to discern whether these proofs are correct? Accordingly, they too make taqleed and rely upon the 'ilm and fahm of their scholars.

There now remain those ghair-muqallideen people who are qualified scholars of the Qur'ān & Sunnah. They too should answer with honesty, whether for every masā'eel that is adjudicated, do they study the whole treasure-house of *tafseer* and Hadeeth to deduce the masā'eel? Obviously not! Moreover, these scholars too are helpless in having to make *ruju* towards the kitabs of the 'Ulama-e-Mutaqadimeen...the only difference is that instead of studying the kitabs of the maslaks of Imām Aboo Haneefah 🌸 or Imām Shāfi'ee 🌸 they analyse the kitabs of 'Allamah Ibn Taymeeyah 🌸, 'Allamah Ibn Hazam 🌸, 'Allamah Ibn-ul-Qayyum 🌸 or Qādhi Shawqanee 🌸.

As these modern-day scholars have no realistic means of studying every proof and masā'eel, they rely on the research of the above scholars - upon the assumption that these 'Ulama-e-Mutaqadimeen were competent scholars of the Qur'ān & Sunnah and their verdicts, in general, are in keeping with the Qur'ān and Sunnah.

In all aspects of human activity, *taqleed* of those who are considered experts in that field is absolutely necessary - if such *blind taqleed* is to be considered *shirk*, then no sphere of Deeni or worldly existence is viable or above such an absurd charge.

3) Hadeeth related by 'Adee bin Hatim 🌸

Those who oppose *taqleed* often present the following hadeeth...

> *'Adee bin Hatim 🌸 relates that, 'When I attended the khidmat (company) of Nabee 🌺, a piece of gold jewellery was around my neck. He 🌺 commented, 'O 'Adee! Remove and throw it away.'*

> *Thereafter, I heard Nabee 🌺 recite this Ayah of Surah Baraat:*

'They (the Jews & Christians) took their ahbarahum (rabbis) and rûhbanuhum (monks) to be their lords besides Allah...'   (Glorious Qur'ān 9:31)

Nabee ﷺ *commented upon this ayah, 'Although these people did not worship their 'ulama and priests, nevertheless, whenever their 'ulama and priests decreed something halāl, they would confirm it as halāl and, whenever their 'ulama and priests decreed something as harām, they too confirmed it as harām.'*   (p124, Taqleed...)

However, there is no connection between this hadeeth and the *taqleed* of the *A'imma-e-Mujtahideen*. The defence for the previous critique also applies here, with the proviso that those Ahl-e-Kitab, about whom Nabee ﷺ commented, they had given their scholars the choice to decree halāl & harām...was not as guardians of their Sharee'ah, but more as totally sinless and infallible personalities with unfettered rights to decide as they please. The *Encyclopaedia Britannica* describes the papacy as...

'the system of central government of the Roman Catholic church, the largest of the three major branches of Christianity, presided over by the pope, the bishop of Rome. The papal system, which has not gone undisputed, developed over the centuries since the early church until 1870 when the first Vatican Council officially defined as a matter of faith the absolute primacy of the pope and his infallibility when pronouncing on 'matters of faith and morals.' According to this definition the pope exercises judicial, legislative, and executive authority over the church as the direct successor of St. Peter, who is thought to

have been the head of the apostles and the first bishop of Rome. His authority rested on the words of Jesus quoted in Matthew 16:18-19 and elsewhere that have been interpreted as giving him authority in Heaven and on Earth in the place of Jesus. The early history of the papacy can be told as the history of the development of this Petrine theory, and the later history as the development of the papal claim to both spiritual and temporal authority over Christian society.

After the demise of effective Roman or Byzantine imperial control over Italy, the Roman pope became the representative of Roman imperial glory to the new Frankish and other German kingdoms. Stephen II (reigned 752-757) and other popes, in linking the fate of the Roman primacy to the support of Charlemagne and his house, gained a powerful protector and, through the Donation of Constantine forgery, temporal power in Italy. However, they did not gain the freedom to exercise the spiritual power over the universal church for which they had hoped, since Charlemagne and his successors ignored the pope's claim to the right to crown the emperor and instead followed in the footsteps of their Byzantine and Roman predecessors by asserting a large measure of control over the Frankish church and the papacy itself. Divested of its temporal power, the papacy increasingly turned to its spiritual or teaching authority to retain control over Catholics, proclaiming infallibility and espousing the Ultramontane position (the idea that the pope is the absolute ruler of the church).

[Kindly Reproduced from the Copyright 1994-1999 Encyclopaedia Britannica]

Now ponder, the 'rank' which Christians have decreed for their Pope, what connection is there between this practice and *taqleed* of the A'imma-e-Mujtahideen?

4) Statement of 'Abdullah bin Mas'ûd ☝

Those who oppose *taqleed* often present the following statement of 'Abdullah bin Mas'ûd ☝...

> *'Nobody should make taqleed of another person in Deen to such an extent that when (the leader) accepts Imān, he (the follower) too brings Imān and should (the leader) commit kufr, (the follower) too commits kufr.'* (p126, Taqleed)

However, the point to remember is 'who has ever advocated such taqleed?' This statement of 'Abdullah bin Mas'ûd ☝ makes clear that in *imāneeyat*, taqleed is not permissible and this is also a fundamental belief of the *muqallideen*. However, regarding making *taqleed* of our *aslaf* in *ahqāms* of the Sharee'ah, we present this statement of Ibn Mas'ûd ☝...

> *'Whomsoever wishes to make Ittiba' should make Ittiba' of those (pious people) who have passed-away, because of those who are living...it is not possible to guarantee that they will never fall into fitnah (trials and deviation). Undoubtedly, those (worthy of Ittiba') are the Sahābāh: the highest ranking personalities of this Ummah... therefore, appreciate their rank, follow their Āthar (statements) and as far as possible cling unto their akhlāq and lifestyle because they were on Sirātul Mustaqeem (the Straight Path).'* (p127, ibid.)

5) Statements of the A'imma-e-Mujtahideen

Some *ghair-muqallideen* people also claim that the A'imma-e-Mujtahideen themselves have stated, 'Do not act upon our statements until their proofs are known,' basically, 'If our statement is against hadeeth, then forgo it and act upon hadeeth.' However, if an honest appraisal is made, one will realise that this teaching is not for laity; who lack the ability to make *ijtihad,* rather it is only for those (Mutabbahir 'Alim's) who possess the prerequisites. 'Allamah Ibn Taymeeyah ﷺ comments accordingly,

> '*Imām Ahmad bin Hambal ﷺ advised laypeople to seek masā'eel from Imām Ishāq ﷺ, Imām 'Ubayd ﷺ, Imām Aboo Thur ﷺ and Imām Aboo Mus'ab ﷺ. Moreover, from amongst his associates, those who were 'Ulamā, for example, Imām Aboo Dawood ﷺ, 'Uthmān bin Sa'eed ﷺ, Ibrāheem al-Harbee ﷺ, Aboo Bakr al-Asram ﷺ, Imām Muslim ﷺ, etc., he would prohibit them from making taqleed of anybody and advised them, 'It is incumbent upon you to firstly make ruju towards Kitabullah and Sunnah.'* (p130, ibid.)

6) Is Taqleed some form of inferiority?

We have already studied how *taqleed* was in existence during time of the Sahābāh, for whichever Sahābee was unable to make *ijtihad* would make *ruju* towards a *Faqeeh* Sahābee. However, some people have objected and interpreted this as a form of inferiority, which displays a persons lack of 'ilm:

> '*Accordingly to claim that the Sahābāh made taqleed is to besmirch their rank. What dishonour of the Sahābāh! All the Sahābāh were lofty and fuqaha...and to differentiate as faqeeh and ghair-faqeeh between the Sahābāh is a great shame.*'

This is merely an emotional accusation, for it is not a fault for a person not to be a *faqeeh* or *mujtahid*...nor is it the worth of a person's true rank. The Glorious Qur'ān decrees the true standard and rank of a person...

'Verily, the most honourable of you with Allah is that (believer) who has taqwā...' (49:13)

Thus, the real *ma'yar* (standard) is *taqwā*, not whether a person has only 'ilm and understanding. Should a person possess true *taqwā*, yet be lacking in fiqh and ijtihad, then he is not at fault or inferior. Nevertheless, all the Sahābāh had reached such a lofty stage and degree of *taqwā*, that they have been described as...'The most elevated in creation after the Prophets.' However, to claim in matters of fiqh and 'ilm that all the Sahābāh were equal is in conflict with the Glorious Qur'ān and Ahadeeth. Allah ﷻ mentions...

'And it is not (proper) for the believers to go out to fight (Jihād) all together. Of every troop of them, a party only should go forth, that they (who are left behind) may get instructions in (Islāmic) religion, and that they may warn their people when they return to them; so that they may beware (of evil).' (Glorious Qur'ān, 9:122)

This differentiation within the Sahābāh (of fuqahas, mujahids, etc.,) was ordained by Allah ﷻ. This is further substantiated by a hadeeth of Nabee ﷺ...

'May Allah Ta'ālā enlighten the person who has heard my statement, learnt, memorised and propagated it to others. Because, some people are such that although possessing some point of fiqh yet they are not personally a faqeeh. Whilst some people are such that possessing some point of fiqh, they pass it unto people more faqeeh than themselves.'

(p137, Taqleed...)

Remember, numerous types of people benefited from the company of Nabee 🌸. These pure souls ranged from Aboo Bakr 🌸 and 'Umar 🌸 to simple though esteemed bedouins such as Iqra' bin Habis 🌸. As far as respect is concerned, even the simple bedouin Sahābee is greater in rank than a thousand later scholars and mujtahids. However, in matters of fiqh, scholars such as Aboo Bakr 🌸 and 'Umar 🌸, 'Ali 🌸 and Ibn Mas'ûd 🌸 were undisputed authorities. According to 'Allamah Ibn Qayum 🌸, of the 124,000 Sahābāh, the fatawa's of approximately 130 companions remain. This is ample proof of the others making *taqleed* of the fuqaha Sahābāh and in no way implicates the rest to be imperfect in any sense.

Excesses in Taqleed

One final point to remember is that just as objecting to *taqleed* and adopting personal desires in Sharee' *masā'eel* is detestable, so too are excesses in making *taqleed*. For example,

1) *It is incorrect to consider the A'imma 🌸 to be sinless or on par with the Ambiya 🌸.*

2) *To forgo any Saheeh Hadeeth because of lack of comment from an A'imma 🌸. For example, it is confirmed by many ahadeeth to raise the finger in Tashahhud. However, some people have refused this sunnah merely on the basis that Imām Aboo Haneefah 🌸 did not appear to make a statement on this issue.*

3) *To distort hadeeth in order to strengthen or collaborate a statement of an A'imma.*

4) *To consider only one's own Imām to be on Haqq whilst regarding the madhab of other Imāms to be batil is also a grave error.*

5) *It is also erroneous to extend and consider the differences between the madhabs to anything beyond 'ilmi hudoods. To resort to slanging, abusing and fighting is totally wrong.*

Final Appeal

After presenting these few words and realities of taqleed, we would like to stress that the purpose behind this publication is not to initiate disputes, arguments or debates. Rather, we wish to bring to attention the proofs behind the stand of the majority of this Ummah - who are following one of the four A'imma-e-Mujtahideen. If, out of naivety, we have used words which have hurt anybody, then we request forgiveness.

One should remember, that at a time when the Ummah is being buffeted on all sides by fitnah and fasad, what greater destruction is there then to resort to in-fighting and squabbling over furu'ee (peripheral) issues and label epithets of kufr & shirk over apparently trivial matters and differences.

The pages of history are full of anecdotes wherein enemies have not been able to harm us as much as we have harmed ourselves by mutual fighting. History shows that whenever we have highlighted and exploded these mutual differences beyond all bounds then the only people who have benefited have been the enemies of Islām.

May Allah ﷻ guide all of us upon the Straight Path, grant us Tawfeeq to consider Haqq as Haqq and act upon it, give us the understanding to consider batil (falsehood) as batil and grant us the strength to steer clear from it; moreover, may He grant us the Tawfeeq to save ourselves from mutual in-fighting and expand our energies and lives to propagate Deen. Ameen.

Shaykh Mufti Taqee 'Uthmānee dāmat barakātuhum relates: 'One should endeavour to remember and act upon the following Naseehat (advises) of 'Allamah Shabbir 'Uthmānee ...

'Haqq (true) speech or dialogue, with a haqq niyyat (intention), delivered with haqq method is never without effect and never creates fitnah or fasad (strife and dissension).'

Three pre-requisites have been formulated: firstly, whatever one is relating must be haqq; secondly, our intention for relating must be haqq (sincere); finally, the method we employ to deliver must be haqq.

For example, a person is submerged in some sin, if one feels pity for him, with genuine affection try to make him understand in order to extricate him from this sin. This should be our niyyat; not to display our superiority or to disgrace him. Similarly, our method must be correct, speak to him with mildness and affection.

If these 3 conditions are present, Inshā'Allah, fitnah will not arise. Moreover, whenever in relating any haqq matter, dissension does arise, immediately conclude that one of these conditions is lacking: either the niyyat, dialogue or the method employed is not haqq.

Remember, the Muslim did not arrive in this world as the soldier of Allah , our mission is only to constantly relate to others haqq dialogue, with haqq niyyat and haqq method. Never become despondent in doing so, but also do not behave in any way whereby fitnah is initiated.

May Allah through His infinite Rahmat and Mercies grant all of us Tawfeeq. Āmeen.

(Islaahi Khutabat, Vol. 8, p294)

Chapter Seven

Schemes
of
Enemies

Edited & Abridged From the
Autumn 1421/2000 Urdu Lecture Series
of

Shaykh Muhammad Saleem Dhorat

dāmat barakātuhum

*W*hen we say we follow one of these four Great Imāms, we imply we follow the Qur'ān and Hadeeth under their guidance. They are followed because the Ummah unanimously agrees that their works are in total harmony with the Qur'an and Hadeeth. One who follows any of the four Great Imāms is, in reality, following the Glorious Qur'ān and Hadeeth, as every ruling of these great luminaries is in accordance with the Ahādeeth of the Prophet ﷺ.'

(p7, Sunnah & the People of Sunnah)

With the Name of Allah, the Most Merciful, Very Merciful
Salāt and Salāms upon Nabee ﷺ

Allah ﷻ mentions in the Glorious Qur'ān:
'And whomsoever seeks a religion other than Al-Islām, it will never be accepted of him, and in the Hereafter he will be one of the losers.' (3:85)

If we were to reflect upon the prevalent conditions in this world, it would appear that all forms of *kufr* (disbelief) have united to destroy Islām and the Muslims:

'If a good befalls you, it grieves them, but if some evil overtakes you, they rejoice at it. Nevertheless, if you remain patient and become pious, not the least harm will their cunning do to you. Surely, Allah surrounds all that they do.'

(Glorious Qur'ān, 3:120)

Within the Ummah, *Jamā'ats* (movements) have been instigated, with an apparent Islāmic and Muslim label - whose activities or angles of attack may be summarized as follows:

Jamā'at 1 - Those who deny the Glorious Qur'ān

Jamā'at 2 - Those who deny the Ahadeeth.

Jamā'at 3 - Those who belittle the Sahābāh ﷺ

Jamā'at 4 - Those who vilify the A'imma & Fuqahā-e-Ezām ﷺ

Jamā'at 5 - Those who denigrate the 'Ulamā

The schemes employed by kufr to destroy Islām fall into two broad categories; two angles are being used. The first mode of approach is to strive so diligently that not a single person remains on the surface of this world to mention the Glorious Name of Islām. No individual or body should be visible who may claim they are Muslims. Wipe Islām off the surface of this earth! This would be the *kuffars* ultimate success. Should they be unsuccessful in this first conspiracy and Muslims *have* vowed never to forsake their Deen; that we shall forever remain Muslims, then *modus operandi* number two of the *kuffar* is to ensure, that if we do remain Muslims, our Deen be weak and incorrect. This poor Muslim may consider himself a true Muslim, whereas in reality, in the List of Allah 🌿, he is no longer a Muslim.

> '...but honour, power and glory belong to Allah and to His Rasool (🌺) and to the believers, but the hypocrites know not.'
> (Glorious Qur'ān, 63:8)

As the first scheme (to obliterate Islām) appears impossible, all efforts of the *kuffar* are towards this second approach.

Jamā'at 1 - Those who deny the Glorious Qur'ān

A group has arisen its ugly head who deny the meaning of Ayahs of the Glorious Qur'ān as related by our Nabee 🌺, his Sahābāh 🌺 and the 'Ulamā of the Ummah. This Jamā'at attempts to transpose its alternative version, a clear-cut *tahreef* (manipulation). Yet, these people still claim to be Muslims, propagators of Islām and those who live a life in accordance to the Glorious Qur'ān! However, the meanings of the Ayah are being altered to satisfy their scheme. This is the first attack.

Jamā'at 2 - Those who deny the Ahadeeth

A second group, also claim to be Muslims and members of the Ummah of Rasoolullah 🌺. However, with a very sweet, shrewd and cunning tongue, they attempt to separate the Ummah from Hadeeth by claiming, *Hasbunā Kitābullah* (Allah's Book is sufficient for us), and when this is present, what need is there for us to make ruju (incline) towards the statements and actions of any created being? People are stupid...forgoing the Book of Allah to follow the book of a creation!'

Jamā'at 3 - Those who belittle the Sahābāh

Another group who also claim to be Muslims and members of the Ummah of Nabee 🌸 hold a grudge and bear *bad ghuman* (evil opinions) against the Sahābāh 🌸. This group does not accept Aboo Bakr 🌸, 'Umar 🌸 and 'Uthmān 🌸 as Muslims. In their hatred, these people even claim that after the death of Rasoolullah 🌸, besides four to five Sahābāh, all the others became *murtad* (renegades) - Allah Forbid!

Now, when such people have no confidence in the Sahābāh 🌸, of a surety they do not harbour *Imān* (faith) upon the Treasures of Hadeeth: Bukhāree, Muslim, Tirmizee, Ibn Majah, Aboo Dawood or Nasa'ee. When association with the Sahābāh is cut so is the connection with Hadeeth and subsequently with the Glorious Qur'ān. These people now audaciously ask, 'Are there 30 or 32 Juz of the Qur'ān?' They claim to be Muslims, yet in the List of Allah 🌸, they are not Muslims.

Jamā'at 4 Those who vilify the A'imma & Fuqahā

Muslims who fail to yield to the above groups are bombarded by the sweet poison of the fourth *Jamā'at* - those who vilify the *A'imma-e-Mujtahideen*. These people contest, 'To understand the Qur'ān and Hadeeth, what need is there for Imām-e-Azām Aboo Haneefah 🌸, Imām Mālik 🌸, Imām Shāfi'ee 🌸, Imām Ahmad ibn Hambal 🌸? Directly study and understand the Qur'ān and Hadeeth. When the Qur'ān and Hadeeth are present, what need is there to make *ittiba* (follow) any of these Imāms 🌸?' Understand well, our *Salaf* (pious predecessors) have concluded and decreed that without perfect *Ittiba-e-Sunnah*, it is not possible to achieve success in dunya or the

Akhirah. 'Hold on, if you claim to only make perfect *ittiba* of Rasoolullah 🌸, then why is it at all necessary to make *ittiba* of Imām-e-Azam Aboo Haneefah 🌸, Imām Mālik 🌸, Imām Shāfi'ee 🌸, Imām Ahmad ibn Hambal 🌸?'

In reality, those who are *muttabe* (followers) of any of these four Imāms are not making *ittiba* of any of the *A'imma* 🌸, rather they are making *ittiba* of Rasoolullah 🌸 under the guidance of one of these four Imāms! Why? Because, whatever each of these four Imāms has related was with the Light of Hadeeth and the Glorious Qur'ān. These Imāms 🌸 are from *Khairul Quroon...*

> *'In my ummah, those people are the best who have met me*
> *(i.e. my Sahābāh), thereafter, those who have met them*
> *(the Tābi'een), then those who have met them (the Tabe'*
> *Tābi'een).'* (Vol 7, p11, Seerah Sahābāh)

It is an undisputed fact that Imām Aboo Haneefah 🌸 was a Tābi'een who met and learned Hadeeth direct from the Sahābāh. How could those who experienced *Khairul Quroon* possibly forsake the Glorious Qur'ān and Sunnat?

Jamā'at 5 - Those who denigrate the 'Ulamā

The final attempt in this 'kufr master plan' is to separate the Ummah from the inheritors of the Ambiya, the 'Ulamā...

> *'The 'Ulamā are the inheritors of the Ambiya and the*
> *inheritance of the Prophets is neither dinars nor dirhams,*
> *rather they leave behind 'ilm.'*

It is therefore the 'Ulamā and not the laity who are the inheritors and *Muhāffiz* (protectors) of the 'Uloom of the Glorious Qur'ān, Hadeeth and Sharee'ah. Therefore, should the Ummah become detached from the 'Ulamā, they will, of a surety, become separated from Deen. This is why such vigorous and hostile attempts are being made to separate us from the 'Ulamā and *Fuqahā-e-Ezām* and consequently the Sahābāh. Such people will then claim, 'this is only the statement of 'Umar ⚬ or Aboo Bakr ⚬ or 'Uthmān ⚬ or Aboo Hurayrah ⚬...show us the words of Prophet Muhammad ﷺ.' At first, such a person becomes *munharif* (disenchanted) with the *A'imma-e-Mujtahideen,* slowly yet surely his venom and hatred turns towards the Sahābāh.

Whilst the first three *Jamā'at's* are quite obviously outside the Pale of Islām, when a person makes hatred of the *A'imma-e-Mujtahideen* his preoccupation, his *Imān* too is in peril. Allah ﷻ relates in a Hadeeth Qudsi:

'Whomsoever harbours enmity towards any of My Walee (Friends), I proclaim a state of war with him.'

When Allah ﷻ proclaims war against anybody, how may his Imān remain protected? Imām-e-Azam Aboo Haneefah ⚬, Imām Mālik ⚬, Imām Shāfi'ee ⚬, Imām Ahmad ibn Hambal ⚬ - all were high-ranking *Awliyaa,* therefore anybody who waggles his tongue and besmirches these lofty personalities is declaring war against Allah ﷻ.

Kufr schemes & the Muslim Response

For the last fourteen centuries, this *Yahoodi* lobby and *kufr* conspiracy has been waged, a crusade, to separate the Ummah from the 'Ulamā. Dear reader, understand and grasp the reality of this conspiracy. For a considerable period in the history of Bukhara and Samarkand there was 'ilmi excellence, but when communism took hold (and turned these areas into southern U.S.S.R provinces), even mentioning the name of

Allah ﷻ was considered a crime. How did the communist atheists achieve this scheme? Study history, it will reveal how the Russian propaganda machine detached the Muslims of these areas from their 'Ulamā. At the outset of communism, around 1920 CE, no restrictions were placed on Masājids, Deeni Madārris or Da'wah work, nor was any anti-Islāmic literature or lecture programmes initiated, but what the communist did instigate was a subtle scheme to tarnish the image, standing and esteem of the 'Ulamā from the hearts of Muslim laity! These atheists were fully aware of the consequences, Muslims would then become separated from Deen. This is precisely the same technique and approach employed today by the world of *kufr* to destroy Islām. They have established commissions and bodies to study how the Muslims were separated from their Deen in Spain, Russia and the Indian sub-continent. They are fully aware and are implementing these same methods to weaken and destroy Islām today. Just as they are researching and studying history to plot our downfall, it is incumbent upon us Muslims to study history and these techniques of the *kuffar* in order to counter their threat and protect our Deen and future.

In Islām, there is no place for negligence, baseless joviality, love for materialism, fame and dunya. These fleeting glories of the world have totally blinded us. Even today, if we Muslims make a firm intention in our hearts to stand firmly as living examples of the Deen of our Nabee ﷺ and thereafter strive to spread this Message of Peace to all corners of the world in the Light of the Glorious Qur'ān and Hadeeth, under the guidance of our 'Ulamā, then Inshā'Allah, millions from mankind will enter Islām and achieve everlasting success in the Ākhirah.

Indifference to Contemporary 'Ulamā

Nowadays another misconception has become embedded in our hearts. When somebody tries to detach us from the Fuqaha-e-Ezām or our Akabireen: Shaykh Ashraf 'Ali Thānwi; Shaykh Rasheed Ahmad Gangohi; Shaykh Muhammad Qaseem Nanotwi; Shaykh Husain Ahmad Madanee; Shaykh-ul-Hadeeth Zakariyya, Shaykh Hifzul Rahman; Shaykh Muhammad Ilyas (🌸), with great gusto we take offence and launch an intellectual boycott of the criticiser. However, dear reader, how do we behave, when somebody spits venom, mocks, criticises or belittles our living 'Ulamā, Ahlullah and Akabir? Why, are we any different to outsiders and enemies?

'Ghair (outsiders) are ghair, what is the surprise?

It is upon the behaviour of friends that my tears arise!'

Should any outsider criticise or revile any of our Akābir or 'Ulamā-e-Haqqa, it is nothing to be surprised about. However, when we are on Haqq, what right do we have to create and fester an atmosphere of disparagement, hatred, gossip, innuendoes, ridiculing and belittling the worth of our own 'Ulamā? Should any person, *Jamā'at* or body, whether on an *infirādi* (individual) or *ijtimā'ee* (collective) basis, attempt to distance the masses away from the company of the 'Ulamā-e-Haqqa, then understand this group to also be a victim of the *kuffar* conspiracy. No other conclusion may be drawn for any *Jamā'at* which connives in this way to separate the Ummah away from the Inheritors of the Ambiya. May Allah 🌸 grant us the Tawfeeq to appreciate the rank of our Fuqaha and 'Ulamā and to derive benefit from them. Āmeen.

Shaykh Muhammad Saleem Dhorat

Fitnah of Doctorates & Hostility towards the 'Ulamā of Islām

haykh Mufti 'Ashiq Ellahi Madanee ❁ narrates, 'Amongst the schemes initiated by enemies of Islām, one ploy is to encourage Muslims to enter universities to study and write such views about Islām which are in total conflict with the teachings of the Glorious Qur'ān and Hadeeth. All this because of the greed for degree's and doctorates. For whatever length of time these people with Muslim names study, their thinking and appearance is corrupted and made anti-Islāmic. Such people with high sounding doctorates are wrongly regarded as 'Alims whose works are studied with awe and respect. However, such university Islāmic degree products are full of arrogance; they have only viewed the college environment and wrongly regard what they have studied to be 'ilm. They consider themselves to be unique and to have traversed all the stages of 'Uloom. When their tutors are Christians and Jewish, these post-graduates are groomed to raise objections towards Islām and be distanced from '*aqāids* and *āmals* (deeds). Thereafter these protégés are dispatched to Muslim lands.

My friend, Shaykh Abdul Hafeez Makki once visited Egypt to print a kitab by Shaykh-ul-Hadeeth Zakariyya ❁. Whilst sitting down to 'proofread,' a young Egyptian would sit down and start commenting. Shaykh Abdul Hafeez commented, 'Why do you keep needlessly interrupting?' He replied, 'I am a doctor!' Shaykh asked, 'Well what have you studied in hadeeth?' When he related his studies, Shaykh replied, 'You have studied nothing of hadeeth, therefore why object?' He thereafter proceeded to explain how in the ('Alim-Faadhil Courses in traditional Darul Ulooms) the *Saheeh Sittah* (six authentic and comprehensive books of hadeeth—each consisting of numerous volumes) are studied, in-depth, together with lectures on other hadeeth kitabs like *Mu'attā*. Upon this, the doctor replied, 'Yes, you have a right to be preoccupied in hadeeth studies.'

Whilst these doctors of philosophy are full of pride, they also pose a threat to Muslims. A student of mine in USA informs how for weekly gatherings, such doctors who are dressed in suit & tie and who go out to appease their non-muslim mentors are invited to speak...and should a Muslim doctor be unavailable, then any Christian or Jewish doctor is asked to address the gathering on Islām! What absurdity! The reason they do not invite an Muslim 'Alim is because he does not have a doctorate from a *kafir* university.

Moreover, university departments in Muslim countries are unwilling to employ even pious *Muhadditheen* who have taught hadeeth with great diligence for over forty years. Why? They are happy to pay huge salaries to doctors of philosophy (whether they be male or female) who have arrived from western colleges brandishing degrees yet are quite unwilling to pay even a meagre stipend to a Muslim 'Alim. The reason is *hubb-ud-dunya* (love of the world) and not true service to Deen or the propagation and acquisition of real 'Uloom of the Glorious Qur'ān and Hadeeth from expert 'Ulamā.

This is precisely why these modernists harbour an innate grudge against Deeni Madāris and the 'Ulamā: desiring these

Deeni institutions be annihilated; whereby the entire Ummah becomes entrapped in their grip. This scheme of enemies of Islām is being aided and abetted by doctors of philosophy, who have no real knowledge of the Glorious Qur'ān and Hadeeth nor have any intention of acquiring it. Some time ago, a female doctor of philosophy was despatched to tour Africa to propagate her poison, sitting upon the *mimbar* in a Masjid on Jumu'ah! It is surprising that Muslims should even allow such a scenario and there are other examples also. Currently, another female doctor of philosophy from Scotland is propagating audiotapes wherein the 'Ulamā are specifically targeted and accused (by misinterpreting Ayahs of the Glorious Qur'ān) of having brought the Deen from the jungle!

However, what these people fail to realise is that just as the Glorious Qur'ān and Hadeeth will be preserved until Qiyāmah, so too will the *Hamil* (bearers of the Glorious Qur'ān, the Ahl-e-'Ilm). History bears witness, that whomsoever has aligned themselves against the *Hamil-e-Qur'ān*, they have been destroyed in the process. Our Nabee ﷺ has prophesised:

> *'The bearers of this 'ilm, amongst whom will later appear such noble souls, who will correct the tahreef (deliberate interpolation) by transgressors; ward-off the effects (of peddlers) of batil (deviation) and purify the interpretations of ignoramuses.'* (Mishkhāt, 36, p959, Al-Balagh)

These *Hamileen* of the Glorious Qur'ān and Hadeeth have striven, toiled, suffered hardship yet always remained to *sar kobi* (smash the brains) of every *batil* movement that has raised its ugly head: *M'utazilah, Jahmiyah, Qādareeyah,*

Jabareeyah, etc., etc. Even today, new revolutionist in the form of male and female doctors of philosophy are graduating from universities beaming with poison acquired from enemies of Islām. However, how may these deviated souls possibly harm or negate the role of the 'Ulamā?

The Ummah is well-aware of the *'ilmi khidmat* (service), *fikr* (concern) for the Ākhirah, *ikhlas,* lack of concern for dunya and the numerous other attributes possessed by pious 'Ulamā, this is precisely why ordinary people incline towards them. Therefore, for the modernists to try and smirch this confidence of the laity towards the 'Ulamā is nothing but an exercise in futility and self-destruction. Rather than worrying about others, these doctors of philosophy should ask themselves whether they possess Imān? Whether they have fikr for the Ākhirah? Whether they believe in Qiyāmah? Allah ﷻ warns such misguided people:

> *'And whomsoever contradicts and opposes the Rasool (ﷺ) after the right path has been clearly shown to him and, follows other than the Believers way, We shall keep him on the (wrong) path he has chosen and burn him in Hell, what an evil destination!'* (Glorious Qur'ān, 4:115)

Remember, whomsoever claims to be a Muslim, then such a person has to compulsorily follow the *ahqāms* and laws of the Glorious Qur'ān and Sunnah. Nobody has the right to change or discard any aspect of Deen. This is precisely the error committed by the Jews and Christians; they changed the Deen brought by Sayyidina Moosaa عليه السلام and Sayyidina 'Esaa عليه السلام...and now it appears as if the *mulhids* and *zindiqs* of this era also wish to follow suit. (Based upon original article in Vol. 36, p959, Al-Balagh)

Chapter Eight

Kitãbullah

&

Rijãlullah

Abridged & Edited From the

Urdu Islaahi Khutabãt

of

Shaykh Mufti Taqee 'Uthmãnee

dãmat barakãtuhum

An introductory Hadeeth Lecture delivered to Students of Tirmizee Shareef at Darul 'Uloom Karachi in Shawwal 1410 AH - 1990 CE. Herein the fadheelat (virtues) and rank of 'Ilm-e-Hadeeth are related together with emphasis upon the fact that no knowledge or skill - no matter how trivial or even if it relates to dunya is acquired without the services of a teacher or mentor. By mere self-study of books, neither may a person become an Alim of Deen, Doctor of Medicine, or an engineer, etc.

The lecture was originally transcribed in Urdu by Shaykh Muhammad Tayyib Atkee - then a student attending this Dars.

May Allah ﷻ grant him jazaa'ikhair.

بسم الله الرحمن الرحيم

Salāt and Salāms upon Nabee ﷺ

A̶llah ﷻ mentions in the Glorious Qur'ān:

'Indeed Allah conferred a great favour on the Believers when He raised in their midst a Rasool from amongst themselves, who recites unto them His Verses (the Glorious Qur'ān) and makes them pure and teaches them the Book and Hikmah, whilst earlier, they were in open error.' (3:164)

A̶llah ﷻ has established two arrangements for the *islah* (reformation) of man, firstly, *Kitābullah*, i.e. the Heavenly Books; Torah, Zaboor, Injeel and finally the Glorious Qur'ān. Secondly, *Rijālullah*, i.e. the patronage and mission of the Prophets' ﷺ. This system of *Rijālullah* was concurrent with *Kitābullah* so that the Prophets ﷺ could elaborate, explain and practically display the message and meaning through their actions and speech. This was the prime purpose in sending Prophets' ﷺ...

'With clear signs and Books (We sent the Prophets). And We have also sent down unto you (O Muhammad ﷺ) the Dhikr (the Glorious Qur'ān), that you may explain clearly to people what is sent down to them and, that they may give thought.' (Glorious Qur'ān, 16:44)

Without the patronage of the Prophets ﷺ, it is impossible for us to derive benefit from this Kitab. Without the services of a teacher, mere reading of books is not sufficient nor may anybody acquire expertise in any field. For this, one must humbly sit in front of an *Ustadh*.

Rapid Increase in Cemetery Population

In-depth books on medical science are available in numerous languages. Should the most talented, intelligent, astute, understanding, determined and industrious student decide to become a doctor by merely studying books and thereafter commence medical practice, what will happen? Obviously, he will rapidly increase the population of the cemetery. Despite having understood the books, because he lacked training from an expert, he fails to qualify as a doctor. No country, institute or hospital will recognise his claim to medical competence nor allow him license to take the lives of others in his hands.

Allah ﷻ has created a few differences between animals and humans, one of these is that animals are not in such need of a *murrabee* (tutor) as humans. For example, immediately a fish hatches from its egg, it begins to swim unaided...without being instructed by a teacher. This is a natural trait created by Allah ﷻ. In complete contrast, should anybody conclude, 'if a new-born fish is able to swim without being taught, I too shall throw my baby into the water!' Such a person will be labelled a fool and wholly irresponsible. A human needs to be trained to swim.

Similarly, the moment a chick hatches from its egg, it begins to peck for food...without any instructions. However, a new-born human will not eat bread, for this it requires patient nurturing and practical training. This is the natural *fitrah* (trait) of humans created by Allah ﷻ, that without the services of a *mu'allim* they are unable to acquire mastery in any field or activity. If anybody disputes this reality, let them attempt to construct a piece of furniture from natural wood following the instructions in a D-I-Y manual. What will be the result? Sawdust! However, spend some time in the company of a carpenter...one will become a competent woodworker.

Heavenly Kitabs were always Accompanied

This requirement of a tutor is a Divinely Appointed Sunnah for every human activity, whether it relates to Deen or dunya. This is why no Heavenly Kitab was ever sent without a Nabee. There are many citations of a Nabee arriving without a new Kitab, but there is not a single instance of a Heavenly Kitab without a Rasool. Why? We humans are unable to understand and grasp (for purpose of *islah nafs*) without the services of a Prophet. This was a concept lost upon the *mushrik* (idol worshippers)...

> *'And those who disbelieve say, 'Why is not the Qur'ān revealed to him all at once...?'*   (Glorious Qur'ān, 25:32)

It was no difficult task for Allah ﷻ, had He wished, there would a gilded hardback copy of the Glorious Qur'ān upon the bedside cabinet of every human when he awoke in the morning with a heavenly voice proclaiming, 'This is Allah's Kitab, act upon it!' However, Allah ﷻ chose to send the Kitab with a Rasool, a *mu'allim*, a *murrabee*, why?

Two Nûrs (Spiritual Lights) & Slogans

It is not possible to understand the Kitab until *Nûr* from the Rasool's *Taleem* is not present. No matter how outstanding the Kitab, if I am sitting in pitch-blackness, will I derive benefit from this Kitab? No, unless two *Nûrs* are present; firstly, the internal *Nûr* of my eyesight; secondly, the external *Nûr* of either the sun or electricity. Should either of these be lacking, it will not be possible to derive benefit from the Kitab. From this allegory, understand the two concurrent systems of *Kitābullah* and *Rijālullah* created by Allah ﷻ.

It is failure to appreciate this concept which is the cause of deviation. Accordingly, one modernist group has raised the rather fancy sounding slogan, *Hasbunā Kitābullah* (Allah's Book is sufficient for us). On face value, it appears a very noble cry, for it is mentioned in the Glorious Qur'ān (16:89), '...*As an exposition of everything...*' However, ask the very votaries of this slogan, 'if medical books are present at home, will it be possible to achieve medical competence without the training of an expert?' Similarly, to take *only* the Glorious Qur'ān and to claim 'we have no need for the Rasool's Taleem,' is pure folly and ignorance. In reality, to forgo *Rijālullah* is also to forfeit *Kitābullah*, because the Glorious Qur'ān itself is stating:

> '*Indeed Allah conferred a great favour on the Believers when He raised in their midst a Rasool from amongst themselves, who recites unto them His Verses (the Glorious Qur'ān) and makes them pure and teaches them the Book and Hikmah, whilst earlier, they were in open error.*' (3:164)

It appears in medical encyclopaedias, guides and home remedies, 'do not administer medicine without the advice of your Doctor.' Why, because if you resort to self-diagnosis and self-prescription, instead of tomorrow, you will most likely die today! Similar is the position of those who raise the hue of '*Hasbunā Kitābullah*' (Allah's Book is sufficient for us).

Yet another modernist movement are those who have become so short-sighted as to consider only *Rijālullah* as necessary, they blissfully ignore the Qur'ān and take from *Rijālullah* what they consider to be appropriate. They too are deviated.

The *e'tidal* (ideal) is to cling firmly to both *Kitābullah* and *Rijālullah*. To acquire *hidayat* (guidance), study *Kitābullah* in the Light of the *tāleem* and *tarbiyyah* of *Rijālullah*. This is collaborated by the meaning of this Hadeeth of Nabee ﷺ...

'Cling firmly unto this Kitab and my Ashāb (Sahābāh).' (p319)

Should this concept be understood, then the root of all modern-day deviation will be cut. Many modernists 'self-study' kitabs and thereafter self-appoint themselves as experts; the next Imām Aboo Haneefah ﷺ. To justify their claim, they argue, 'He (i.e. Imām Aboo Haneefah) was a human, we too are humans. In the same way he made *ijthihad* from the Qur'ān and Hadeeth, we too shall adopt *ijthihad* and formulate masā'eel.'

The fallacy and absurdity of this claim is akin to a butcher comparing himself to a doctor. Both are humans and both cut, one to kill and the other to cure. Understand well, to follow an untrained and unqualified person, no matter how well read and educated is nothing but folly. Why? Because the danger always exists of him making such a fundamental and basic error which will destroy his follower. Even if a handful of people have benefited from him or his publications, the danger of deviating people is immense and very real.

From Bosom to Bosom

One distinguishing feature of our Deen, created by Allah ﷻ, is that it passes from bosom to bosom - it does not come from mere reading of books. It must pass from the bosom of the teacher to the one being taught. Why, did the Sahābāh read any kitābs? Did they acquire a *sanad* or degree? Nothing of the sort, they humbly sat at *Sufa* (the first maktab in Masjid-An-

Nabawee in Madeenah). No apparent syllabus or timetable... but the personality and practical *Taleem* of Nabee ﷺ. This *Nûr* from Nabbuwwat, which thereafter they passed unto the *Tābiʿeen* (the Great Imām included) and they onto the *Tabe-Tābiʿeen* and so on, through the great chain of successive generations of 'Ulamā - from one bosom to another.

Allah's ﷻ Sunnah to grant through an Ustadh

There are two ways of studying a kitab: firstly, self-study, using a dictionary to look up words you do not understand. Secondly, study the same kitab sitting in front of an *Ustadh*. The difference between both methods is as if the distance between the heavens and earth. The *Nûr* and *barakah* one receives from an *Ustadh* is supplemented with the *Tajaleeyat* of 'Ilm from Allah ﷻ - blessings unavailable in self-study. Why? In reality, the *Ustadh* is only a medium, it is Allah ﷻ Who grants; moreover, it is His Sunnah to grant through an Ustadh.

Allah ﷻ could have revealed *Wahee* direct to Nabee ﷺ, yet He chose Jibraʿeel Ameen عليه السلام as an intermediary. Similarly, when He spoke to Prophet Moosā عليه السلام it was via. a tree, why? Only He knows, however, it is His Sunnah to grant through an *Ustadh* (medium). Therefore, although *Kitābullah* comes first and *Rijalullah* follows, nevertheless in order to understand the Glorious Qur'ān we will need the practical *taleem* of Hadeeth (from an *Ustadh*). May Allah ﷻ grant us the Tawfeeq to study the 'Ilm of Hadeeth with *Ikhlaas* and correct Adab (etiquettes). Āmeen,

Shaykh Mufti Taqee 'Uthmānee

dāmat barakātuhum

haykh Ashraf 'Ali Thānwi ﷺ writes in *Tuhfatul Ulama*, *'The ghair-muqallideen falsely claim that Imām Aboo Haneefah ﷺ only knew 17 Hadeeth. I aver that even if a less number were known by the Great Imām, it would be a display of his excellence. Why? Because, any person who supposedly possessed such little 'Uloom of Hadeeth yet was able to derive so many thousands of masā'eel's in complete confirmation to Ahadeeth; then what doubt is there in him being a Mujtahid?'*

(p433, ibid.)

haykh Mufti Taqee 'Uthmānee *dāmat barakātuhum* relates, *'The Great Imām's Kitab-ul-Āsār is ample testimony to his enormous 'Uloom of Hadeeth. Accordingly, Imām Suyûtee ﷺ narrates, 'Imām Aboo Haneefah ﷺ is no less in virtue for he had compiled the first systemised Fiqhee kitab based upon Hadeeth. No other person enjoys this honour; it is equal in rank to Imām Mālik's ﷺ Mu'atta...'*

'Yahyā bin Nasrahee ﷺ relates, 'Once I visited the Great Imām ﷺ and noticed his room was full of kitabs. I inquired to be informed, 'These are kitabs of Hadeeth.'

Another student related, '(Thousands of) hadeeth narrations appear in the works of the Great Imām ﷺ.' If this appears far-fetched...remember because he had dedicated his life to deducing masā'eel from hadeeth rather than only relating hadeeth, this is why such a large number of narrations based upon hadeeth are not at all unconceivable. Numerous Muhadditheen (throughout history) have written commentaries (some stretching to 20 volumes) upon this Kitab-ul-Āsār. This is sufficient testimony of their acceptance of the Great Imām's 'Uloom of Hadeeth.'

(Vol. 1, p 97-8, Darse Tirmizee)

Chapter Nine

Istiftā'

The Seeking of Legal Advice in Religious Matters from Scholars

Shaykh Mufti Muhammad Shafee 🌼
Shaykh Mufti Azeez-ur-Rahman Qasimee 🌼
Shaykh Muhammad Qāsim Nanotwee 🌼
Shaykh 'Abdullah Albarnee Madanee
Shaykh Muhammad Saleem Dhorat

What is the Command of Kitabullah and Hadeeth of Rasoolullah ﷺ to the following questions O 'Ulamā-e-Kirām? May Allah's Rahmat be upon you...

1) Question: Is taqleed of an Imām Mujtahid Fardh, Wājib or mubah?

$\bigcirc\!\!\!\!\!\mathcal{S}$haykh Mufti Azeez-ur-Rahman Qasimee ﷺ replies: Taqleed is fardh because Allah ﷻ mentions in the Glorious Qur'ān...

'*Ask the People of Knowledge if you do not know.*' (21:7)

'*O you who believe! Obey Allah and obey the Messenger (ﷺ) and those of you (Muslims) who are ulul amr (in authority)...*'   (4:59)

Jabir bin 'Abdullah ﷺ, 'Abdullah Ibn 'Abbas ﷺ and other Sahābāh, Tābi'een & Tabe Tābi'een scholars have interpreted *ulul amr* as the 'Ulamā. Shaykh Siddeeq Hasan Khan, former Ameer of the Ahl-e-Hadeeth accepts this commentary in his publications. It appears in hadeeth... '*The cure for ignorance is to ask those of knowledge.*' (Vol. 1, p122, Jawahir...) However, this begs the question, 'in everyday terminology, are all the persons who are known as 'Alim able to discharge this responsibility or is a *Khas* (extraordinary) 'Alim and Faqeeh implied?' Shāh Waleehullah's ﷺ reply has already been related and comprehensively answers this query.

2) Question: Why is taqleed made of only the Four Great Imāms - is there any proof for this? Are there no other Imām's of this rank whose taqleed may be made?

$\mathcal{S}$haykh Mufti Azeez-ur-Rahman Qasimee 🏵 replies: 'For the chain of taqleed to end upon the Four Great Imāms is not an intellectual matter, but is the product of Divine Judgement which Decided to perpetuate these four *madhabs* and annihilate all other schools of fiqh. Even though (a few) statements and rulings of the now defunct schools *may* remain, nevertheless they do not constitute a separate *madhab* which people would be able to follow. Even if 100 *ahqāms* were still present to be followed, what of the other thousands of daily masā'eels?

This is like the example of a family with numerous children. The majority of whom have died and only four are living when the parents too pass-away. Obviously, inheritance will be distributed amongst the four remaining children, notwithstanding the fact that numerous other children were also born. But, have you ever heard anybody object as to why only these four have inherited? Even if somebody should, the simple and only answer will be, 'Brother, this was the divine decree!' Moreover, will you also ask, 'which Qur'ānic Ayah or hadeeth substantiates this distribution to the four specific children by name.' Obviously, the Commands of the Sharee'ah are general, specific names of personalities are not always mentioned. Otherwise, where is your name mentioned whereby it is permissible for you to sleep, arise or sit?

If it was necessary to mention names for all commands of the Sharee'ah, then it would not be possible for anybody to practise upon any fardh, wājib, harām or makruh! Which āyah or hadeeth will you display to show that salāh is compulsory upon you by name?'

3) Question: Is Imāmat (leading of Salāh) of a person who does not make taqleed of any of the Four Great Imāms permissible?

haykh Mufti Azeez-ur-Rahman Qasimee 🐝 replies: 'Although the Imāmat of such a person is *fee nafsah* (by default) permissible. Nevertheless, in this day and age, people who do not make *taqleed* of any of the Four Great Imāms and claim to act upon hadeeth have a general habit of practicing acts which are *mufsid* (break) salāh. For example, they do not make (proper) *istinjā*...and the flowing of drops of urine is well-known in this era, accordingly, the clothes of such people are often impure. Consequently, it is best to abstain from their Imāmat.

haykh Muhammad Qāsim Nanotwee 🐝 commented, 'Undoubtedly, the true religion is Islām and all Four *Madhabs* are *Haqq*. Ponder, medical science is a field within which all qualified and competent doctors are allowed to treat. However, despite the differences of opinion and approaches within the medical profession, whichever doctor one is connected to, only his diagnosis, judgement and treatment will be adhered to. The advice of other doctors will not be considered. Whilst this is the general scenario, sometimes it does become necessary to move away from one's own doctor and consult another specialist and thereafter heed only his advise. Similarly, it was necessary for some Saints to forgo their *madhab* and follow another *mu'ayin* (specific) Mujtahid...Imām Tahāwee 🐝, a very high ranking *Muhaddith* and *Faqeeh* was initially a Shāfi'ee and thereafter became a Hanafee. Despite his own 'Uloom, he remained a *muqallid*... for without *taqleed* it is not possible to progress. Imām

Tahāwee 🌸, Imām Muhammad 🌸 and Imām Aboo Yousuf 🌸 all made *taqleed* of Imām Aboo Haneefah 🌸. Another example is the renown Imām Tirmizee 🌸 - a great 'Alim, Muhaddith and Faqeeh. *Tirmizee Shareef* is his publication, yet despite this excellence, he was still a *muqallid* of Imām Shāfi'ee 🌸. Therefore, which 'Alim today is beyond *taqleed?* Even if some great 'Alim (in the past) had not made *taqleed,* so what? Any intelligent person will conclude, that the actions and practise of the majority of any group constitutes their consensus...

There now remains the question of *tarāweeh,* which certain half-baked people claim to be only 8 rakaahs instead of 20. Obviously, this is pleasing to the *nafs,* but what is conveniently overlooked is that the 8 rakaahs which appear in hadeeth applies to *tahajjud salāh.* There are 20 rakaahs for *tarāweeh.* There were thousands of Sahābāh during the time of 'Umar 🌸, yet not a single person from that time until recently had questioned the need for proofs as to why there are 20 rakaahs for *tarāweeh?* However, lately, some quacks have decided they have the right to question the authority and decisions of 'Umar 🌸 and other senior Sahābāh. For such 'enlightened' people, we conclude with some hadeeth of Nabee 🌸...

'Make incumbent upon you my Sunnah and the Sunnah of the Khulafaa-e-Rāshideen who will come after me.'

'Iqtidā' (follow) those people who will appear after me.'

'My Sahābāh are like guiding stars; whomsoever amongst them you follow, you will be guided on the right path.'

(V. 1, p135, Gems of Fiqh)

ഇൗന്ദ്ര

Fitnah of Refuting Hadeeth

'Say (O Muhammad ﷺ them), 'Tell me, of the provision Allah has sent down to you, you have made some of it halāl and some of it harām. Say (O Muhammad ﷺ to them), 'Has Allah permitted you (to do so), or do you invent a lie against Allah?' (Glorious Qur'ān, 10:59)

Shaykh 'Abdullah Albarnee Madanee *dāmat barakātuhum* narrates, 'Wahee (Divine Revelations) which descended upon our Nabee ﷺ is classified into two categories. Firstly, those Glorious Qur'ānic Ayahs, which are known as *Kalāmullah.* The words and meanings of this form of *wahee* are both from Allah ﷻ and have been protected in the Glorious Qur'ān in such a way that until today and unto Qiyāmah, not a single word or letter will change. In the terminology of the Ahl-e-'Ilm, this form of *wahee* is known as *Wahee Matlû,* i.e. the *wahee* which is recited.

The second form of *wahee,* which although not part of the Glorious Qur'ān, was also a means whereby Allah ﷻ bestowed many *ahqāms* to our Nabee ﷺ. This type of wahee is known as *Wahee-ghair-matlû,* i.e. the *wahee* which is not recited. This type of *wahee* has been preserved in the form of Saheeh ahadeeth and generally after revelation to Nabee ﷺ were elucidated upon in his own blessed words. Shaykh Mufti Taqee 'Uthmānee writes in *Uloom-ul-Qur'ān...*

'From Ayahs of the Glorious Qur'ān itself it is evident that Wahee-Illahee is not munhasir (restricted) to the Qur'ān-e-Kareem. Many matters were revealed unto Nabee ﷺ via

Wahee besides the Ayahs of the Qur'ān. To support this claim, a few Qur'ānic Ayahs are presented:

1) '...And We made the Qiblah (prayer direction towards Bayt-ul-Muqaddas - Jerusalem) which you used to face, only to test those who followed the Rasool (   ) from those who would turn on their heels...'   (2:143)

Every Muslim is aware that for a period in Madeenah Tayyibah, our Nabee   faced Bayt-ul-Muqaddas as qiblah during Salāh. Thereafter, when the command arrived to once again face Baytullah (Ka'bah in Makkah), this ayah was revealed. The point to ponder over is that in this Ayah, the Command to face Bayt-ul-Muqaddas is also assigned as from Allah   ...Now, study the entire Glorious Qur'ān from beginning to end and you will not find a single reference, 'face Bayt-ul-Muqaddas as Qiblah during Salāh.' It is evident this command was revealed via such Wahee which is not contained in the Qur'ān - this is precisely Wahee-ghair-matlû.

2) 'And (remember) when the Prophet (   ) disclosed a matter in confidence to one of His wives and she told it to another. And Allah made it known to him; he informed part thereof and left a part...'

(Glorious Qur'ān, 66:3)

The circumstances to this ayah was that one of the Umm-ul-Mu'mineen attempted to keep a matter hidden from Nabee   , however, by way of Wahee, Allah   revealed it. Upon this the Umm-ul-Mu'mineen inquired, 'How did you become aware of this?' Nabee   replied, 'This matter was revealed unto Me by 'Aleem and Hakeem (i.e. Allah ﷻ).' However, no mention of this is found in the entire Qur'ān - again, it is evident that this revelation was via Wahee-ghair-matlû.' (p41-43, Uloom-ul-Qur'ān)

In this era, wherein many *fitnahs* have reared their ugly heads, one such *fitnah* is *inkār* (refuting of) Hadeeth. These deviated people claim, 'Through only the Qur'ān we are able to deduce all Islāmic *ahqāms*, whether they are Fardh, Wājib...' They neither recognise, accept or consider it compulsory to follow *Hadeeth-e-Nabawee*. Despite the glaring and obvious discrepancies of this claim, many gullible and westernised Muslims have fallen into the snare of this group. We ask them, 'The command to perform Salāh is related in the Glorious Qur'ān, however show us where is the method, number of rakāhs, items to be recited, etc., mentioned?' These matters are only available from Saheeh Hadeeth. Similarly, the *nisab* of Zakāt is not mentioned in the Glorious Qur'ān, again one will need to study Saheeh Hadeeth. Accordingly, *munkareen-e-hadeeth* (refuters of hadeeth) should make *taubah* and refrain from propagating deviation.

May Allah ﷻ grant all of us respect, confidence and esteem for the Hadeeth of Nabee ﷺ.

Based upon original Urdu article in Al-Balagh (Vol. 35, Issue 6)

ॐ

Conclusion

haykh Muhammad Saleem Dhorat *dāmat barakātuhum* concludes, 'When the names of all the Fuqahā-e-Ezām are compiled in a list, the name of Imām-e-Azam Aboo Haneefah ﷺ stands out boldly. Imām Shāfi'ee ﷺ, an inhabitant of Makkah and undisputed authority in fiqh and Hadeeth commented,

'*The people are all children (dependants) of Imām Aboo Haneefah* ﷺ *in the field of fiqh.*'

(p9, Sunnah & the People of Sunnah)

A very large percentage of the Ummah is today acting upon the teachings of Imām Aboo Haneefah ﷺ and will forever remain indebted to him. As Islām is the Deen of Allah ﷻ, it follows that every facet of its Tāleem, from 'A to Z' is a creation and presentation from the Creator of the Universe. This system is not some man-made fad, but a perfect concept from Allah ﷻ, therefore the question of even an iota of error therein is inconceivable.

Accordingly, the *shuqooq and subahāt* (doubts) which are being raised (by the media and modernists) is not because of any deficiency within the system, but is an attempt to create uncertainties in the hearts and minds of people like us who are weak in Imān. When these false doubts are raised, because of our weakness, we fall into perplexity... 'How is this possible?' 'What type of hukm is this?' Sometimes, an aspect of the rights of women is distortedly publicized; the practice of *hijāb* (purdah); the concept of *hudood & qisās* (capital punishment); all are misconstrued. However, through the Grace and Favour of Allah ﷻ, our Ulamā-e-Kirām have, with their pens waged an untiring *Jihād* (intellectual crusade) and comprehensively answered all possible objections to the pure *tāleem* of Islām. When Nabee ﷺ departed from this world, there existed only one *kitab* in the library of Islām, i.e. the Glorious Qur'ān...and that too *muntashir* (in parts and dispersed). Whilst many of the Sahābāh ﷺ had preserved the whole Qur'ān in their hearts, nevertheless, in written format, parts and pages were scattered amongst them. Hifz of the Glorious Qur'ān and Ahadeeth, at a highly impeccable degree and level, existed amongst the Sahābāh ﷺ. However, even the scattered written format was devoid of symbols, signs and *sukoon* (jazm). Now ponder, if from the time of the Sahābāh, our Ulamā had not toiled, forget about other Ibādāhs, we would not be able to even read Surah Fātihah! Accordingly, this Ummah is greatly indebted to our Ulamā-e-kirām, therefore we should look upon and remember them with the utmost of respect and reverence. Make du'aa of *khair* (goodness) for them, this too is a haqq of theirs upon us. Analyse the history of the past fourteen centuries and, you will notice how our Ulamā-e-kirām have engaged and confronted every single *fitnah* that has arisen. This is an unique feature of the Ulamā-e-kirām, that Allah ﷻ has specifically chosen them to protect the Deen; no other profession enjoys this distinction. Whatever fitnah has arisen against the Glorious Qur'ān, Hadeeth, Aqaaid, Khutme-Nabbuwwat (Finality of Prophethood), Inkār-e-Hadeeth (refuting and denying Hadeeth), whatever *fitnah* has arisen, examine the history of the last fourteen centuries and you will not find any other group besides the Ulamā who have confronted these *fitnahs* and protected the Deen.'

Selflessness of our Akābir 'Ulamā

*T*o conclude, let us relate an episode from *Seerah Sahābāh,* 'During the time of the famous Tābi'ee Ibrāheem Nakha'ee 🌸, there lived in Kufa another pious though less famous scholar by the name of Ibrāheem bin Yazeed Taymee 🌸. The notorious Governor Hajjaj bin Yousuf had ordered a warrant for the arrest and life imprisonment of Ibrāheem Nakha'ee stipulating a deadline for his officers to capture him by a certain date or face severe punishment. One day, the police (unaware of his appearance) entered a Masjid in desperate search of Ibrāheem Nakha'ee to find Ibrāheem Taymee 🌸 delivering a lecture. The latter to save Ibrāheem Nakha'ee contented, 'I am Ibrāheem!' Immediately, the police apprehended him and informed Hajjaj, who without a trial ordered that Ibrāheem Nakha'ee be imprisoned in a dungeon. Unknown to anybody but himself and his family, Ibrāheem Taymee 🌸 was serving the sentence on behalf of Ibrāheem Nakha'ee in the most horrendous conditions imaginable; wherein there was no light, warmth, water or fresh air.

Within a few days, Ibrāheem Taymee's 🌸 condition had so deteriorated, that even his mother was unable to recognise him. However, in order to ensure the Ummah derive maximum Deeni benefit from his contemporary and name sake, Ibrāheem Taymee 🌸 maintained silence and adopted tremendous *sabr.* He died in this state and his *janāzah* was taken out of the dungeon. That very night, Hajjaj dreamt that a *Janatee* had died in Kufa.

When he made inquiries in the morning, he was informed that 'Ibrāheem' had died during the night in the dungeons. Unable to bear this news, he dismissed the dream as shaytānic and ordered the body be thrown onto a rubbish heap.

These are the superhuman and selfless sacrifices which servants of Allah ﷻ have undertaken to ensure that true Deen reaches us in its pristine and pure state.

May Allah ﷻ grant us tawfeeq to appreciate & act accordingly,

Āmeen, Was-salām, Ashraf's Amānat©, Dewsbury

৪০০৪

References

- **Ma'āriful Qur'ān** (Original)
Shaykh Muhammad Shafee' ﷺ ....Darul Ishā'at

- **The Noble Qur'ān** (Arabic with English translation)
Shaykh Dr. M. Taqi-ud-Din & Dr. M. Muhsin Khan .... Maktaba Dar-us-Salām

- **Mazāhir Haqq** (Original)
Shaykh Muhammad Qutbuddeen Khān Dehlwi ﷺ ....Darul Ishā'at

- **Ma'āriful Hadeeth** (Original)
Shaykh Manzoor Nu'maani ﷺ ....Darul Ishā'at

- **Mu'attā Imām Mālik** (Original)
Shaykh Allahmah Waheed-u-Zaman ﷺ .... Maktab Rahmaniyyah

- **Riyadus Sāliheen** (Original)
Shaykh Muhyuddeen Abee Zakariyya ﷺ ....Darul Ishā'at

- **Al-Hidāyah** (Arabic)
Shaykh-ul-Islām Burhanuddeen ﷺ .... Makatab Shirkatul 'Ilm

- **Aimma Arba'a** (Original)
Shaykh Qadhi Athar Mubarakpoori ﷺ .... Shaykh-ul-Hind Academy, Deoband

- **Tazkiratul No'amān** (Original by Allamah Muhammad bin Yousuf Salehee)
Shaykh Abdullah Bastawee Madanee ﷺ................................... Kutub Khana Mazharee

- **Episodes (Hikayat) of Imàm Azam** ﷺ (Original)
Shaykh 'Abdu'l-Qayyum Haqqānee.. Kutub Khana

- **Fadha'il A'mal & Fadha'il Sadaqah** (Original)
Shaykh Zakariyya Khandalwi ﷺ .... Kutub Khana Faidhee

- **Dawah Azeemat** (Original)
Shaykh Abul Hasan Ali Nadwee ﷺ .... Majlis Nashreeyat Islam

- **Taqleed Kee Shar'ee Haysheeyat** (Original)
Shaykh Mufti Muhammad Taqee 'Uthmānee .... Makatab Darul Uloom Karachi

- **Dars Tirmizee** (Original)
Shaykh Mufti Muhammad Taqee 'Uthmānee .... Makatab Darul Uloom Karachi

- **Lectures of Hakeemul Ummah** (Original)
Shaykh Ashraf 'Ali Thānwi ﷺ.. Idārah Taleefāt Ashrafeeyah

- **Sawtul Haqq** (Original ~ Audio/CD)
Shaykh Muhammad Saleem Dhorat..Da'wah Book Centre

- **Majālis** (Original ~ Book & Audio)
Shaykh Maseehullah Khān ﷺ .... Jāmea Miftāhul Uloom

- **Islāhi Discourses** (Original 13 Vols.)
Shaykh Mufti Taqee Uthmānee ....Mayman Islāmic Publishers

- **Islāhi Lectures** (Original 4 vols.)
Shaykh Mufti 'Abdur Ra'oof Sakhrawee......................................Mayman Islāmic Publishers

- **Statements of Pious Elders** ﷺ (Original)
Shaykh Mufti Muhammad Taqee Uthmānee .... Idārah Tāleefat Ashrafeeyah

- **Jawahir-ul-Fiqh** (Original)
Shaykh Mufti Muhammad Shafee ﷺ ....Makatab Darul Uloom Karachi

- **Fiqh-ul-Faqee'** (Original)
Shaykh Aboo Yousuf Muhammad Shareed ﷺ .... Fareed Book Stall

- **Hālat Musanifeen** (Original)
Shaykh Muhammad Haneef Gangohee ﷺ..Darul Ishā'at

- **Encyclopaedia Britannica** (CD Version)
Britannica© CD 99, 1994-1998. ....Encyclopædia Britannica, Inc.

Certain advises/episodes are those heard directly from the lectures and company of Scholars, Mashāikh and Huffaz. May Allah ﷺ grant all of them the best of rewards.

Other Ashraf's Amānat Books for the Whole Family

Set A: Ashraf's Beloved (Ideal for Early years)

1 Ashraf's Colouring Book 1
2 Ashraf's Nursery 1
3 Ashraf's Nursery 2
4 Ashraf's Alphabet
5 Ashraf's First Words
6 Ashraf's First Sentences

Set B: Ashraf's Classics (Series for ages 5-14 yrs)

- *Classics 1:* A Town Named Injusticebury
- *Classics 2:* Beautiful Reward of Patience
- *Classics 3:* Moosaa عليه السلام
- Ashraf's First Maktab
- Ashraf's Beautiful Muaasharat

Set C: Nabee's Roses (Graded Series for ages 6-18 yrs)

1 Allah Ta'ālā's Rasool ﷺ
2 Khadeejah ﵐ
3 'Ā'ishah ﵐ
4 Daughters of Prophet Muhammad ﷺ
5 Mothers' of the Believers ﵐ
6 Sahābeeyāt ﵐ

Set D: Ashraf's Roses (Graded Series for ages 6-18 yrs)

1 Aboo Bakr ﵁
2 'Umar ﵁
3 'Uthmān ﵁
4 'Ali ﵁
5 Guiding Stars (Senior Sahābāh) ﵁

Set E: Ashraf's Readers (For the whole family)

- Ashraf's Blessings of Marriage
- Great Imām's of Fiqh ﵜ
- Ashraf's Advice upon Death of a Muslim
- Ashraf's Advice upon Tazkiyah (Due Soon, Inshā'Allah)
- Ashraf's Orchard
- Ashraf's Blessings of Ramadhān

Ashraf's Amānat©,

PO Box 12, Dewsbury, W. Yorkshire, UK, WF12 9YX
Tel: (01924) 488929
email: info@ashrafsamanat.org ~ www.ashrafsamanat.org